Secret Manoeuvres in the Dark

SECRET MANOEUVRES IN THE DARK

Corporate and Police Spying on Activists

Eveline Lubbers

PlutoPress
www.plutobooks.com

This book is a joint project of
SpinWatch in the UK
www.spinwatch.org

and

Buro Jansen & Janssen in the Netherlands
www.burojansen.nl

First published 2012 by Pluto Press
345 Archway Road, London N6 5AA

www.plutobooks.com

Distributed in the United States of America exclusively by
Palgrave Macmillan, a division of St. Martin's Press LLC,
175 Fifth Avenue, New York, NY 10010

British Library Cataloguing in Publication Data
A catalogue record for this book is available from the British Library

ISBN   978 0 7453 3186 7   Hardback
ISBN   978 0 7453 3185 0   Paperback
ISBN   978 1 8496 4640 6   PDF eBook
ISBN   978 1 8496 4642 0   Kindle eBook
ISBN   978 1 8496 4641 3   EPUB eBook

Library of Congress Cataloging in Publication Data applied for

This book is printed on paper suitable for recycling and made from fully managed
and sustained forest sources. Logging, pulping and manufacturing processes are
expected to conform to the environmental standards of the country of origin.

10   9   8   7   6   5   4   3   2   1

Designed and produced for Pluto Press by Chase Publishing Services Ltd
Typeset from disk by Stanford DTP Services, Northampton, England
Simultaneously printed digitally by CPI Antony Rowe, Chippenham, UK and
Edwards Bros in the United States of America

For Felipe Rodriquez

Thanks

Geert Lovink for guiding me through the wilderness,
Buro Jansen & Janssen for all those years,
David Miller and Will Dinan
Dienke Hondius, Monique Verrijcke, Sheila O'Donnell, Andy
Rowell, Maja van der Velden, Rob Dover, Rick van Amersfoort
and all the other friends who knew that I was going to get there.
The ladies' gym for their support and courage,

and of course, most of all, to Marq, my love, and Castor,
Franka and Renzo, my kids,
for making this possible and still loving me,
and everybody at Omega and Villa Spijker for taking
so much weight off my shoulders.

Contents

Preface: Corporate Spying Today   viii

1. Introduction: The Waste Paper Man   1
2. Covert Corporate Strategy in the Past   23
3. Rafael Pagan, Nestlé and Shell: Case Study   45
4. McSpy: Case Study   82
5. Cybersurveillance and Online Covert Strategy: Case Study   109
6. Hakluyt and the Jobbing Spy: Case Study   135
7. The Threat Response Spy Files: Case Study   159
8. Conclusion: Secrecy, Research and Resistance   195

Appendix 1: Manfred Schlickenrieder Documents   207
Appendix 2: Evelyn le Chêne Documents   210
Notes   211
Bibliography and References   215
Index   241

Preface
Corporate Spying Today

The exposure of Mark Kennedy as an infiltrator of activist groups made headlines in early 2011. Confronted by friends and fellow campaigners in the UK, Kennedy admitted to having been a spy for seven years. Using the name Mark Stone, he had embedded himself in the environmental movement, while widening his scope to protests against the summits of world leaders, anti-fascism campaigning and animal rights advocacy. His nickname was 'Flash' because of the money he had available. He offered transport to set up climate camps and volunteered his climbing skills to add spectacular effects to, for instance, the occupation of power plants.

The Mark Kennedy case could have been a chapter in this book. It is an exemplary case, with the infiltrator providing transport and money, and sometimes crossing the thin line between facilitator and agent provocateur. It is an extraordinary case, not only for the span of the operation, the many years, and the amount of countries in Europe. The coverage in the press was huge, and as a result of public pressure, half a dozen official reviews are now under way.

The fact that he was a police spy would not have made a difference. On the contrary, the Kennedy case reveals the increasingly blurring boundaries between public and private policing and puts the grey area of corporate intelligence in the spotlight. The set of secret units Kennedy worked for was founded explicitly to satisfy the needs of companies targeted by activists. What is more, the companies involved – such as electricity suppliers and airline companies – also hire former police and intelligence staff to deal with security issues.

The fact that none of the official reviews into the Kennedy case investigates the aspects of corporate spying underlines the urgent need for a book putting the spotlight on similar secret manoeuvres in the dark.

BLURRING BOUNDARIES

The exposure of Mark Kennedy put the spotlight on secret police units making a profit from selling information, and showed that the police cooperate with private security services founded by former intelligence staff with long track records in monitoring activist groups.

As an undercover agent, Kennedy reported to a secret unit founded to deal with 'domestic extremism' run by the Association of Chief Police Officers (ACPO). Its organization reflects the culture of secretiveness and the aversion to any public scrutiny of intelligence work. The unit Kennedy worked for was one of three. His was the National Public Order Intelligence Unit, created in 1999. The other two ACPO branches are the National Extremism Tactical Coordination Unit, set up in 2004, which advises thousands of companies on how to manage political campaigns, and the National Domestic Extremism Team, added in 2005, which pools intelligence gathered by investigations into protesters across the country. The units report to ACPO's Terrorism and Allied Matters Committee. Although it is responsible for some of the more sensitive national operations, ACPO is not a public body of any sort.[1] It is a limited company, sharing its data with clients such as energy companies running power plants and airline companies involved in the expansion of airports and flights. In its 2008 'statement of purpose', ACPO vowed 'to develop our business activities to ensure that the ACPO brand name is recognized globally as a mark of excellence in policing' (ACPO, 2008). A *Daily Mail* investigation into its activities and assets revealed that ACPO was selling information from the Police National Computer for up to £70 – even though it pays just 60p to access those details. It offers, among other services, so-called police certificates that reveal whether someone has a criminal record – a service over which it has a monopoly. For a 'not-for profit', the company accounts show a significant annual surplus, still according to the *Daily Mail*, with £15.8 million in assets, including £9.2 million 'cash at bank and in hand' (Lewis, 2009). In a response, the organization defended their activities, claiming that 'all funds to ACPO are employed in the interests of public safety and the police service' (ACPO, 2009).

The national infrastructure for dealing with 'domestic extremism' was set up with the backing of the Home Office in 1997 in an attempt to combat animal rights activists. It started in Huntingdon, as a section of Special Branch, the Animal Rights National Index (ARNI). At the time, the Home Office was 'getting really pressurized by big business – pharmaceuticals in particular, and the banks' about the 'extreme criminal behaviour of some people within the animal rights movement', according to Superintendent Steve Pearl, head of National Extremism unit. Later, the units incorporated ARNI altogether (Evans, Lewis and Taylor, 2009; for more background, see Mobbs, 2009). Since the criminal activity associated with these groups has receded, the secret units have expanded their remit to incorporate campaign groups across the political spectrum engaged in peaceful direct action. Special Branch colluded with private investigators hired by McDonald's to spy on activists in the 1990s, as Chapter 4 shows. More recently, according to Pearl, the focus shifted to the Climate Camp and Plane Stupid campaigns because environmental protesters had started 'shutting down airports and coal-fired power stations'. A freedom of information request by the Liberal Democrats in 2009 revealed that the police and the Department of Business, Enterprise and Regulatory Reform (BERR) exchanged information with E.ON over the Climate Camp demonstrations at Kingsnorth power station. According to correspondence between civil servants and security officials at the company (seen by the *Guardian*), police intelligence and the Department's strategies on protesters, including their names and whereabouts, were passed to E.ON. 'David Howarth MP, who obtained the emails, said they suggested that BERR had attempted to politicise the police, using their intelligence to attempt to disrupt a peaceful protest. "It is as though BERR was treating the police as an extension of E.ON's private security operation,"' he said (Taylor and Lewis, 2009).

While some of the information gathered comes from police spies like Kennedy, the ACPO database also contains 'information supplied by companies that hire private investigators to spy on protestors, sometimes by infiltration', according to the national co-coordinator for domestic extremism, Anton Setchell (Evans, Lewis and Taylor, 2009).

For instance, Kennedy secretly taped the discussions of a group of people from all over the UK to take over the Radcliffe-on-Soar power station the next day, on Easter Monday 2009. Just before everybody went to sleep, a large police force surprised the group and arrested 114 people.

However, the energy giant E.ON, which runs the Radcliffe-on-Soar plant, also turned to private security firms. The energy giant claimed that it happened 'on an "ad hoc" basis as its executives wanted to know when environmentalists were going to demonstrate at or invade its power stations and other premises' (Lewis and Evans, 2011a).

One such firm was Vericola, which worked for several companies targeted by climate campaigners, such as Scottish Resources Group, Britain's second biggest coal producer. Their information on activists also went to Gordon Irving, security director of Scottish Power, one of the UK's largest electricity generators. He joined the firm in 2001 after 30 years with Strathclyde police, where he had been head of Special Branch.

The other security firm hired by E.ON was Global Open, a company that, according to its website, 'maintains a discreet watch on groups that may present a risk to a corporation's reputation or safety' and offers to assist in 'intelligence gathering'. Its clients include BAe, England's largest arms producer, whose spying operations feature in Chapter 9.

Global Open's director is Rod Leeming, another member of the so-called old boys' network. He left the police, where as head of the Animal Rights National Index he regularly infiltrated undercover operatives into protest groups, in 2001 (Evans et al., 2011). With the ACPO unit's history of countering animal rights activism and its subsequent shift of focus towards climate campaigners, the extent of its link with companies like Global Open remains relatively unknown.

Mark Kennedy was also connected to Global Open. In February 2010, he set up Tokra Limited, acting as 'logistics officer' and sole director. The company was registered to the address of Heather Millgate, a director of Global Open at the time. Kennedy started using Tokra contact details in the period after he stopped working for the police, but before he was exposed as a spy. He did so at an Earth First! gathering in August 2010, taking part in a workshop on resisting police infiltration. Mark was by far the most vocal and enthusiastic contributor (Gifford, 2011).

Whether Kennedy pursued a career in corporate intelligence to continue his spying work after the police had pulled the plug, or whether the contacts with private security started earlier on, is not known. As we have said, the official reviews of the Kennedy case have failed to investigate the links between the special police units, the heads of security of the companies involved (such as power plants and airports) and the private agencies providing corporate intelligence. Mapping out these links is crucial to understand the current version of old boys' networks – male and female today – and their formal and informal sharing of information. *Secret Manoeuvres* provides the first collection of case studies in activist intelligence and corporate counterstrategy, depicting close cooperation between public and private forces.

NOT UNIQUE

With the many surprising twists in the story still unfolding, it is easy to forget that the Kennedy case is in no way unique. On the contrary: it is just the latest exposure in a long line of similar stories of intelligence operations in the UK and elsewhere, conducted either by the police or by private contractors. Several infiltrators have been exposed since; their stories show just how difficult it is to find out for whom they were working.

Just a few years ago, in 2007, someone calling himself Ken Tobias joined the protests of Plane Stupid, a loose network that takes action against the aviation industry's climate impact. He spent a year covertly gathering information on Plane Stupid, attending meetings and participating in protests. Tobias' infiltration was exposed when Plane Stupid fed the Oxford-educated 'activist' false information that found its way back to the aviation industry and journalists. When he was confronted, he denied being a spy, but failed to produce a passport or a photo ID. Following up his supposed Oxford connection, students shown a photograph recognized Ken as Toby Kendall, an Oriental Studies student from Wadham College. A quick Google search then revealed that Ken claimed to be an analyst at C2i International, a company advertising itself as 'Specialists in Security Crisis Risk Management' with 'aerospace' at the top of the client list. However, since BAA denied any contacts with C2i, it remains a mystery as to who paid for Ken Tobias' spying (Webster, 2008).

C2i was founded by Justin King, another example of an ex-police officer now working with his former colleagues. He had been a helicopter pilot in the Special Forces, and was trained to 'British police special operations standards' in surveillance and counter-espionage. The agents for the company – now called Lynceus Consulting Ltd – are 'hand-picked from Special Operations at New Scotland Yard', according to the company website.

After Plane Stupid Scotland had managed to close down Aberdeen Airport for a day in March 2009, several activists were approached for information on the group's activities. Among them was Tilly Gifford. She was offered cash in return by two men, of whom one claimed to be a detective constable, the other an assistant. Plane Stupid decided to expose the police's recruiting tactics in the media, using a spy-cam and recording conversations on a mobile phone. Gifford recorded almost three hours' worth of talks with the two men before she ended the contact.

In an attempt to identify the two spies, Gifford has been locked in a bureaucratic maze ever since. Strathclyde Police confirmed that the names of the two police officers did not feature on their databases at the time they approached her. After Gifford's request for the officer's date of commission in the Strathclyde force was refused, her case went all the way to the Scottish Information Commissioner, but she still does not know who the men were or even if they were police officers (Gifford, 2011). Her lawyer, Patrick Campbell, is not sure whether the covert operation is being run with Strathclyde police, or just using its name. Either way, he says, 'the methods employed are disturbing, and more worrying yet is the lack of any clearly identifiable body responsible for this' (Lewis, 2009).

As it turned out, Gifford was not the only one. More members of Plane Stupid in Scotland have been separately approached by what they thought to be plainclothes police in early 2009. The *Sunday Herald* reported that in addition to environmental protest groups, individuals protesting against the Faslane naval base on the Clyde were offered cash for intelligence. Some, arrested for protesting, were taken out of their cells for 'cosy chats' with two female MoD police officers. Others were approached by Strathclyde Police and had similar problems tracing the officers. However, Assistant Chief Constable George Hamilton confirmed the police action, saying: 'Officers from Strathclyde Police have been in contact with a number of protesters involved with the Plane Stupid protests, including Aberdeen Airport. The purpose of this has been to ensure any future protest activity is carried out within the law' (Edwards, 2009).

NOT WITHOUT PRECEDENTS

Outsourcing surveillance and employing spies to monitor public protest is not a new phenomenon, and the present cases should not be seen in isolation. The climate change movement has its roots in the direct action campaign against the Tory road-building programme in the early 1990s. The state employed a whole range of tactics against protestors, including surveillance, legal and physical intimidation, and disinformation. But contractors were also involved. For many the defining anti-roads campaign was that of Twyford Down, where the route for the M3 was bulldozed through the chalk downs of Hampshire. In what was believed to be the first time a government department, rather than the security services, had spied on environmental protestors, the Department for Transport hired the Brays Detective Agency from Southampton. Brays ran up a bill of £700,000 spying on the protestors for the government, a move condemned by the organizations involved, including Liberty. 'We believe that collecting information on people solely because they are protestors is a breach of their privacy under international law,' said Liberty (cited in Rowell, 1996: 347), in a statement that has ramifications for the Mark Kennedy case.

Another defining anti-roads battle was that over the Newbury bypass. Thames Valley police later admitted paying for someone to spy on the protestors. Further intelligence was collected on Newbury activists for the security company Group Four and for the police by Evelyn le Chêne, the security consultant featured in Chapter 7. At the time, it was known that security companies were in regular contact with Special Branch, which had started compiling a list of environmental and animal rights activists. Fed by Special Branch, the press started a disinformation campaign against the protestors, often labelling them as violent and extremist (Rowell, 1996). The road protests marked the beginning of political policing as we know it today in the UK.

SECRET MANOEUVRES

As with most of the other cases related in this book, exposing Mark Kennedy would not have been possible without the unremitting efforts of a few of the activists involved, their research and the cooperation of committed *Guardian* journalists.

The story is typical in terms of the damage done and the trail of ruined friendships and relationships Kennedy left behind. The feelings of loss and betrayal on both the political and the personal levels tend to hamper crucial investigations by those involved in an attempt to map out what happened in more detail, and to understand the impact and the full consequences of the operation. Several of the stories in this book relay similar experiences. The ongoing exposure in the media, with the undercover police officer flawlessly recasting his character to the duped victim, did not help those involved to acquire the necessary distance from their object of investigation.

The Mark Kennedy case is more than a sensational scoop. The focus on his person and his personality obscures the underlying development of corporate spying on activists. *Secret Manoeuvres in the Dark* aims to address this trend of conjunctions between the state and the corporate world aimed at suppressing the critical voices that are indispensable in a democratic society.

1
Introduction: The Waste Paper Man

This book is about intelligence and activism. It addresses the ways in which large corporations seek to manage and manipulate public protest, and it reveals the informal dimension of information-gathering hidden behind the politics and practices of public relations and reputation management. It brings together a set of case studies examining corporate espionage, based on exclusive access to previously confidential documented sources. Each story is systematically unravelled to map the different aspects of the spying process. Detailing chronology, agents and strategy, each case is analysed as an actual intelligence operation, creating a new perspective on the events.

To make a proper risk assessment, first and foremost a company needs to know what is coming its way. Nowadays business intelligence has gone beyond details about the world economy, overseas wars and news about the competition. It must also include an evaluation of the risks of becoming the target of campaigners, boycotters or net activists. Publicly available information is not sufficient for this task. Informal data, however obtained, are invaluable. Desirable information is not limited to concrete action scenarios but can be as broad (and vague) as long-term strategy discussions, impressions of the mood inside a campaigning group, connections between organizations, networking possibilities, funding details, and so on. As it turns out, corporate issue management is evolving into more than an occasional exercise of 'damage control'. *Secret Manoeuvres in the Dark* shows how intelligence gathering facilitates covert strategies designed to frustrate and undermine the critics of corporations.

Globalization and neoliberal politics provide the contexts for this investigation. The stories in this book highlight the privatization of intelligence, and the increasing value of information as capital in power relations. The research reveals increasingly blurred boundaries between public and private in secret operations, which, in my opinion, represents a potential danger to democracy. The importance of the issues at stake calls for a more active role for social scientists, investigative journalists, politicians and non-governmental organizations (NGOs), and others concerned about the role of public protest in society. This book seeks to broaden the understanding of the policies of large corporations in their pursuit of power, and their efforts to avoid public debate and silence critics.

BATTLING BIG BUSINESS

The first time I encountered a case of corporate spying was in 1994, when I was involved in exposing a spy called Paul Oosterbeek. At the time, I was working with buro Jansen & Janssen in the Netherlands, monitoring police and intelligence. Founded in 1984, the buro investigated the ways in which social movements were curtailed and undermined, by supporting people and groups who had become involuntarily targeted by the police, intelligence agencies or their corporate counterparts. Buro Jansen & Janssen has since developed a broader perspective on monitoring and intervening in debates on issues like repression and privacy. For me, the shift of focus included an increasing interest in private intelligence agencies.

The case of the Waste Paper Man serves as a typical illustration of the issues at stake. It shows how an individual infiltrating activist groups can work for long periods of time collecting information in several different ways. It also illustrates how the information gathered is processed into 'intelligence products' and used by clients to undermine activist groups. The case reveals how the intelligence can end up in the hands of the press. When used to incriminate activist groups, this can work to the advantage of prosecuting authorities.

Oosterbeek was active in groups I worked with, and had tried to get involved in a network of activists investigating intelligence-related topics in the Netherlands. Although several people did not trust him, it took years to act upon the plans to screen Oosterbeek's background. Only when several campaigners compared experiences was it discovered that he had used a variety of cover stories to hide his true identity. It emerged that Oosterbeek had created quite a network of information sources, and had worked for several activist organizations and NGOs. Going by the name of Marcel Paul Knotter, he posed as a volunteer and managed to stay under cover for more than seven years. He promoted his computer skills – rare in the late 1980s and the early 1990s – and offered to install software and set up computer databases. He would handle the input of contact addresses, new subscribers and possible sponsors into

IT systems, and also assisted with archiving work. To explain his background Oosterbeek claimed to be engaged in investigating large corporations and their involvement in apartheid, child labour or other human rights violations – tailoring the details of his cover to the needs of his audience. Meanwhile, he took advantage of his position to collect the groups' discarded paperwork, pretending he would sell it to a pulp mill and donate the proceeds to a charity project of the groups' choice. At the time of his exposure, no fewer than 30 organizations, ranging from small activist groups to big church-affiliated research foundations like Pax Christi, knew Oosterbeek as their 'Waste Paper Man'. In fact, Oosterbeek delivered boxes of faxed originals, photocopies and printouts to the offices of ABC, a small security consultancy owned by Peter Siebelt. There, behind a high wall and a sharp-spiked iron fence and under guard of security cameras, the data were processed. Every sheet was carefully combed for information, from financial data to the details of internal strategy discussions. The networks between organizations and the overlap in personnel were mapped, and the special interests of groups' individual members scrutinized. ABC thus compiled numerous files on activists and NGOs, supplementing them with information available from public sources such as magazines, annual reports and other records filed with the Chambers of Commerce, the Dutch equivalent of the UK Companies House (Lubbers, 1994a, 1994b, 1995a, 2002a).

What we had discovered was a new, cleaner form of *garbology* – which is detective slang for a particularly dirty kind of research. Activists and advocacy groups in the Netherlands knew their waste paper was being gathered, but not what it was being 'recycled' into: intelligence files for companies those groups were criticizing. Little did they realize how interesting their paperwork could be to the companies they campaigned against, to the tabloids, and occasionally even to the police, the public prosecutor and the secret service.

Siebelt maintained good contacts with the Dutch daily *De Telegraaf,* a newspaper with a reputation for mudslinging and activist bashing. Over the years, the paper frequently published articles based on internal documents that could be traced back to the Waste Paper Man (see, for instance, De Haas and Koolhoven, 1993a, 1993b; Koolhoven, 1996, 1997; de Haas and Sanders, 1997a, 1997b). In one case, an article randomly linking alleged networks of progressive organizations to terrorism served as the sole piece of evidence to launch a criminal investigation. The paper claimed to know that the Dutch secret service BVD identified this network as potentially terrorist (De Haas and Koolhoven, 1993b). Based on a small quote in a *De Telegraaf* article, freelance journalist Hans Krikke ended up as the main suspect of two bomb attacks aimed against authorities responsible for the contentious Dutch asylum policy. According to the police, Krikke 'doesn't rule out the practice of bomb attacks.' The police conveniently left out the rest of the quotation: 'in times of severe oppression, like World War II' – which qualifies the statement somewhat. Krikke and his colleague were arrested and their offices raided; it took months before the case was dismissed. The two received 230,000 in Dutch guilders (worth €136,000 or more than £11,000 today) in compensation, but their non-profit company did not survive (Lubbers, 1996, 1997a, 2002a).

The Waste Paper episode also demonstrates how inside information can give companies a strategic advantage. Used at the right moment, it can be an effective weapon. The formula industry, for instance, had acquired some internal correspondence of Wemos, a Dutch group monitoring pharmaceutical companies and the marketing of infant formula products in the Third World. In 1994, Wemos tried to convince the infant formula industry that it was not targeting specific companies. Dutch formula maker Nutricia (now Numico) produced a letter Wemos had sent to its partners in the Nestlé boycott campaign. The request for examples of companies circumventing the WHO code that restricts advertising infant formula in Third World countries was an example that proved otherwise in the eyes of the industry. Wemos had been a long-time client of the Waste Paper Man (Lubbers, 2002b).

Companies do not necessarily acknowledge that they have inside information on their critics. Using the information to anticipate future actions can be sufficient. In 1990, the Clean Clothes Campaign started a protest action against the use of child labour by clothing chain C&A. Customers were encouraged to ask shop assistants where their clothes had been manufactured. No sooner had the campaign begun than C&A came out with printed fact-sheets, and a booklet explaining the company's CSR policy. Until then, C&A had been known as a closed, family-run company that never even published annual reports – and did not do so until 2005 (van der Hoff, 2006; NDH, 2006). Its rapid response to the Clean Clothes Campaign was remarkable. In fact, Oosterbeek had joined the Clean Clothes Campaign as a regular volunteer just before the campaign was launched. Oosterbeek's inside information permitted C&A to anticipate and facilitate the rapid response.

The exposure of the Waste Paper Man revealed that there is a market for informal information about activists. It brings up questions about the kinds of information required, how this intelligence is gathered and how it may be used in subsequent strategizing. This book seeks to answer these questions by presenting a set of detailed well-sourced case studies. To address the blind spots in investigating corporate spying I will outline a specific field of research best described as *activist intelligence*, focused on the gathering of information, the methods used and the people professionally involved. It also includes the processing of the information into intelligence, and the strategic planning by corporations to make use of it: the *covert corporate strategy*.

The Impact of Infiltration

My commitment to do the research for this book originates from my work with buro Jansen & Janssen. Investigating cases of infiltration by either the state or private spies hired by corporations, I discovered the impact of such intrusions for the groups involved. The result, as explained below, was a quest for a wider and deeper understanding of what was behind the stories I encountered.

Buro Jansen & Janssen was rooted in the same network as the movements it sought to support. Although this made us a trusted party, our investigations were sometimes hampered by differences of opinion about the implications of infiltration, and the need for security awareness. Exposing stories was part of the Jansen & Janssen strategy, challenging the power of the responsible authorities. However, this strategy was not always seen as being in the best interests of the people involved. Some of the infiltrated groups preferred to avoid publicity, afraid that it would affect the perceived trustworthiness and reliability of their work.

A group that has experienced infiltration often wants to return to business as usual sooner rather than later. Dealing with surveillance and infiltration is not part of their core activities; it is often regarded as a waste of time and contrary to the aims of the group. It can also be uncomfortable, even painful, as it involves profound breaches of trust. Feelings of unease at the personal level are matched with fears that the effects of exposure are counterproductive for the group at the organizational level. To have their experiences with spying and infiltration made public could suggest that they had been careless or sloppy with security; it could keep possible allies or whistleblowers from sharing crucial information. For similar reasons, groups often refrain from taking legal action. Of course, in the absence of a legal framework, the option to file a complaint or to report a crime is rare. The remote chance of success fuels the reluctance to allocate money and energy to activities regarded as counterproductive for the organization.

A clear conflict of interest emerged that sometimes hindered cooperation in investigations. While groups had understandable reasons not to go public, sometimes Jansen & Janssen's intervention was regarded as yet another disturbance. In order to help a group understand what had taken place and what it meant, and to advise them how to prevent it from happening again, an in-depth investigation of each case of infiltration was required. Exposing well-documented cases seemed consistent as a next step. Instead of acknowledging the existence of conflicting interests, the problems between an activist group and buro Jansen & Janssen were occasionally dealt with as irritations on the personal level, or – worse – as political differences.

During my time with buro Jansen & Janssen, I also worked as a consultant for NGOs to raise security awareness. The work involved screening organizations on a variety of levels, ranging from their access control to personnel management and recruitment policies, using methods such as in-depth interviews covering different parts of the organization. However, plans to raise security awareness within these groups proved to be difficult to put into practice. For many activist groups and NGOs, openness and inclusivity are highly respected principles, as the need for new members is an essential condition for survival. Security measures are often viewed as superfluous or counterproductive.

In a broader context, these experiences show that infiltration as a strategy to undermine corporate critics has damaging effects regardless of the sensitivity of the information gathered. Essentially, the fear of being publicly associated with infiltration is harmful in itself. At the personal level, people are hurt, while at the organizational level the work of the groups is disrupted. The fear of press coverage keeps people from making a serious assessment of the actual damage of an information-gathering operation. Moreover, the perception of publicity as counterproductive leads to a form of self-censorship. The reluctance to expose detailed findings implies abandoning the opportunity – waiving the right – to hold corporations accountable for their practices of abusing power. Few political organizations that have been the victims of infiltration are willing to take official action that might disclose the extent of the operation. Patrice Brodeur of the University of Montréal, who studied the policing of political activities, confirms this. From 1979 to 1981, he was involved in the Keable inquiry into police wrongdoing in Québec, and he concluded that for political groups, revelations about the extent of infiltration are 'liable to drastically reduce their credibility in the eyes of other movements and their membership' (Brodeur, 1983: 510). Ironically, he argues, this makes the victims partners in secrecy with the police, politicians, the courts and the press (ibid.). The police, well aware of this reluctance to expose experiences, deliberately spread rumours of infiltration to destabilize political groups.

The issues that arise regarding the exposure of cases of infiltration illustrate the chilling effects of covert corporate strategy. The fear of being associated with espionage keeps the groups involved from addressing the issue in a public debate. This indicates a need for evidence-based research, as substantiation is essential on the road towards comprehending the meaning and effects of infiltration and espionage. Furthermore, in order to comprehend the significance and the implications of this issue, corporate spying needs to be understood in the broader context of corporate strategy.

Undercover Operations

To explain the dangers of infiltration and espionage, only strong arguments and evidence will persuade people to consider any form of security. To substantiate my arguments, I felt the need to put my experiences and knowledge into context. I set out to understand the broad range of corporate strategies for dealing with critics. A key event in this was the 1999 Next 5 Minutes conference in Amsterdam, where I brought together experts in the field, mostly people who identify themselves as researchers, activists and freelance journalists. The panel discussion on corporate counterstrategies was the beginning of a network, which eventually resulted in the book *Battling Big Business, Countering Greenwash, Infiltration and other Forms of Corporate Bullying* (Lubbers (ed.), 2002a) and the founding of *SpinWatch.org* in 2004.

Battling Big Business was inspired by the work of Naomi Klein (2000), who also wrote the preface to the book. Her own book, *No Logo*, investigated how corporations experienced growing pressure from their critics over the last few decades. In an effort to manage the adverse publicity their environmental, labour and consumer records so often attract, many giant corporations looked for new strategies to counter the activities of their opponents. Klein identified two important developments that characterize the current timeframe. Today, brand identity and corporate image are key to a corporation's value, over and above its actual products or services. The more companies shift towards being all about brand identity, the more vulnerable they are to attacks on this image. At the same time, corporations are becoming less restricted by national laws or unilateral treaties. In some cases, they are more powerful than governments, and must expect to be held to account in the same way (Klein, 2002). Consumers are demanding sustainability, accountability and transparency. Losing control in the media arena as a result of activist pressure has become a public relations nightmare for the modern multinational. The industry learned that lesson the hard way. Shell's lost battle over Brent Spar in 1995 and the human rights situation in Nigeria haunt the oil company to the present day. These cases have become landmarks in the field of corporate responsibility. Likewise, Monsanto gained damaging notoriety for its underestimation of European resistance to the introduction of genetically engineered products.

The power of spin cannot easily protect big business's growing vulnerability. This was the starting point of *Battling Big Business*. Public relations (PR) departments struggle to deal with today's complicated stakeholder demands. Accordingly, reputation management now includes the gradual embrace of mostly voluntary and non-binding corporate social responsibility (CSR) guidelines. This embrace is often predicated on the idea that repositioning the corporation via PR is sufficient, suggesting an unwillingness to establish a more substantive corporate accountability regime.

Companies under fire are in need of other strategies to counter their critics. They attempt to influence political processes by means of a variety of tactics. It is useful to conceive of these as public and open on the one hand, and secretive and covert on the other. The former encompass marketing communications, CSR and PR including maintaining stakeholder relations with, for instance, investors, employees or specific communities. The latter includes lobbying, regulation and covert activities. The past two decades have witnessed the development of a wide range of such tactics. *Battling Big Business* discussed overt strategy such as PR, greenwash and sponsorship. It showed that dialogues and partnerships with NGOs are often used to separate the more moderate organizations from their radical counterparts, in an attempt to undermine cooperation and solidarity. The book also explored the more covert tactics, such as hiring specialized PR consultants to fight activists on all fronts, corporate lobbying behind the scenes, the use of libel laws to silence critics (including scholars) and think-tanks influencing decision-making processes in both the USA and the European Union. Additionally, *Battling Big Business* contained a section on undercover operations, examining spying and infiltration as a strategy to undermine the work of activist groups.

It was not until I had finished editing the book that I realized that this classification was slightly inaccurate. Corporate spying and infiltration should not be considered as *just* another set of counterstrategies, grouped alongside greenwash or lobbying. Corporate spying and infiltration *can* be used as such, but there is more to it. Spying also involves the gathering of intelligence that *precedes* the development of corporate counterstrategy. Or – vice versa – a corporation does not spy on its critics just to know what is going on: it does so to be prepared and to defend itself. The connection between surveillance and the gathering of intelligence on the one hand, and subsequent corporate strategy on the other, is crucial. This connection constitutes the point of departure for this book.

Essentially, in *Battling Big Business* I explored the *broad range* of possible corporate counterstrategy. The book before you now is a more strictly focused *in-depth* investigation into intelligence gathering on activist groups and the covert strategy that corporations use to undermine criticism. The underlying question is how such counter-strategies function in safeguarding the interests of large corporations in the context of a globalizing world. Consequently, research into this aspect of corporate power needs to be situated within the wider context of globalization, governance and democracy.

SECRET MANOEUVRES IN THE DARK

Confidential sources are the starting point for this book. My research material included notes taken by infiltrators after each undercover operation, surveillance reports and communications between private intelligence agencies and their clients. Starting from this basic level provides an extraordinary insider view of the methods and routines of private investigators. The case studies describe how the agents collect information, what kinds of detail are considered important and how the results are presented to the client companies. Further research shows how the intelligence is processed and used in proactive strategies – in other words, how corporations use the information and act upon the perceived threats. The studies examine why even publicly available information about campaigning groups can be of interest to their opponents. They also demonstrate how infiltrators work their way into the groups, and how they manipulate operations once they have gained a group's trust.

Another aspect of importance highlighted in the case studies is the impact of corporate spying and covert strategies on the targeted groups and on individuals. Chapter 3 includes examples of attempts to break the boycotts against Nestlé and Shell by driving a wedge between the moderate and the more radical members of coalitions. Members of church groups, for instance, felt deceived after they found out that the dialogue set up with the company turned out to be part of a strategy to divide and rule. The McSpy story in Chapter 4 shows the overkill effect of several infiltrators of an activist group with a relatively small membership. Chapter 5 on cybersurveillance has an example of people who lost their jobs after an online monitoring agency identified them as the initiators of a so-called 'sick-out' – flight attendants disrupting the Christmas traffic in the United States in an ongoing conflict about wages. And two Californian scientists had trouble gaining tenure after an online campaign damaged their professional reputation. As it turned out, Monsanto and its viral campaign agency had set up digital identities merely to attack them because of their research critical of genetic engineering.

When the *Sunday Times* exposed spy files composed for arms manufacturer BAe, the Campaign against Arms Trade (CAAT) had the difficult task of finding out who was the mole. Chapter 7 reveals the difficulties of such research, and the problems people within CAAT had in accepting that one of the core activists was a spy.

Zooming in on the agencies hired by corporations to protect their reputation reveals another important aspect of the field of activist intelligence and covert corporate strategy. The consultants and private investigators share a background of former careers with the police, intelligence services or the military, and see this as a selling point in their present line of business. To quote the former MI6 agent who founded Hakluyt, the agency featured in Chapter 6: 'the idea was to do for industry what we had done for the government' (Overell, 2000).

Intelligence for the Market

The blurring boundaries between public and private spying point to a growing field of 'grey intelligence' where corporate spies take care of the interests of big business. This is nothing new, as Chapter 2 makes clear. Private policing has a long history, starting with the notorious Pinkerton's in the United States, while the link between propaganda and covert action goes back to the beginning of the twentieth century, with people such as John Hill (later Hill & Knowlton) amplifying the voice of business ever since. In the UK, the Economic League was founded around the same time against a similar background, and continued its activities until very recently.

The McSpy story confirms close cooperation between McDonald's security department, private investigators and Special Branch in an operation set up to find out who was responsible for leafleting branches of the fast food chain. This cooperation raises several questions. Was it aimed only at gathering evidence to stop the campaign against the fast food company? Or did Special Branch use the private investigators to get closer to animal right activists?

After the *Sunday Times* exposed Evelyn le Chêne for spying on CAAT, BAe hired someone else to collect information. After he got hung out to dry as well, it turned out that they had a common background in conservative circles, with mutual acquaintances and friends in intelligence circles. Further research revealed that Le Chêne had a long history in intelligence and covert operations going back to the Cold War. She headed a propaganda organization linked to NATO and the CIA aimed at fuelling fears of the dangers of communism, and she herself was actively involved in covert actions in Southern Africa directed against the ANC, and in supporting Jonas Savimbi. After the end of the Cold War, Le Chêne increasingly focused on activists and campaigners – although, in her worldview, this was more a matter of continuity than of a major change.

This background sketch adds several layers to the issues discussed in *Secret Manoeuvres*. It links corporate intelligence more closely to a deeply conservative and capitalist ideology aimed at keeping critical voices down, at undermining protest and resistance, both with 'propaganda' and covert action, and at conserving the status quo. It shows us a glimpse of today's old boys' network, the blurring boundaries between intelligence and its privatized branches, as a distinct aspect of globalization and neoliberalism wherein the state provides the optimum conditions for business and capital to accumulate.

History of the Present

Research into activist intelligence and covert corporate strategy is almost by definition historical, for the simple reason that ongoing operations are hardly ever exposed. Cases of corporate spying are typically concealed beneath a cloak of secrecy. Source material is difficult to access. The passing of time sometimes makes discovery slightly easier, with political and personal sensibilities losing their significance little by little. Most of the case studies researched for this book would not have been revealed but for the persistent investigations of activists targeted by corporations, through complicated and lengthy court cases, and with the help of dedicated investigative journalists and their whistleblowers.

This work can, however, be described as a 'history of the present'. My concern is both archival and analytical. As the field of study is new, there is a need for well-sourced case studies to describe and outline the matters at stake. However, as Garland (2000: 2) put it, the history proposed is 'not motivated by a historical concern to understand the past, but by a critical concern to come to terms with the present'. The point is to use the history to rethink the present. But the practices of activist intelligence and covert corporate strategy need to be described and mapped first, to understand how this field is currently constituted and situated between other fields of study. Apart from that, the fact that most of the case studies in this book took place several years ago, and some in the 1970s, does not mean the subject is out of date – on the contrary, as the Mark Kennedy case discussed in the Preface shows.

By mapping various cases of covert corporate strategy, in both the past and present, at several locations in Europe and the US and in the real word as well as on the internet, *Secret Manoeuvres* details at least some of the different ways in which activist groups are infiltrated, undermined and contained. The main criterion for the selection of case studies was the availability of original source material, which allows the research to go beyond the publicly known version of the various cases. The documents include surveillance reports and intelligence assessments, court transcripts of private investigators' evidence, and internal strategy plans prepared by specialist consultants for large corporations targeted by boycott campaigns.

The choice of case studies was influenced by the desire to cover as much of the playing field as possible. Several cases have come to light in recent years; to initiate more investigations was – unfortunately –

beyond the scope of the project (see e.g. Ridgeway, 2008; Schlosser, 2008). Not included for similar reasons are cases that have already been extensively documented by other investigative journalists, researchers, activists and academics. *Secret Manoeuvres* is situated in a tradition of existing work on related issues (for example, Stauber and Rampton, 1995, 1998, 2001, 2003, 2004, 2006; Helvarg, 1994; Rowell, 1996, 2003; Beder, 1997; Dinan and Miller, 2007; Miller and Dinan, 2008; Hager and Burton, 1999; Committee on Interior and Insular Affairs, 1992, O'Donnell, 2002).

The covert strategies discussed here are among the strategies used in the wealthy countries of the Western world. Whether they are applied elsewhere in the world is beyond the current focus (for work on corporate strategy that includes corporate use of armed force, torture, rape, kidnap or even murder, see Swanson, 2002; Drohan, 2003; Martens and Schürkes, 2004; redflags.info, 2008). That said, the intelligence gathered from groups in Europe and Northern America, may include information about people involved in resisting or opposing the work of TNCs in the South. Such information may have serious consequences in countries where people are killed for taking part in protest actions. An example of such a link is now being investigated in court, and discussed in Chapter 3. Nestlé had the Swiss chapter of Attac infiltrated in 2003–4 (Losa and Ceppi, 2008). One of the activities of Attac is supporting people in their struggle against Nestlé in Colombia. Early in 2005, Luciano Enrique Romero was brutally murdered shortly after he filed a wrongful termination lawsuit against the company over there. His widow joined a lawsuit against Nestlé in the US; the company is charged with acting in complicity with the paramilitary (Bussey, 2006). A court case could reveal whether there are connections between the infiltration in Switzerland and the murder in Colombia.

PR, Propaganda and Issue Management

The stories related in this book are each typical examples of public relations, unless, however, one is prepared to understand PR and promotion as 'all the activities which corporations engage in to exert influence' (Miller and Dinan, 2003: 194). Nevertheless, the term 'public relations' is misleading. 'An essential characteristic of corporate PR – or corporate propaganda, as it used to be called – is that it is concealed' (Richter, 2001: 146). In this context, it is all the more important to remember, 'public relations is also the art of camouflage and deception' (Kunczik, 1990: 1). The growth of corporate-led globalization has prompted the fine-tuning of corporate communication and its more widespread use with the aim of influencing international politics in favour of corporations. If PR can also be seen as the sum of political activities of corporations, one would expect it to include strategies to counter their critics. However, covert action is a topic that many corporations prefer to avoid, while academic research does not address it either. The only place where such counterstrategy is sometimes discussed is under the generic category of *issue management* (IM). W. Howard Chase coined the term in 1977. An influential consultant since the 1950s (he died in 2003), he recommended a new kind of corporate communication response to the critics of business activities who were gaining influence in the 1960s and 1970s. His *Issue Management Council* uses a very broad characterization: 'Think of an issue as a gap between your actions and stakeholder expectations. Issue management is the process used to close that gap' (Crane, 1977). Agreeing on a more detailed definition of this form of corporate communication and strategy is difficult. Heath (1997) devoted a lengthy chapter to the definitional question, assessing 20 years of available literature, starting in the late 1970s. He quoted Miller (1987) to summarize the lack of consensus:

> Issue management is not quite public relations. Neither is it government relations, nor public affairs, nor lobbying, nor crisis management, nor futurism, nor strategic planning. It embraces all of these disciplines and maybe a few more. (Heath, 1997: 12)

PR and IM both grew out of the same reality and recognition of the necessity for corporations to defend themselves – currently against 'protest groups who gain public support by striking public chords'. While acknowledging the importance of IM, many experts on PR do not elaborate on how information on activists, their ideas and surroundings should be gathered, how it should be assessed and what – if any – action taken. Given the emphasis on 'proactive, constructive problem–solving' as preferable to 'combat', the lack of scholarly attention to the information-gathering phase is remarkable.

> To avoid unpleasant surprises, organisations should scan, monitor and track external forces. […] These forces should be analysed in terms of their effects on an organisation's image, profit and ability to act. Based on that analysis, an organisation's policy must be

developed, strategy planned, and action implemented. (Baskin, Aronoff and Lattimore, 1997: 80)

But what that 'action' implies is not discussed in any further detail. Renfro is one of the few authors to mention the intelligence character of IM.

> With the focus on the intelligence aspects, issue management consists of at least four, interlocked stages: (1) scanning for emerging issues, (2) researching, analysing, and forecasting the issues, (3) prioritising the many issues identified by the scanning and research stages, and (4) developing strategies and issue operation (or action) plans. (Renfro, 1993: 64)

Heath explains that issue management should track the coalescence of individuals and unorganized publics into organized activists. The aim would be to provide insight into how and where corporations 'can constructively intervene to reduce the strain that motivates activism' (Heath, 1997: 165).

The various authors elide the question of intelligence-gathering as such. While emphasizing the importance to corporations of proactively managing public opinion at formative stages, they do not elaborate on corresponding covert corporate strategy. Confronted with matters that might raise wide discussion and scrutiny, private corporations under fire often decide to deal with those matters in secret. Such secrecy might be understandable from a corporate point of view; however, the studied silence about IM in advanced industrial societies is disconcerting. Moreover, it seems to overlap with a similar silence about covert action in intelligence studies, as will be detailed below. The concluding chapter addresses the dangers of secrecy in governance more in general.

In an attempt to get rid of vague and evading language, Richter (2001: 146) proposed abandoning the term 'issue management' in favour of 'engineering of consent' (as a variation on the phrase manufacturing consent, coined by Chomsky and Herman in 1988). Such strategy, typically concealed, usually has three, sometimes overlapping, components, she said:

- intelligence gathering and an assessment of the sociopolitical climate in which the particular company is operating;

- attempts to manipulate public debates in a direction favourable to the company; and
- attempts to exclude what the industry perceives as diverging or antagonistic voices from the public debate. (Richter, 1998: 5)

But like Renfro, Richter outlines a typical intelligence operation here, from the beginning to the end. That is why, although the aim might be the engineering of consent, I would rather describe this specific subject as activist intelligence and covert corporate strategy, as explained above.

In his work on the risk society, Ulrich Beck explored issues of agenda setting and engineering of consent in a manner that is more pertinent to the subject of this book. The issues are, Beck argues, who gets to decide, and on the basis of which legally defined norms of liability and proof, what counts as a 'risk', who counts as the 'responsible party' and who therefore, is to pay if the worst comes to the worst? An important aspect of corporate PR is the promotion of the policies of rational and responsible leaders versus the short-term goals of 'emotional' protesters. Directors of multinational corporations, politicians and governments tend to consider conflicts over risks – such as protests against oil drillings, child labour or genetically modified food – as 'single-issue' affairs. In weighing environmental costs against economic growth, they consider themselves to be the ones to see the bigger picture and to reach a 'rational' view (Beck, 2005: 105–6).

Secret Manoeuvres examines several specific aspects of the connection between risk and power, in order to, as Beck put it, 'get some indication how changes in the power relation of definition [...] can influence the political dynamic of risk conflicts' (ibid.: 106). The gathering of intelligence about campaigning groups is an indicator of what the corporation employing the investigators considers as a risk, and how the corporation interprets the balances of power. Subsequent covert corporate strategy can be understood as an attempt to determine the definition of what is best for society as a whole.

INFORMATION WARS

Those who have power also have capital and vice versa, as Marx and Engels pointed out in 1848. Among the first to identify the growing importance of information as a new form of capital were Alvin and Heidi Toffler. In their book *Power Shift* (1990), the Tofflers[2] argued that the very nature of power was changing. Throughout history, power has often shifted from one group to another; however, in the 1990s, the *dominant form* of power was changing. During the Industrial Revolution, power shifted from nobility acting primarily through violence to industrialists and financiers acting through wealth (as is further detailed in Chapter 2). A new wave of shifting power is taking place, with wealth being overtaken by knowledge. Even without accepting that information is now the most important form of capital, the relevance of the Tofflers' ideas is evident. For management today, whether in the financial world or public bureaucracy, in the retail trade or manufacturing, information is an important asset. Companies need information on clients, competitors, consumers, workers, regulators and others. They need information for market research, product adaptation, marketing, control of the production process, restructuring of the organization, for protection against economic espionage or internal fraud. In what the Tofflers named *The Third Wave* (1980), they saw the rise of a new branch dedicated to the collection and selling of information (marketing bureaus, head hunters, scientific and other research bureaus). Such information has economic value. The information society also changes the nature of military conflict. As Cronin and Crawford (1999: 64) summed up, the Tofflers anticipated 'the growing significance of economic warfare as, in some instances, a replacement for, and in others, a complement to, conventional forms of international aggression'. Instead of arms stockpiling and force augmentation, the focus today has shifted to the management of intangible assets such as know-how, techno-economic intelligence and foresight (of course, the Tofflers were writing before the Gulf war, the Balkan conflicts, before 9/11, the war in Afghanistan and the invasion of Iraq). In this framework, the exploitation of intelligence becomes a multiplier of power. In 1990, they predicted that 'as the stakes rise in global trading rivalries, intelligence rivalries will heat up in parallel' (Toffler, 1990: 313). Consequently, the Tofflers concluded that 'the development of strategic intelligence capability, both offensive and defensive, will be a sine qua non of successful organisation, military and market, in the next millennium' (Cronin and Crawford, 1999: 64).

It is in this context that the Tofflers speak of information wars. They predicted growing 'total info wars' within and between the public and the private sector about the access to data and the possibility of connecting disparate databases. The informatization of our society is not just about social and economic changes, but also about a major power-shift. The financialization of society in the past two decades is built on this shift, and substantiates the increased importance of information. He (or she) who controls and regulates information will be able to consolidate his political, commercial and/or organizational position (Toffler, 1990: 129). Among other things this would – and this is of specific interest for this book – invoke a growing fusion between the public and the private sector in intelligence. 'The line between public and private espionage will continue to blur' (ibid.: 312). As multinational corporations proliferate, many grow their own private intelligence networks – 'para-CIAs' – as the Tofflers called them. Because these business firms hire former spies and analysts from the ranks of government, the informal links with government intelligence increase. 'Such incestuous relationships will multiply as a consequence of the restructuring of world business now taking place, which is leading to complex cross-national business alliances' (ibid.: 313). This shift in power, from public to private, can be seen as an aspect of globalization and the changing position of transnational companies (TNCs) in the world, and constitutes the setting against which the case studies in this book should be understood.

As the Tofflers predicted, multinational corporations have developed their own private intelligence networks, hiring former spies and analysts from the ranks of government. This complex network of formal state and private structures and processes would benefit from network analysis. In order to stimulate research into these phenomena, Dutch scholar Hoogenboom (2006: 373) introduced the concept of *grey intelligence*:

> 'Grey' here refers to the blurred boundaries between public and private spheres, and to the increasing importance of private, 'informal' initiatives and provisions in the gathering, circulation and distribution of intelligence.

Hoogenboom built on his earlier concept of 'grey policing' (1994), developed to analyse the field of the legal use of coercion no longer exclusively in the hands of state authorities. State monopoly is replaced by an informal information market with a wide variety of private entrepreneurs. Their primary aim is loss prevention: the gathering of intelligence is supposed to minimise damage for the client company. As mentioned above, the Tofflers also pointed to business espionage as a growing force, in addition to the more legitimate ways of gathering information. Meanwhile, the changing position of the TNC in the globalizing world and the accumulating risks to reputation increase the corporate demand for intelligence on activists and campaigners. However, it would be too easy to read such developments in an instrumental way only. In order to move beyond the dominant academic focus of policy by proxy, O'Reilly and Ellison re-introduce the concept of 'high policing'. The concept originates in the French Absolutist state, and for Brodeur (1983) it involves the promotion of state authority. But O'Reilly and Ellison (2006: 641) detach it from its roots in the public domain and propose 'a more complex relationship of obfuscation whereby both public and private high policing actors cross-permeate and coalesce in the pursuit of symbiotic state and corporate objectives'. They use high policing to reflect the 'more complex contemporary security field in which dominant interests within corporate power structures, as well as in state ones, are protected' (Johnston, 2007: 15, fn.18).

The movement towards privatizing government work has created more opportunities for coordinated groups of individuals to take over public policy agendas in pursuit of their own interests. Janine Wedel introduced the terms 'flex groups' and 'flex power' to describe how Washington's neoconservatives differ from other influential individuals passing through the revolving door, serving serially in government and the private sector. The difference shows in their political goal, which is increasing their influence. Operating on both sides of the door, 'they are continually working to further the shared agenda *of the group*' (Wedel, 2004b, emphasis in the original; see also Wedel, 2009). Flex groups are in fact a living example of why labels such as 'conflict of interests' no longer suffice.

Wedel emphasizes their skill at both relaxing the government's rules of accountability and businesses' codes of competition, and at conflating state and private interests.

> A flex group can use the ambiguity of its members' roles to its advantage, making their activities difficult to define, let alone monitor. In this lies the potential for corruption or abuse of power. Yet our system of government today is providing increasing opportunities for such groups to arise. (ibid.)

In security governance the network concept is, as yet, under-theorized. Johnston emphasizes the need to analyse the functioning of security networks, to map the nodes and analyse the dynamics. There is a tendency, he says, among those writing about both domestic and transnational commercial security to take this for granted. It is necessary to go beyond 'what we know about the operation of the "old–boys" network (linking public police and private security) and the "old–spies" network (linking state and commercial security services)' (Johnston, 2007: 21). Flex groups and flex power seem useful concepts to understand the dynamics of high policing and corporate intelligence.

> By examining relationships among formal and informal institutions, organisations and individuals, [social network analysis] is ideally suited to map mixes of organisational forms, the changing, overlapping and multiple roles that actors within them may play and the ambiguities surrounding them. (Wedel, 2004a: 220)

All in all, intelligence should never be studied as an isolated activity (Gill, 2009: 83). It is an integral part of government, or rather governance, and it has a 'peculiarly intimate relation to political power' (Cawthra and Luckham, 2003: 305). 'Much of the study of intelligence concerns the relationship between power and knowledge, or rather', as Scott and Jackson (2004a: 150) point out, 'the relationship between certain kinds of power and certain kinds of knowledge'. Dover (2007: 19–20) also emphasizes the power issue when posing the question of whether corporate intelligence can be included in general definitions of intelligence activity:

> The central question within intelligence studies should not be merely the production of knowledge, but the power context in which it is produced, and what the information is used for. [The criteria would be] the structural advantage of the knowledge producer over the surveyed, and the ends to which the intelligence product has been used.

Corporate control of intelligence (to be understood as a specific form of knowledge) serves as a guiding tool for action, to shape a response to public protest, or to prepare lobbying strategies, for instance, or in the field of covert action. Ultimately, in the Tofflers' words, knowledge is used as an instrument of power.

SPYING AND RESISTANCE

A useful framework to study activist intelligence and covert corporate strategy can be found in the work of Peter Gill. He proposed some core concepts (which are applicable well beyond Anglo-American intelligence studies): *surveillance, power, knowledge, secrecy, and resistance* (Gill, 2009: 85).

Surveillance relates to the gathering and storing of information as well as to the supervision of people's behaviour. In other words, it is concerned with the relationship between knowledge and power. It is not a linear relationship, Gill warns; 'sometimes "knowledge is power" while at other times knowledge may inform the exercise of power. Yet, as we have seen in the case of Iraq, at other times power may determine what is "knowledge"' (ibid.).

Secrecy distinguishes intelligence structures and processes from many other aspects of governance. It applies to power, according to Gill, because some actions make sense only with an element of surprise. But more often, actions are carried out in secret because of their controversial character. The secrecy helps to avoid or disguise responsibility, involvement is often 'plausibly denied' (ibid.) – as will be confirmed in most of the stories in this book.

Gill's work is interesting for his unorthodox approach to intelligence, which differs from the authors in the more traditional state-related field of international relations policy (see, for instance, Kent, 1946; Laqueur, 1985; Shulsky and Schmitt, 2001). Instead of the restricted perspective of theory *for* intelligence, his research – and mine – underlines the need to develop theory *of* intelligence (ibid.: 212). While most efforts to find a proper definition of intelligence include a reference to how 'gathered information' transforms into 'intelligence' – they fail to mention a crucial part of the intelligence process. Remarkably enough, the step that connects intelligence to actual strategy seems to be absent in most suggested definitions. Scholars have frequently ignored covert action in their analyses of intelligence (Scott and Jackson, 2004a: 142; see also Schlesinger, 1977; Rositzke, 1977). The fact that this step is not mentioned relates to the reluctance to acknowledge this part of intelligence work, and to the avoidance of addressing covert action – just as most management literature fails to go into the details of issue management.

Gill's conceptual framework relates to his recent attempt to define intelligence, which explicitly includes action; he stresses that a full understanding of intelligence without acknowledging the integral connection with action is impossible. Furthermore, Gill and Phythian have added a practical description of 'covert action' in their latest work (2006: 102):

Covert action is a kind of institutionalised hypocrisy in which ethics and the rule of law are subjugated to the achievement of short-time political gains, when the costs are borne by some national or political 'other'. In the long term, of course, such policies may come back to haunt the perpetrators.

The connection between surveillance and the gathering of intelligence on the one hand and the subsequent corporate strategy and covert action on the other, is crucial – and not just in this book. Action is an essential element in any conceptual framework of intelligence.

The case studies in this book present examples of infiltration and expose secret documents. The research goes beyond verifying the original sources and profiling the private investigators and their respective clients. The aim is to understand how spying or infiltration is used as a tactic to gather intelligence as well as to undermine the targeted groups. *Secret Manoeuvres* aims to provide an oversight of the various techniques used. The case studies illustrate the different kinds of information they were interested in, and how the intelligence informed strategy to damage the work of activist groups and other corporate critics.

Analysing the case studies within Gill's framework allows answers to the central question of this book. Should the cases of infiltration be recognized as covert corporate strategy in relation to the exercise of power? Once we understand the workings of activist intelligence within the framework of surveillance, power, knowledge, and secrecy, we can start to appreciate the value and the necessity of the last – and rather underdeveloped – part of the framework: resistance.

2
Covert Corporate Strategy in the Past

Modern corporations exist to make profit, and to promote and defend their core interests, while modern states seem to be organized to suit the demands of business – in part, at least. This symbiotic relationship has a long history, as is shown below in two examples of corporate strategy and political tactics in the USA and the UK. Of course, the targets of corporate strategy have changed, and the use of armed force has diminished, but there are similarities between the strategies and tactics used then and now.

At the end of the nineteenth century, the United States saw agencies like the notorious Pinkerton's provide armed guards and strikebreakers to deal with social unrest. Later, during the Depression and the New Deal reforms in the 1920s and 1930s, employers hired PR professionals to defend the need for violent confrontations and for covert operations such as espionage and infiltration.

In the UK, the government as well as organizations of employers had learned to appreciate the value of propaganda and internal surveillance during the First World War. They continued to use such practices because they were afraid of revolutionary outbreaks in the early 1920s. The Economic League (discussed below) was a long-running project set up by British industrialists to defend corporate interests. This organization spanned most of the twentieth century and existed until it was officially disbanded in the mid-1990s. Recent discoveries revealed that people involved in the Economic League continued their blacklisting work until early 2009.

The cooperation between the state and the private sector in gathering information about people potentially posing a risk to the stability of society or of the economy can be dated back to the beginning of the Industrial Revolution. This supports the hypothesis that public and private intelligence derive from the same set of circumstances and represent the same social practice divided into distinct areas of responsibility.

THE UNITED STATES: THE VOICE OF BUSINESS

At the end of the nineteenth century, the steel industry was a rapidly growing sector of the economy in the United States. Early industrialization and the expanding railroads required growing supplies of steel and associated products. Steel factories set up in smaller towns often became the largest local employer, with a corresponding influence on local affairs. On a national level, the steel industry was a powerful force in the economy. Most employers in the steel industry fiercely denied workers their rights, and outbreaks of worker militancy brought forth a varied corporate reaction. When threats, armed guards and violent confrontations did not stop workers from asserting collective rights, American corporations sought strategies that were more sophisticated. Propaganda and covert operations were used in conjunction with violence. Workers responded creatively to these onslaughts. Just as modern social movement organizations have developed a variety of responses to corporate covert action, they developed ways to take on strikebreakers and to make it difficult for spying to be effective.

In the developments discussed below, the Memorial Day Massacre in 1937, a violent confrontation that left ten people dead on the street, became a turning point. The US Congress quickly set up a committee to investigate the role played by industry in undermining and attacking organized labour. Chaired by Senator Robert La Follette, this subcommittee of the Education and Labor Committee held an impressive series of hearings over the course of five years to question those involved. This inquiry inspired several authors to write detailed accounts of what had happened (Silverberg, 1941; Tedlow, 1976; Auerbach, 1966; Miller, 1999; Norwood, 2002; Smith, 2003). The Committee specified four strategies that were used to frustrate the organization of labour: espionage, strikebreaking, industrial munitions, and private police.

The following account provides a description of these strategies and the accompanying use of propaganda around the turn of the last century.

Union Busting

Perhaps the best-known exponent of union-busting and strikebreaking is Allan Pinkerton. A Scottish immigrant in the United States, he moved from providing watchmen for the protection of banks and merchants to supplying guards for labour disputes. Pinkerton wrote in his memoirs *Strikers, Communists, Tramps and Detectives* in 1878 that he regarded union activity as not only criminal but also contrary to American values (Smith, 2003: 7). Pinkerton's Protective Police Patrol, battling angry workers at a miners' strike in Illinois in

1866, marked the starting point of two decades of unprecedented levels of violence. The use of armed guards against strikers and the constant harassment of union organizers provoked violent reactions, resulting in many injured and some mortally wounded. The end of the nineteenth century showed a growing antipathy towards the agency, with various unions denouncing what they called 'Pinkertonism'. A first petition to outlaw the private guard industry was presented to Congress in 1890. However, it would be another two years before Members of the House started an official investigation. As a result, lawmakers across the country enacted bills that became known as 'anti-Pinkerton' laws.

> For the image-conscious Pinkterton National Detective Agency, the realisation that many Americans questioned the presence of private armies for hire in a modern republic provided the impulse it needed to end its armed guard service. (Smith: 20–1)

The nation's leading detective agency could not risk further condemnation on this front. Others were ready to take over, however. By 1893, Chicago alone counted more than 20 such agencies. Private police agencies flourished for years to come. In isolated mining communities, major employers demanded near-complete control over the small towns and their residents (ibid.). The private armed forces established by mine corporations in Pennsylvania in the early years of the twentieth century profited from the state's Coal and Iron Police Acts of 1865 and 1866. These laws permitted railroad and coalmining corporations to hire as many policemen as they desired. Coal and iron policemen were supervised and paid only by the employers; however, they were uniformed and equipped with revolvers, nightsticks and, sometimes, Winchester repeating rifles. Later, during the 1920s, they also carried machine guns and tear gas (Norwood, 2002: 120–1).

Strikebreaking took a new form in the early decades of the twentieth century. In addition to physically protecting plants and non-striking employees, various firms furnished workers to take the place of those on strike. Pinkerton and another very successful firm, Bergoff Brothers and Waddell, dominated the business. Not only did they supply personnel and guards, but they assumed control of all operations from the employer during the strike, housing the strikebreakers on company property. Bergoff's top aide, Harry Bowan, explained: 'We have our own baggage system. We carry our own portable shower baths. We carry along a physician, a boot-black, a barber, a lawyer' (ibid.: 65). An army of 5,000 men could be ready for action, on 48 hours' notice. Speed was critical, as an employer tended to hire from the agency that delivered most rapidly.

The strikebreaking business needs to be understood against the enormous unemployment between 1870 and the early 1920s. Each year several hundred thousand persons were unable to find work for at least a few months, even in relatively prosperous periods. Aging also contributed significantly to unemployment. In the eyes of many employers, men over the age of 35 lacked the capacity for endurance required of heavy physical labour. Besides, before the New Deal, there were no welfare or pension schemes. This permanently unstable situation created 'a great industrial reserve army' of potential strikebreakers (ibid.: 7–8). Their often violent behaviour led to excesses that were justified as the defence of free enterprise.

Propaganda

The American elite discovered the power of propaganda when President Wilson launched a campaign on America's entry in the First World War in 1917. The result, an intense anti-German hysteria, impressed American business with the potential of large-scale propaganda to control public opinion. Edward Bernays led the transfer of wartime propaganda skills to business' peacetime problems of coping with democracy. Born 1891 in Vienna to Jewish parents, and a nephew of Sigmund Freud twice over (his father was Ely Bernays, brother of Freud's wife Martha Bernays; his mother was Freud's sister, Anna), he was one of the first to attempt to manipulate public opinion using the subconscious. At the time of his death in 1995, he was widely considered the originator of modern public relations (Carey, 1995: 22). The old justifications for economic power – the Christian virtues of thrift and hard work, the law of the survival of the fittest, and the routine workings of the free market – no longer satisfied a more sceptical public (Tedlow, 1976: 25). The Great Steel Strike of 1919, over the right of wage earners to bargain collectively, was the first big confrontation. At the outset, public opinion favoured the strikers, who worked an 84-hour week under very poor conditions. The Steel Corporation launched a campaign of full-page advertisements denouncing the leaders of the strike as 'trying to establish the red rule of anarchy and bolshevism' and the strike as 'anti-American'. One advertisement even suggested, '[t]he

Huns had a hand in fomenting the strike' (Commission of Inquiry of the Interchurch World Movement, 1921: 97, 99, cited in Carey, 1995: 22). This propaganda assault on public opinion widened until it produced an anti-communist hysteria about an invented plan by workers to overthrow the government. In retrospect, this can be categorized as a precursor of McCarthyism, shorter, but more severe (Post, 1970, cited in Carey, 1995: 23).

The onset of the Great Depression in the 1930s brought another period of labour conflicts. The 1935 Wagner Act guaranteed workers the right to organize without employer involvement. However, the new law did not impress the leaders of Little Steel, who strongly believed maximizing profitable production was the company's only responsibility. This left no room for democracy in the production process, as – in their vision – only hierarchy would lead to efficiency (Miller, 1999: 15). Little Steel comprised of several, formerly independent steel companies, such as Republic and Bethlehem. With more than 185,000 workers, Little Steel was only relatively 'little' compared to US Steel, the other American steel giant. The company's influence in the ongoing labour conflicts was critical. Because of Little Steel's rigid position, numerous strikes ended in violent confrontations. The worst confrontation was during the Little Steel Strike of 1937, the Memorial Day Massacre mentioned earlier; most of the ten people who died that day had been shot in the back (Auerbach, 1966: 121–8).

To manage its reputation, Little Steel hired one of the first PR consultants, John Hill. Hill started his 'corporate publicity office' in 1927, and was joined by Don Knowlton in 1933 in what was to become one or the largest and most influential public relations agencies in the world, Hill & Knowlton. Hill proclaimed that his sole aim was to persuade the public that business leaders were best equipped to govern economic policy, thus fending off government regulation of the economy. His biographer Miller summarized his views. Hill worshipped the principle of the sovereignty of the free marketplace of ideas, where public opinion would judge the worthiness of his client's position and products. The PR practitioner's factual, responsible statements about the client would make

> the average citizen realise what contribution private enterprise has made to American society, and how important its preservation is to the material and spiritual welfare of all the people. (Miller, 1999: 25)

Hill's mission was 'amplifying the voices of business' and providing them with a rationale for their behaviour (ibid.: 5, 192). The Congressional Committee chaired by Senator Robert La Follette investigating the industry suppression of workers' rights was more critical about the work of Hill & Knowlton. The Committee detailed four anti-union practices that had frustrated labour organization for decades: espionage, strikebreaking, industrial munitions and private police. Little Steel's Republic had employed all four, and it was Hill & Knowlton's job to help the company explain why (ibid.: 17). 'The corporate public relations apparatus [...] had been used in tandem with the most vicious anti-union tactics in order to protect the public opinion flank of the conservative corporation' (Tedlow, 1976: 43). Thus, we see Republic Steel hiring Hill & Knowlton to look after its reputation while it was 'equipping a private army, employing an extensive espionage network, and locking workers out of plants' (Bernstein, cited in ibid.).

Espionage and Strikebreaking

The La Follette Committee discovered espionage 'to be common, almost universal, practice in American industry' (US Senate, 1937, cited in Auerbach, 1966: 97). Espionage became more important since the 1935 Wagner Act prohibited other union-busting strategies. The detective agencies 'preferred to place emphasis on its undercover work which being secret, created less antagonism' (Aikins, 1935, cited in Smith, 2003: 75). In 1936, more than 200 agencies offered their clients undercover operatives. Examining five such labour detective agencies, the Committee found a correlation between the decline of labour unions and company expenditures on espionage, and concluded that collective bargaining could not succeed while the industrial spy plied his trade (US Senate, 1937, cited in Auerbach, 1966: 98).

Companies also engaged the services of their own workers, which were cheaper and more difficult to detect because they seldom reported in writing. Workers were driven into espionage by financial distress; they believed it would improve their chances of promotion or help them avoid redundancy. The company preferred to approach workers at home, in the presence of the wife, who might – it was thought – favour the opportunity for some extra income (Norwood, 2002: 205–6). Nearly one-third of Pinkerton's undercover agents held high positions in the unions, and used those to create factions and disagreements. Spies reported on union meetings behind closed doors, and workers seen as less than loyal were fired. The detective agencies also employed a number of undercover men skilled at destroying unions from within. They used a wide variety of dirty tricks, such as whispering campaigns spreading false rumours – not only among the workers, but also directed at their spouses, or at local merchants who extended credit to workers in support of their strikes. 'Missionaries' would pose as sales agents for furniture or vacuum cleaners, anything that a man on strike could not afford to purchase for his wife. Women 'missionaries' would try to convince the wives of union members that the strike would destroy the family's ability to survive. Pretending to sell face cream door to door, they claimed this work was their fate because their husbands had lost their jobs by participating in a strike (ibid.: 205). Labour spies further tried to undermine confidence and divide the labour force by stirring up ethnic and racial conflict. In addition, the Pinkerton Agency was involved in setting up 'spontaneous' less threatening company unions – in fact inspired and controlled by spies.

A local union at the General Motors stamping plant in Lansing, Michigan, built up a substantial membership, until management began sacking workers who had joined it. After a while, only seven members remained, all officers. The La Follette investigation established that every one of them was a labour spy. As they were all working for a different detective agency, none of them realised that any of the others were in the spy business too (ibid.: 3).

Eventually, the fear of spies effectively killed many unions. Testifying before the Congress Committee in 1937, the chair of the National Labour Relations Board reported:

> The mystery and deadly certainty with which this scheme [espionage] operated was so baffling to the men that they each suspected the others, were afraid to meet or talk and the union was completely broken. (cited in Smith, 2003: 87)

The vocabulary to justify espionage lingers. Employers and hired detectives claim that their strategies are indispensable for protection against radicalism, for prevention of sabotage and the detection of theft. Above all, it is necessary for the improvement of labour–management relations – euphemistically called 'human engineering' (Auerbach, 1966: 99). And those who admit using espionage show few ethical doubts. The general manager of the Associated Industries of Cleveland insisted:

Spying will always be an essential part of warfare [...] When a man has reason to fear that the work of a lifetime is going to be struck at by some attack [...] he is going to forewarn himself in order to forearm himself if he can. (US Senate, 1937, Hearings, pt. 22, 9457, quoted in Auerbach, ibid.)

Industrial Munitions and Private Police

Ehen espionage alone failed to deter organization, companies invested in arms, such as tear gas, machine guns, gas bombs and billy clubs. Between 1933 and 1937 five of the Little Steel companies each purchased more gas equipment than did any law enforcement agency in the country. Republic, with 52,000 employees, purchased more than ten times as many gas guns and more than 26 times as many gas shells and projectiles as did the Chicago police department – responsible for 3,300,000 people.[3] These munitions were placed in the various plants of Republic Steel in preparation for an anticipated strike. Munitions companies and corporation officials agreed that gas provided 'the most human way' of handling labour disputes (Auerbach, 1966: 101). In Detroit, in the 1930s, the auto companies were very close to the police department. During the 1935 Motor Products strike, the company provided stables for the policemen's horses within the gates and set up a dining room for the police. Strikebreakers got police protection to go home, and in return the company re-plated 1,300 police badges and pairs of handcuffs. During the strike, the police, or 'company thugs', killed a striker, fractured another's skull, and seriously injured 24 men (Norwood, 2002: 200).

Private policing became fashionable, for local police departments could not always meet the special needs of railroads, mines, or lumbering districts. Private forces as instruments of corporate economic policy were not accountable to anyone but their employers.

During strikes, company police and hired strike-guards constantly usurped the public police power by venturing away from company property, weapons in hand, to maintain 'law and order'. They scattered picket lines and disrupted union meetings. (Auerbach, 1966: 100)

Again, the Republic Steel Corporation provided what Auerbach (ibid.: 105–6) called 'a dismal example of the perversion of police power in private hands' – they used private police as the chief instrument of the company's labour policy. New recruits got the instruction that union activity was detrimental to company interests. Consequently, company police tapped telephone wires, read personal mail, confiscated union literature, and intimidated and attacked organizers, bystanders, women and children. The La Follette Committee concluded 'that violations of civil liberties ensue whenever private police systems are used as instruments of labour policy to thwart self–organization of workers' (ibid., 106–7), and issued a vigorous indictment of private police systems, charging that

> they abridged civil liberties; violated the statutory rights of workers; spawned violence and bloodshed; endangered public safety; fostered labour–management bitterness; encouraged private usurpation of public authority; and perverted representative government. (*Private Police Systems*, 1937: 214, cited in Auerbach, ibid.: 107)

Like espionage, munitions stockpiling and strikebreaking, Auerbach concluded, private police systems testified that industrial autocracy was incompatible with civil liberty (ibid.; see also *Harvard Law Review*, 1939).

Public Opinion and Citizen Committees

The steel companies added a modern refinement to traditional anti-union practices: the organization and manipulation of public opinion. At first it was difficult to convince employers that advertising was worthwhile as an anti-strike weapon. The National Association of Manufacturers circulated a March 1937 *Printers Ink* article to all its members, stating that if employers would just invest

> one-tenth of the money in advertising preparation that they are apparently quite willing to invest in labour spies, tear gas and other methods, which have proved worse than useless, they will stand a far better chance of winning public support than is possible under the present circumstances. (cited in Tedlow, 1976: 43–4)

To place anti-union messages in the news media, the American Iron and Steel Institute and individual Little Steel companies paid Hill & Knowlton a sum of $323,000. The PR agency employed a variety of strategies to reach this goal. The Hill & Knowlton representative in Birmingham, AL, Edgar S. Bowerfind, tried to make local newspapers see the rectitude of Republic Steel Corp's position on labour problems. Personal and confidential documents discovered by the La Follette committee showed that his technique consisted of visits to local editors and pressure 'judiciously exerted' through advertisers (Miller, 1999: 18). Furthermore, Hill & Knowlton paid George Sokolsky large sums of money in the period from June 1936 to February 1938 – nearly $40,000 plus fees and expenses, according to the La Follette inquiry (ibid.). Sokolsky, an author and a lecturer, was paid for his columns in the republican *New York Herald Tribune* and for commentary on government, economics, and business in a weekly radio programme sponsored by the National Association of Manufacturers. In 1938, *Time* described him as 'a one-man intellectual front for conservative capital and subtlest performer for Hill & Knowlton' (*Time*, 1938). Most of the money was for consultancy for the American Iron and Steel Institute. Some of Mr Sokolsky's lecturing was done at 'civic progress meetings' arranged and paid for by local employers while publicly sponsored by 'neutral' groups.

Another weapon of choice was the formation of a citizens' committee, ostensibly neutral but in fact the mouthpiece for corporate policy. As an executive explained before the La Follette Committee that

> [t]he old method of using strike breakers and violence and things of that kind were things of the past [...] The way to win or combat a strike was to organise community sentiment. (Silverberg, 1941: 27)

In industrial districts, the life of the community is largely dependent on a single or several corporations. Dependency on the corporations extends beyond workers on the payroll, and includes other professionals and small businessmen. In such social conditions, according to Louis Silverberg, who studied the role of citizens' committees in industrial conflict, law and order leagues flourish. They function through a pattern of contradictions: 'seeking peace, it creates violence; in protecting law and order, it resorts to disorder; in preserving democracy, it denies its every corollary' (1941: 18).

These committees could accomplish what companies would not risk doing openly. This 'new alignment of forces' in the words of the La Follette Committee was intentionally not entirely non-violent. As Silverman put it, projected, organized propaganda may take shape as organized public opinion, and thus become an instrument for controlling the community. "Furthermore, propaganda is not only a weapon used in conflict, it is a means of intensifying the conflict. It thus serves to prepare the ground for the injection and justification of violence into the dispute" (ibid.: 27).

As reported at the time in the edited volume *Industrial Conflict*, this tactic 'envisaged a public opinion aroused to the point where it will tolerate the often outrageous use of force by police or vigilantes to break a strike' (Chapman, 1939, cited in Carey, 1995: 25). The committees claimed to advocate law and order, constitutional liberty, and conciliation and mediation between parties to the dispute. However, according to the disillusioned Rabbi A.M. Granowitz, who was a member of one such committee in Johnstown, PA, testifying before the Senate Civil Liberties Committee

> the actual objectives [...] were, first, to get as many men back to work as possible, and to get them back as soon as possible. Second, to break the strike. Third, to break the union. (Silverberg, op. cit.: 23)

In Johnstown, Bethlehem Steel financed the local citizens' committee that worked closely with a crowd of 500 vigilantes. The company had the support of the mayor, who chose to defend the interests of capital instead of supporting his citizens in their fight for the right to organize. He deputized the vigilantes, armed them with nightsticks, and instructed them to patrol the neighbourhoods. His use of propaganda further increased feelings of fear amongst the community. In a radio address, the mayor told his constituents: 'communism and anarchism are in evidence in our city today'. The La Follette Committee concluded that 'the rights of workers to strike and to picket were at no time the concern of the mayor' (Little Steel Strike, pp. 255–69; Hearings, Pt. 19, pp. 8394, 8639, cited in Auerbach, 1966: 135–6).

Hill & Knowlton was suspected of involvement in the various citizens' committees that sprang up in many Ohio steel towns promoting back-to-work movements. During the hearings, Senator La Follette returned several times to mysterious funds Hill & Knowlton had created during the strike periods. The agency had been hired by six corporations – allegedly to describe the history of the strike and the labour movement. Each corporation paid $1,500 per month and H&K kept track of these funds in a separate account book. The project began in July 1937, shortly after the Memorial Day Massacre on 30 May, and involved hiring five new employees. One year later and having paid $13,499 each, none of the corporations had received anything from the agency. However, when questioned about this by the La Follette Committee, all executives involved claimed they were satisfied with the progress of the work. Their statements were prepared with the help of H&K. In spite of the suspicions, and the secret money, the Committee was not able to substantiate that Hill was indeed connected to underhand activities (Miller, 1999: 18–9).

Unsurprisingly, the companies were not willing to cooperate with the Senate investigation. These refusals to cooperate with official investigations provide yet another similarity with employers' tactics today – as we will see below. When La Follette asked the largest detective firms and their most important clients to turn over all documents relating to the use of anti-union agencies, the Committee encountered duplicity, evasion and open defiance. The Pinkerton Agency refused to submit its files, particularly those containing the names of its secret operatives. Several agencies tried to destroy records before – or while – the subpoenas were served. Investigators pieced together scraps of bills and secret reports retrieved from trash bins. La Follette was not surprised that agencies 'whose very business is founded on deceit, should attempt to conceal their activities' but he was shocked to discover that 'influential and respectable industrial corporations' like General Motors resorted to 'such devices' (Hearings, cited in Smith, 2003: 90–1). The revelations of the La Follette Committee forced the Pinkerton board to put an end to the spying business in April 1937. As a result, the agency's income dropped to an all-time low in the first full year after this announcement. Many others in the business related similar stories (ibid.: 93).

Public relations was closely connected with covert strategy in the early days of industrialisation. Talk, after all, rather than violence, was what public relations was all about, Tedlow (1976: 44) concluded, and 'with talk begins responsibility'. Nevertheless, the La Follette Committee did not trust the ulterior motives for corporate communication. Victory over the unions, rather than rational dialogue, was the goal, the Committee believed. To achieve this goal, propaganda and PR are crucial. According to Silverberg (1941: 27):

If it utilises sufficiently significant symbols and is effectively projected, organised propaganda may take shape as organised public opinion, and thus become an instrument for controlling the community. [...]

Furthermore, propaganda is not only a weapon used in conflict; it is a means of intensifying the conflict. It thus serves to prepare the ground for the injection – and justification – of violence into the dispute.

The targets of the propaganda are obvious, the techniques copied from wartime situations. The first target is befriending the neutrals and gaining their support, attempting to win over certain elements, and demonstrating their identification with the employer or the corporation. The second is alienating the enemy by discrediting their objectives, leadership, and tactics or approaches. Third, to divide the enemy by driving a wedge between rank-and-file and its leadership, and otherwise to demoralize labour (ibid.: 27–8), as can be seen in Chapter 3.

UNITED KINGDOM: A CRUSADE FOR CAPITALISM, 1919–2009

One of the organizations set up in the United Kingdom to defend corporate interests was the Economic League. It was founded by employers in the interwar years 'to neutralise the growing power of labour' (McIvor, 1988: 631). The Economic League paired propaganda campaigns to teach the public 'simple economics' with covert strategy involving dirty tricks such as strikebreaking and blacklisting. In collaboration with police and intelligence agencies, the League built an extensive system of files with personal details identifying potentially subversive 'agitators'. Although it was not the only anti-socialist organization in the 1920s and 1930s, McIvor argues that the Economic League was significant as it was the only central organization to attempt systematic, national monitoring and labour blacklisting of individuals for their alleged left-wing political beliefs. 'As such, the Economic League was the propaganda arm of big business in Britain and its "dirty tricks" department, keeping constant vigilance for what it regarded as subversive activities' (ibid.: 650).

This was a struggle against popular democracy, which used violence and intimidation alongside persuasion and propaganda. The propaganda was simply an element of the strategy, which also involved intrigue, subversion, bribery and spying. (Miller and Dinan, 2008: 42)

Defending Capitalism

The Economic League was founded in 1919, and known as National Propaganda until 1925. Its establishment must be understood against the turbulent era of the First World War and the Russian Revolution. The accompanying resurgence of socialist, syndicalist and communist ideas resulted in an industrial militancy and rising trade union membership. Britain experienced a profound challenge to the established order. The Cabinet and business leaders feared the potentially revolutionary implications of the industrial unrest and felt the need for an active battle plan to present capitalism in a way that would have popular appeal. The Representation of the People Act 1918 reforming the electoral system gave this need a sense of urgency (Hughes, 1994b). The act had given voting rights to men over 21 and to women over 30, and had thus raised the prospect of a democratically elected Labour Party government in the immediate future. 'No longer would it be sufficient to rely on government to defend elite interests. With voting, governments could change' (Miller and Dinan, 2008: 43). National Propaganda fitted into a strategy 'to ensure that capitalist rule could be defended, whatever government was in power'. It was a campaign in other words, 'to ensure that democracy did not work' (ibid.).

As in the United States, the British government had discovered the value of internal propaganda during the war, and intended to continue using it to secure the support of public opinion in major labour disputes. Duplicating the tactics of revolutionary groups, the Economic League would concentrate on what they called 'educative propaganda'. This, however, was to be combined with blacklisting, or, as McIvor put it, 'an uncompromising, though covert, strategy to ensure that all militant socialists, communists and other loosely defined "subversives" were kept out of employment in British industry' (McIvor, 1988: 634). In their own words, in the pamphlet *Fifty Fighting Years*,[4] National Propaganda was set up not only to 'fight subversion relentlessly and ruthlessly' but also to 'replace it by constructive thought and ideas, by what, for want of a better term, is known as simple economics'. According to Miller and Dinan (2008) 'this account, written by the League itself, indicates how closely intertwined were the propaganda and private intelligence and spying work of National Propaganda'.

The Economic League set out to improve the tarnished image of capitalism, convinced that the success of the socialist message was caused by the ignorance of people and their lack of understanding of economics. Or, as the League put it in their 1926 *Speaker's Notes*: 'What is required is some years of propaganda for capitalism as the finest system that human ingenuity can devise to counteract the forty years of propaganda for socialism' (cited in McIvor, 1988: 634).

This philosophy closely resembles the ideas of the American PR consultant John Hill. According to their own figures in 1938, the League estimated it had held almost a quarter of a million meetings since its foundation. Open-air meetings held at dock and factory gates, marketplaces, street-corners and parks; indoor meetings at welfare institutes, schools, halls and clubs. Special meetings in the afternoons attracted unemployed workers, and some employers gave permission for lectures to workers during their lunch break. Conventions and demonstrations were part of the programme as well; in 1929, for instance, Liverpool saw a 'Women's Demonstration Against Strikes'. To back up the spoken word, the League distributed millions of leaflets, each dealing with a vital economic or social topic and written simply, to be understood by ordinary working people. The material found its way to the public through extensive mailing lists, close relations with the press, small study groups, and special campaigns. To counter the socialist 'clarion vans' for instance, the League toured the regions with 'propaganda vans', devoting a full week to a single town to disseminate their literature and give between 30 and 40 lectures in the area (McIvor, 1988: 640–5).

Blacklisting

Educational activities and propaganda were not the only elements of the anti-labour campaign. The Economic League also ran a confidential service, keeping dossiers of all the revolutionary political organizations in Britain and of the people they regarded as 'subversives'.

Internal surveillance was one of the wartime practices that was difficult to give up. During the First World War the British authorities focused their surveillance mainly on anarchists and Irish nationalists. However, several ministries and sections of the armed services, as well as MI5, reported on members of the Labour movement too. The Army reportedly ended surveillance of industrial workers in early 1920 (Wrigley, 1999: 298). The Economic League, founded by a group of right-wing industrialists and financiers in collaboration with military intelligence experts, was ready to take over (internal Economic League *Annual Report 1925*, cited in McIvor, 1988: 634).

The Conservative MP Sir Reginald Hall, who took the initiative to found the Economic League, had been director of Naval Intelligence at the Admiralty during the First World War, and was a close friend of Basil Thomson, head of Special Branch at the time.

Blacklisting 'may well have been undertaken by the League in an ad hoc fashion from its foundation in 1919' (ibid.: 647). Indeed, the League's chair Sir Auckland Geddes reported in 1925 that he had initiated 'the compilation of a chart and dossier of socialist and subversive organisations and [...] arrangements are in hand for a permanent clearing-house of information in connection with alien organisations and individuals' (*State Research Bulletin*, 1978, cited in ibid.). The League's 'confidential' activities 'demanded at least a crude espionage network with spies and contacts within the Communist Party and other revolutionary groups' (ibid.: 648). Several exposures in the press in 1937 proved that the League operated closely with local police forces, specifically in Manchester and Lancashire. This involved meeting with detectives specialised in subversion, arranging mutual cover of meetings and surveillance, and sending reports to the police on 'radical' activities. In return, the League was allowed access to police files and reports on left-wing extremist activities (ibid.: 648–649). The Economic League supplied the information to employers, on request or on its own initiative.

THE LEGACY OF THE ECONOMIC LEAGUE

The Economic League continued its blacklisting business. Hughes (1994a) extensively documented its involvement in the post-war period, the Wilson years and in what has been dubbed the secret state. More than 2,000 companies once subscribed to the League, which in the 1980s had an annual income estimated at £1million (Norton-Taylor, 1993). In the 1970s and 1980s, the organization accumulated files on more than 30,000 people. The targets included Labour MPs, trade union activists, and many individuals who campaigned on local issues or protested against government policy. The information was held on cards, and thus escaped the provisions of the 1984 Data Protection Act, which only covered information in computer databases. After repeated disclosures in the press in the late 1980s and the early 1990s, the Economic League was forced to close its doors in 1994. But this did not mean an end to blacklisting.

The exposure of the secretive organization in the mainstream media is directly attributable to the laborious efforts of campaigners and the courage of whistleblowers leaking inside information.

With their help, investigative journalists revealed the League's controversial methods and inaccurate files, and how individuals were unfairly blocked from jobs based on hearsay only.

Public concern was initially prompted by a documentary produced by Granada TV's *World in Action* in June 1987 (the first of three on the issue); a result of years of campaigning by LeagueWatch supported by Scottish Labour MP Maria Fife. The BBC's consumer affairs programme *Watchdog* in November 1988 featured the revelations of a whistleblower called Richard Brett, a former regional director of the organization. Mark Hollingsworth devoted two publications to the Economic League, the first with Richard Norton-Taylor (1988) and the second with Charles Tremayne of the National Council for Civil Liberties (1989). The final concerted media assault started after Paul Foot of the *Daily Mirror* got hold of a copy of the whole of the League's blacklist and ran a series of articles in late September 1988.

As a result of the continuing exposure in the media, many clients of the Economic League, such as banks, withdrew their subscriptions. Other large companies, including Ford, left the Economic League and relied on their own personnel vetting (Hughes, 1994d). The League was officially disbanded in 1994.

Within weeks of its closure, former employees started at least two separate security consultancies offering identical services. One was called Caprim Ltd, and was set up by Jack Winder and Stan Hardy. (Companies House, 2007, 2008). They were the two most senior Economic League employees at the time – both had been directors since 1988 (Norton-Taylor, 1994). Hansard (1990: 1081) shows that as the League's director-general, Hardy had been corresponding with MPs to defend its work in the early 1990s.

Caprim could, according to Hardy, 'draw on a network of agents around the world, among them Farleigh Projects, a subsidiary of Group 4, which describes itself as "corporate investigators and security consultants"' (*Europe Intelligence Wire*, 1997). The staff included a former police officer, industrialists and a political adviser. The company's newsletter *Caprim Monitor* invited companies to retain its 'anti-business monitoring service'.

> That service includes tracking down left-wing militants, finding the source of leaks where companies have suffered bad publicity, and vetting potential employees. It also identifies environmental

activists and animal rights campaigners whose information could lead to companies being 'condemned as unethical'. (Osler, 1994)

Through Caprim, Hardy continued warning firms of those he believed could 'weaken a company's ability to manage its affairs profitably'. He denounced, for instance, the Ethical Investment Research Service for 'busybodyness' [sic] in drawing investors' attention to whether firms supplied services to the defence ministry, or whether furniture firms used tropical hardwoods.

> Companies need to be warned what these organisations are saying and planning. Caprim provides this information. And assesses the strength of the threat. And advises on appropriate action. (*Caprim Monitor*, cited in Hencke, 2000)

Today, Caprim is a dormant company with hardly any capital, and 60 shares divided between Mr and Mrs Hardy, both in their seventies.

A second company was started by Ian Kerr of Stoke Heath, in the West Midlands. After the Economic League wound up, Kerr took the files on construction workers and set up the Consulting Association. After the Information Commissioner's Office (ICO) investigated complaints of blacklisting, Kerr was brought before the court in early 2009, and admitted to having run a secret database of 3,200 workers.

Again, it took the work of a freelance journalist and a whistleblower to address the issue of blacklisting before the proper authorities showed any initiative. It started with an electrician, who was convinced he was not getting work because of his union membership. His case was brought before an industrial tribunal and Phil Chamberlain reported it in the *Guardian*. The tribunal heard evidence from Alan Wainwright, a former manager in the construction industry, who testified about his experience with private detective agencies selling lists of workers identified as troublemakers. As the national labour manager at an engineering company, Crown House (then a Tarmac subsidiary), he had run into Kerr and his database for the first time in 1997. Seven years later, Wainwright was a manager for Haden Young (a subsidiary of Balfour Beatty) where he tried to address the blacklisting practices – to no avail. In 2006, Wainwright quit his job and lost an employment tribunal claim. After he had applied unsuccessfully for more than 150 jobs, he started a website to expose blacklisting and linked up with workers in similar circumstances (Evans, 2009).

The evidence provided by Wainwright convinced the industrial tribunal and the electrician was awarded compensation. In its adjudication the tribunal said: 'Disgraceful though it is, the tribunal concludes that a blacklist exists in relation to certain workers in the industry in which the claimants work and that the claimants are all on that blacklist.' Such findings are rare; in most cases the problem is proving blacklisting exists, Chamberlain (2008) concluded.

A member of staff at the Information Commissioner's Office put a copy of the *Guardian* article on the desk of ICO investigator David Clancy. Worried that workers were unfairly being denied jobs through a breach of data protection rules, Clancy's team started an investigation. The documentation Wainwright had collected over the years formed a key part of this. A raid of the Haden Young premises provided the information that led to the office of Kerr and his secret databases. According to the Information Commissioner, no fewer than 40 construction firms – including Balfour Beatty, Sir Robert McAlpine, Laing O'Rourke, Emcor and Crown House – had bought details of the individuals' trade union activities and work record from Kerr. 'Among the entries was one on Wainwright recording how he had helped blacklisted workers' (Evans, 2009).

Some of the files seized by the Information Commissioner turned out to be more than 30 years old; many had been named by the League before it had collapsed. The *Guardian* saw the files and gave some examples.

> One card with the letter 'K' on it – a code used by the league to designate the building industry – records the trade union and political activities of Alan Ritchie, now general secretary of the UCATT construction workers' union. It notes he was a 'leading striker' at the Govan shipyard in Glasgow. (ibid.)

Files dating back to the early 1970s described

> one building worker in Liverpool as 'politically unstable' and 'extreme', while another in Twickenham, London, was sacked after the league named him as a militant strike leader and said he was 'identical' to an Irish communist. A third in Wembley was named as a 'political menace' because he supported 'extreme elements' (ibid.).

Kerr had worked for the organization since the 1970s, infiltrating 'a lot' of trade union and political meetings, recording who had said what and taking away documents such as attendance lists, Michael Noar, the League's director–general between 1986 and 1989, told the *Guardian*. 'He was a key guy. He was one of our most effective research people – his information was genuine and reliable' (Evans, Carrell and Carter, 2009).

Minutes from internal Economic League meetings in 1988, seen by the *Guardian*, show that Kerr liaised with construction companies known as the Service Group. They got help with vetting and covert intelligence gathering on union activists, allegedly left-wing employees and workers who complained about safety or rights at work. A confidential letter from the Costain construction firm to the Economic League in 1988 names Kerr as an important official in the organization (ibid.). When the organization ran into financial problems after the media exposure detailed above, it was Kerr who put forward suggestions about raising more money from the Services Group, minutes of the League showed. After 1994, when the Economic League was forced to close down, Kerr continued to run checks on individuals paid by construction firms – now through the Consulting Association. According to confidential internal documents, the Association was 'collectively' owned by the companies, which paid an annual £3,000 subscription. Between 2004 and 2009, the Court heard, Kerr's agency received £600,000 paid by more than 40 construction companies to record personal and employment details of allegedly troublesome workers. About 90 per cent of the information came from the companies to be shared with other firms to vet workers before they were employed (Evans, Carrell and Carter, 2009; for a full list of the corporations involved, see CorporateWatch, 2009).

This case shows the power as well as the weaknesses of the Office of the Information Commissioner, and this is of interest when thinking about regulation to monitor corporate intelligence. Kerr pleaded guilty to breaking data protection laws at Macclesfield Magistrates Court in May 2009. However, the chairman of the bench felt his sentencing powers under the Data Protection Act were 'woefully inadequate' and passed the case up to the Crown Court (ibid.). In July 2009, Kerr appeared before Knutsford Crown Court for sentencing and was fined £5,000 for breaches of the Data Protection Act. The judge said that Kerr was not the only person responsible, as he was financed by big 'high street' companies. To the disappointment of affected trade unionists, the businesses involved got nothing more than an official warning. The major firms in the construction industry were notified that they would be prosecuted if they set up a new blacklist.

Today, it is unlawful for trade union members to be denied employment through blacklists. The new regulations that outlaw the compilation, dissemination and use of blacklists came into effect in March 2010. Blacklisting had been made illegal under the 1999 Employment Relations Act, but the necessary regulations were never enacted because the government claimed there was no evidence. That changed with the Kerr case, when Business Secretary Lord Mandelson promised 'to stamp out this despicable practice' (cited in Penman, 2009). Announcing the new rules, the then Employment Relations Minister Lord Young (2010) said: 'Blacklisting someone because they are a member of a trade union is underhand, unfair and blights people's lives.' The new regulation also 'enables individuals or unions to pursue compensation or solicit action against those who compile, distribute or use blacklists' (ibid.). The construction union UCATT, however, was disappointed with the new regulations. All their submissions to ensure that blacklisting was effectively stamped out had been rejected. Blacklisting has not been made a specific criminal offence, and the law only protects workers who undertake narrowly defined 'trade union activities'. If a blacklist is discovered workers will not be automatically told their name was on the list, nor will they have an automatic right to compensation. The union fears that the weak regulations could allow employers to continue these practices (UCATT, 2010).

However, the ICO has seen its powers steadily increase since the Kerr case. The Coroners and Justice Act 2009 strengthened its inspection powers (Ministry of Justice, 2009). The original proposal drew criticism from the Confederation of British Industry, which called it an unwelcome burden (Muncaster, 2009). In May 2011 the ICO was given the power to levy fines of up to £500,000 for breaches of the Privacy and Electronic Communications Regulations covering intrusive marketing. It was also given greater oversight of internet service providers (ISPs). Meanwhile the government is considering extending the number of organizations covered by the Freedom of Information Act, which is enforced by the ICO (Ministry of Justice, 2011). That includes organizations such as the Association of Chief Police Officers. ACPO has been involved in infiltrating the environmental movement and exchanging gathered information with energy companies targeted by climate activists, as detailed in the Preface.

Despite these extra powers, allegations from trade unions of continued blacklisting and willingness by the ICO to investigate, no further cases have been uncovered.

The Economic League casts a shadow over the case studies in this book. As the McSpy case in Chapter 4 shows, the Economic League provided McDonald's UK with a newsletter and additional information on possible threats from activists. The Threat Response Spy Files case study is built around infiltration operations led by Evelyn le Chêne. In her reports to British Aerospace about the Campaign Against Arms Trade, she claimed to be able to provide intelligence and confidential details on nearly 150,000 activists. Her history puts her in intelligence circles; her background is one of strong anti-communism and defence of capitalism, as detailed in Chapter 7.

The legacy of the Economic League is not just in the archives, although the question of who is using these databases on British subversives now is an interesting one. There is a historical continuity in surveillance and covert counterstrategy in defence of corporate interests, as the case studies in this book show. Mapping the grey area of overlapping state intelligence services, corporate security consultants and private investigators is now as important as it was in the past, because critical voices need to be heard.

3
Rafael Pagan, Nestlé and Shell: Case Study

The roots of today's activist intelligence can be traced back to the 1980s, when the new phenomenon of worldwide boycotts of multinational corporations required sophisticated corporate plans to counter them. Rafael D. Pagan Jr. was one of the first American specialists to develop such counterstrategies. This chapter examines his work for Nestlé between 1981 and 1985, and subsequently for Shell Oil in 1986–87. Nestlé had been the target of campaigns against the promotion of infant formula in the Third World for many years. Four years after the company hired Pagan, the boycott was broken – though just temporarily as it turned out – and an agreement signed between campaigners and the company. The plan Pagan developed for Shell Oil, known as the *Neptune Strategy* (1986), was designed to neutralize boycott groups campaigning against Shell's continuing involvement with the apartheid regime in South Africa.

This case study analyses the various elements of Pagan's strategy. Dialogue with major constituencies, such as moderate church groups, was of major importance. Each contact with the company's opponents was essentially an information-gathering opportunity too. The strategy was intended to divide and conquer campaigning coalitions.

The analysis of Pagan's work for Nestlé draws on an evaluation of the infant formula controversy by Professor S. Prakash Sethi, published as *Multinational Corporations and the Impact ofPublic Advocacy on Corporate Strategy* (1994). His exclusive access to Pagan himself, as well as to Nestlé's management, their internal documents and communications, gives an extraordinary insight into the company's public affairs strategy. The second part of this chapter is based on the *Neptune Strategy*, developed by Pagan for Shell. This confidential report was leaked to the Interfaith Center on Corporate Responsibility in September 1987 (the ICCR is the corporate responsibility office of a coalition of 234 churches and religious groups in the US, engaged in the anti-apartheid boycott at the time). Buro Jansen & Janssen was one of the many NGOs and activist groups to receive a stencilled copy of the 256-page document. In the publicity that followed, Shell acknowledged the origins of the document and Pagan as its author. In the Netherlands, two investigative journalists interviewed Pagan and Shell staff about the *Neptune Strategy*, and exposed a spy who – on behalf of Pagan and Shell – had posed as a journalist to gather information from representatives of targeted activist groups (Runderkamp and Salverda, 1987). The *Neptune Strategy* offers a rare glimpse into one of the first extended corporate campaigns against civil society critics.

In an attempt to get direct access to Nestlé's confidential material, I contacted Professor Prakash Sethi by email. His book on Nestlé had been published in 1994 after the dust had settled, but his research had started before the end of the boycott was agreed ten years earlier. He had managed to win Pagan's trust, had interviewed him extensively (20 hours spread over 12 months), and had talked to his strategy staff and Nestlé's top management. Sethi, however, claimed access to the material was impossible. It had been, he wrote, a long time since the project was completed, and most of his notes, earlier drafts and interview materials had been destroyed. The second part of his explanation seems to contradict this. Because it was a controversial project, Sethi explained (email to the author, 16 November 2006), all the interviews were done on a confidential basis with the understanding that the materials would not be released without the consent of the people interviewed. Moreover, most of the people involved in Pagan's company and its successors have either retired or died.

Sethi's reluctance is understandable as he had strong ties to Pagan. As I found out, the professor was hired by Pagan as 'an adviser' while he was conducting his research into the Nestlé case. Moreover, the Neptune Strategy named him as the 'project manager' for the 'university strategy' – as will be detailed in this chapter. Effectively, Prof. Sethi was a member of Pagan's team working for Shell. This exposes a serious case of conflicts of interest, one that Sethi has failed to address when he published his research, and still does not talk about today. Notwithstanding the friendly tone and fast exchange of our first emails (with Sethi inviting me to one of his conferences, email to the author, 16 November 2006), when asked about his paid work for Pagan, the communication was over and no further replies were forthcoming. The fact that my attempts to access source material were unsuccessful is not crucial, as Sethi's book on the Nestlé boycot is fully referenced. To be aware of the extent of his involvement is indeed essential, as it explains the way he got access to a wealth of internal sources. Furthermore, it raises questions about big business influencing academic research while part of the corporate strategy is aimed at manipulating 'the phase of the forming of ideas' at the university – as will be detailed below (additionally, Chapter 5 also includes examples of influencing academic discussions albeit in a different context, and attempts to damage the carreer of scientists who spoke out against genetic engineering).

THE NESTLÉ CONTROVERSY

In October 1984, the International Nestlé Boycott Committee announced the end of a seven-year consumer boycott of Nestlé. The boycott against one of the world's largest food companies was created to bring an end to Nestlé's marketing abuses in promoting and selling infant formula products in less developed countries. The Nestlé boycott had become virtually synonymous with the infant formula controversy, and was an important factor in the development, adoption and implementation of the World Health Organization's International Code of Marketing for Breast-milk Substitutes. 'The Nestlé boycott has had a major impact on the interpretation of corporate accountability and the reconciliation of human rights and commercial interests' (Post, 1985: 113).

The coalition against Nestlé consisted of many different groups including health professionals, church groups and anti-corporate activists. Leaders in business sometimes felt the boycott was 'a holy war against the infant formula industry, if not a challenge to free enterprise and capitalism itself' (ibid.: 114; see also Dobbing, 1988).

Hiring Rafael Pagan

The controversy over the marketing of infant formula in Third World countries dates back to the early 1970s. The hiring of Rafael Pagan in 1981 meant a radical shift in Nestlé's strategy for dealing with the boycott (Sethi, 1994: 221). A highly decentralized corporate structure had allowed the head of Nestlé's USA subsidiary, David Guerrant, to maintain his 'ostrich policy' – hoping the issue would go away. The public affairs staff of Nestlé USA lacked experience in dealing with such a very public and controversial political issue, and most of the response from the company's headquarters in Switzerland lacked the understanding of the American mentality and media (ibid.: 70, 218).[5] Until Pagan was recruited, Nestlé USA had resorted to standard PR. The largest agencies had been hired, but to no avail. Edelman, still the largest private PR firm today, had advised the company to continue to ignore the problem. Hill & Knowlton unsuccessfully tried a 'truth squad' strategy, using a massive education campaign including mailing information kits to 300,000 clergy (Campion, cited in Sethi, 1994: 218; also see Johnson, 1981: 65). Several other public relations experts – such as Gerry Raffe and Henry Cioka – were consulted, but none worked for the company very long. Nestlé's top management in the United States were unwilling to consider viewpoints that were different to their own (Sethi, ibid.: 218–19).[6] A critical factor in the decision to hire Pagan was the change in Nestlé's top management in Switzerland. According to Sethi, Helmut Maucher, Chief Executive Officer, and Carl Angst, Managing Director, were willing to try new strategies.

The decision was taken in late 1980, when the boycott of Nestlé products was gaining momentum. In a secret memorandum Vice-President Ernest Saunders expressed his concern over 'the professionalism of the forces involved' and pleaded for a similar operation: 'It is clear that we have an urgent need to develop an effective counter-propaganda operation' (Saunders, 1980). To establish a 'strategic capability' Pagan asked for an office, a staff and a budget, as well as unrestricted access to Nestlé's top management. At his request, the company founded an independent subsidiary, divorced from the day-to-day operations of Nestlé USA. Pagan also negotiated full freedom in selecting his own staff and an independent budget necessary to meet the challenge of his mission (Sethi, ibid.: 221). The new office was located in a prestigious building in Washington DC with no expense spared to provide it with top-of-the-range furniture and equipment (ibid.: 224). Although it was essentially an issue management unit dealing exclusively with the controversy, everything was done to avoid the charge that Nestlé was creating a lobbying and PR group to fight the boycott. Pagan's desk officially had a broader public function: 'to coordinate Nestlé's worldwide efforts in nutrition research' – as was reflected in its name, the Nestlé Coordination Centre for Nutrition (NCCN) (ibid.: 222).

Divide and Rule

To break the boycott against Nestlé, Pagan developed a strategy that can be summarized as *divide and rule*. Pagan's background in the armed forces shaped his worldview, equating issue management with military action and what he called 'corporate combat' (Pagan, 1996: 443). Based on analyses of the key critics' motives, NCCN aimed at 'resolving the boycott by a long process of dialogues and one-to-one discussions designed to achieve what one boycott leader called a win–win result' (Pagan, 1986a: 16).

The campaign was divided into four phases. The first was the *containment* of critics' initiatives by listening to both sides, covering the first six months of NCCN's existence. Phase two, from May–June 1981 to October 1982, explored relations with moderate groups to see whether NCCN could work with any of them (*reaching out*). The third phase was a *breakthrough* that led to the erosion of support for the boycott among moderate critics and to discussions with activist leaders for the purpose of resolving the conflict. This phase lasted from May 1982 to October 1984, when the boycott was lifted. Phase four, *consolidation*, was to be conducted while Pagan was writing his account of the campaign. It aimed at 'the establishment of a stable corporate social environment and public policy implementation' (ibid.).

The following brief chronology contextualizes Pagan's strategy. In spring 1980, the United Methodist Church formed a Task Force (MTF) to examine Nestlé's practices. By October 1982, the MTF was scheduled to advise the Methodist Church on joining the boycott – a date critical to Pagan's planning. In the meantime, in May 1981 the World Health Assembly (the governing body of the World Health Organization, WHO) adopted its code on the marketing of infant formula, endorsed by UNICEF. A year later, in May 1982, the company created the 'independent' Nestlé Infant Formula Audit Commission.

Containment

Pagan's first strategic decision was 'to stop the unproductive shouting match between Nestlé and its critics, and to listen'. Articulate and well-trained spokespersons and scientists were sent 'to the field of the political battle' (as Pagan called it) to meet with church leaders and public interest groups, and to answer criticism levelled against the company (Pagan, 1986a: 14; see also Sethi, 1994: 229). Listening served two purposes, as Pagan explained:

> One, it enabled NCCN to gather information about the critics and their objectives so appropriate strategies could be developed.

And two, it allowed NCCN to earn the right to be listened to by the critics, in turn. Stopping the shouting freed Nestlé from having to defend fixed positions. (Pagan, ibid.)

Damage control and containment in order to prevent the boycott from gaining momentum were important tactics that bought Nestlé time and allowed them to become proactive: 'NCCN also began a well-focused information-gathering effort' (ibid.). Intelligence on critics and their objectives delivered the stepping-stones 'to develop appropriate ways of combating them' (Pagan, 1996: 444). In Pagan's words (ibid.: 445) this phase was to explore the relations with moderate groups by 'hearing out our adversaries'.

Upon listening to the critics, NCCN soon discovered that while the critics were led by skilful political activists, the campaign against Nestlé received its moral authority and most of its popular and financial support from religious groups and critics of conscience. (Pagan, 1986a: 14–16)

Nestlé understood the 'enormous importance' of the influence and support of religious groups to the activists' boycott campaign, according to Sethi. The power base of the professional leadership of the boycott movement was 'very narrow' – but for the fact that they were supported by a wide variety of organized religious groups (Sethi, 1994: 229). Pagan observed that while many of the church-based critics were uncomfortable with profit-oriented multinational capitalism, they also did not like the idea of 'being used for extraneous purposes by activists or of being viewed as clever, amoral, or radical political activists' (Pagan, 1996: 16). 'But these critics were willing to work with Nestlé on behalf of the world's poor and to see if multinationals were as useful and as caring as Nestlé claimed' (ibid.: 14–16). Pagan considered the groups coordinating the boycott – INFACT and the Interfaith Center on Corporate Responsibility – to be more radical. He decided to bypass them and go directly to the National Council of Churches (Pagan, 1996: 437). This strategy was predicated on the actions taken by various church groups independently to investigate issues at stake. Instead of endorsing the boycott right away, the United Methodist Church (UMC) had established the Methodist Task Force in May 1980 to investigate the misuse of infant formula and to instigate a constructive dialogue with the companies involved. Pagan thought of moderate church groups as

a 'very large constituency of thoughtful and concerned people [...]
who would be absolutely necessary if Nestlé were to improve its
credibility and at the same time make a dent in the activists' support
base' (Sethi, 1994: 230). Jack Mongoven, the strategist working
with Pagan, explained why they had strategically chosen to put
pressure on the church community:

> The weakness and the strength of the church institutions are first
> and foremost that they have a conscience, and that, once they
> know the truth, the pressure on them to act accordingly is very
> heavy. Because they are committed to doing that which is ethical,
> they became our best hope. (ibid.: 229)

The 'truth' Mongoven is referring to was the fact that selected
church people had to be convinced that Nestlé was determined
to resolve its critics' legitimate concerns. Likewise, 'doing what is
ethical' in Mongoven's eyes, involved *not* joining the boycott.

Reaching Out

In May 1981, the WHO passed its International Code of Marketing
of Breast-milk Substitutes. Pagan used this moment as an opportunity
to 'begin seizing the moral initiative from the confrontationists'
(Pagan, 1986a: 16; also see Sethi, 1994: 231). At his insistence,
Nestlé immediately issued a statement supporting the 'aim and
principle' of the code. Although many activists saw this statement
as a cosmetic PR ploy, seeds of doubt were sown. What was the
moral basis for a boycott against a company that *did* support the
code, rather than against other companies that opposed it? Pagan's
NCCN and the Methodist Church were then exploring a basis for
dialogue, and Nestlé's statement of support for the code helped them
find common ground (Sethi, 1994: 231). Eventually Pagan brought
together the new managing director of Nestlé and the new head of
the National Council of Churches, James Armstrong, who, until
his election in April 1982, had been on the Methodist Task Force.

However, dialogue alone was not enough. The Methodist Church
demanded that Nestlé demonstrate its compliance with the WHO
code, and provide evidence that it was indeed changing its marketing
practices. 'Having put major emphasis on wooing the Methodists,
Nestlé could not do otherwise' (ibid.). At the Church's suggestion,
Nestlé issued instructions requiring unilateral compliance for
those Third World countries that had no code yet. Further steps

were taken to build trust between the two parties. At Pagan's recommendation, Nestlé shared sensitive internal documents with the Methodists, which helped convince them of Nestlé's bona fides. The Methodists honoured these confidences. A subsequent meeting between Nestlé CEOs and the MTF in 1982 'swept away most of the hidden antagonism and wariness between the two groups and went a long way toward building mutual trust and respect' (Pagan, 1986a.: 16–17; Sethi, 1994: 231–2). As a result, the Methodists took initiatives on their own to persuade other activists to enter into a dialogue with Nestlé.

Pagan increased Nestlé's visibility on other fronts too. The company tried to gain credibility with the scientific community via 'research-supported activities' in the US aimed at Third World health and nutrition. This involved grants made to various universities and sponsoring a number of symposia on the problems of infant nutrition (Sethi, ibid.: 232).

NCCN also targeted public interest groups directly. In early 1982, Pagan set up a database of more than 700 American organizations that had endorsed the boycott. The strategy was, according to Mongoven, to reach out to these groups 'once Nestlé had begun to make solid progress in building credibility' to create a feeling of movement which would 'prepare boycott endorsers for an ending'.

Richard Ullrich, the coordinator of the Justice and Peace office of the Marianist Brothers and Priests in Baltimore, met with Nestlé officials to discuss the boycott. 'By having us hear their [Nestlé's] side, they believed we'd be convinced of their sincerity and then we would call off the boycott', said Ullrich (in Bartimole, 1982). They hoped 'that would be symbolic and they could use that to convince other groups to call off their boycott' (ibid.).

Multinational Monitor obtained copies of a number of long letters Pagan sent to church groups and other organizations. These letters show Pagan and Nestlé intentionally playing one group off against another. Pagan sent two letters on 13 November 1981, one to a group of pastors, the other to priests. Both contained this paragraph:

> We regret that so much strident rhetoric has often characterised the debate on this critically important issue. It is obvious, however, that more and more religious bodies are giving this issue the time, effort, and research it merits. We applaud these efforts. It is only through careful consideration of all the important aspects of this matter that all of us can manifest our concern for the children of poverty in developing countries. (Pagan, cited in Bartimole, 1982)

At the campus of Notre Dame University, Nestlé tried to influence the student referendum on the boycott, criticized the 'biased' editorial line of the *Observer*, the student magazine, and tried to bribe influential students. 'Notre Dame has become known for its interest in Third World and humanitarian issues,' John McGrath, editor of the magazine, told *Multinational Monitor*, and a 'no' to the boycott would thus serve as a victory that could be exploited on other campuses. *Multinational Monitor* concluded in September 1998:

> The tactics Pagan and Nestlé employ with church and educational groups reveal an organised effort to confuse and splinter Nestlé's critics. This suggests the company may be more interested in altering the public perception of its practices than in changing those practices themselves. (Bartimole, 1982)

This analysis is confirmed by the fact that *Nestlé News*, the newsletter published to publicize Nestlé's many constructive efforts in the Third World, 'almost always led with a positive story about progress in resolving the boycott issue or partnership with a responsible organisation' (Sethi, 1994: 232). PR was always more important than real change.

Outside Validation

Another strategy to secure an end to the boycott was to seek outside validation. To overcome public distrust in early 1982, Pagan established the Nestlé Infant Formula Audit Commission (NIFAC). Its official mission was to answer inquiries from the public and to monitor the company's application of WHO Codes (see NIFAC Charter, article II, cited in Sethi, ibid.: 26). The Commission was chaired by former US Secretary of State Senator Edmund S. Muskie, who was considered strong enough to withstand public pressure. He had a reputation for integrity and a commitment to the disadvantaged. Muskie insisted on independence for NIFAC, and full control of the finances and staff (Sethi, ibid.: 267).

Public reaction to the commission was mixed, for many different reasons. Although it had been established to investigate Nestlé's marketing practices in the Third World, none of the members had any direct expertise in those fields. Doubt was cast over the commission's impartiality, because Nestlé financed it. Its legalistic and bureaucratic approach was criticized too. The creation of

NIFAC neatly shifted the burden of proof; as if it were a court of law, Nestlé was now innocent until proved guilty. According to Johnson of INFACT this meant that 'the responsibility for establishing violations was unduly placed on those organizations that had the least capacity and the fewest resources to pursue them' (ibid.: 272). The complicated juridical requirements kept many organizations from filing complaints, especially those in developing countries unfamiliar with the procedures NIFAC applied. The boycott movement was primarily rooted in the USA and Western Europe, while the field of operation concerning infant formula marketing was in Africa, Asia and Latin America. The movement lacked a structure of field offices and networks to collect complaints and the additional detailed paperwork the procedure involved (ibid.: 274) – this was before the age of the internet.

The creation of NIFAC served as an effective deflection shield for Nestlé. Rather than having to deal with complaints directly, the company could plausibly claim that NIFAC was studying the situation (Chetley, 1986: 120–1).

Pagan and Mongoven explained how the Commission served as an instrument for damage control and containment. Muskie's operation created a regular 'event hook' for news media. The media focus on the new commission also put some boundaries around the issues that activists might raise, and the manner in which they were addressed (Sethi, 1994: 269). Pagan pointed out that the establishment of the commission 'created much disarray and confusion amongst the activist leadership' (Pagan, 1986a: 17). The Muskie Audit Commission was to

> [...] cause an erosion of the rationale for boycott, narrow the differences between the opposing groups from broad generalities to specifics of content and process. [This Pagan saw as] one of the conditions for a satisfactory negotiation of the boycott termination. (Sethi, 1994: 233)

In short, the commission was a key component of the divide and rule strategy.

Breakthrough

An important moment in breaking support for the boycott was when the *Washington Post* changed its editorial line on the issue. The newspaper had been a key outlet supporting the boycott; in the first six months of 1981, it published 91 articles critical of Nestlé. The paper had exposed secret internal Nestlé documents on several occasions that had seriously damaged the corporation's reputation (see, for instance, Mintz, 1981). But in November 1982 the *Post* published an editorial arguing that international health policy 'needs a broader perspective' than the 'anti-formula crusade' (*Washington Post*, 1982). Pagan had persuaded the management of the paper to assign its science editor to the issue. Nestlé 'kept him *so* informed of our activities he tired of us' (Pagan, cited in Nelson-Horchler, 1984; emphasis added). The editorial included critical assessments of evidence presented by the campaign: 'Upon closer inspection, the data linking formula marketing and infant mortality turn out to be sketchy at best' (*Washington Post*, 1982).

The shift had started a few weeks earlier, when Pagan had achieved a crucial victory in separating the 'fanatic' activist leaders from those who are 'decent concerned people' (Pagan, 1982: 3–4). 'As scheduled' Pagan proudly noted, the Methodist Task Force recommended the Church should *not* join the boycott (Pagan, 1986a: 17; and Sethi, 1994: 232). Why was the United Methodist Church decision so significant?

The Infant Formula Action Coalition (INFACT) had a leading role in the Nestlé boycott. The group had strong ties with the National Council of Churches, and tried to mobilize support from larger religious communities. The UMC was – and still is – one of the largest mainline Protestant denominations, representing a mix of moderate and liberal theologies. Guided by their 'social principles' they are usually open to new ideas and societal changes:

> The United Methodist Church believes God's love for the world is an active and engaged love, a love seeking justice and liberty. We cannot just be observers. So we care enough about people's lives to risk interpreting God's love, to take a stand, to call each of us into a response, no matter how controversial or complex. (United Methodist Church, 2004)

To gain the UMC's official support for the boycott would have exerted strong pressure on Nestlé to negotiate a settlement with the campaigners. Instead, the Council on Ministries, the Church's chief programme coordinating agency, asked two other Methodist agencies – the Board of Church and Society and the Board of Global Ministries – and the more than 30 Methodist annual conferences that backed the boycott to 're-examine their position and consider concluding their participation' (Anderson, 1982).

According to Sethi, the activists at INFACT saw the establishment of the Methodist Task Force in (too) narrow political terms. They were afraid that because of the Methodists' inexperience, the Task Force would be manipulated – or at least confused and overwhelmed – by Nestlé and others. Yet, the chair of the MTF, Philip Wogaman, then Dean of the Wesley Seminary, seemed well aware of the issues at stake:

> The real issue was not whether the company was using us; but whether it was using us to find a way into a more responsible relationship with its public, or whether it was using us as a device to maintain the status quo. (Sethi, 1994: 247)

Doug Johnson of INFACT confirmed the vital importance of the Church's decision when Sethi interviewed him:

> Had the Methodist Church joined (the boycott) there would have been a lot less internal problems with the churches as a whole. We would have been able to press the boycott harder. We would have gotten settlement sooner. […] Because they were out [of the boycott] and because Nestlé was stroking them, it took away the will power of the other churches to be seriously involved in the boycott as they should. (ibid.: 247)

The activists had made the mistake of taking the support of the religious institutions for granted, Sethi concluded. 'They were quite willing to work with the Church subunits as long as they could wrap themselves with the moral authority of the church' (ibid.: 248, see also 230).

Sethi's observations – although clearly containing a moral judgement – emphasize the significance of Pagan's assessments. For the strategy of creating divisions within the boycott campaign, targeting the moderate church groups proved to be a wise choice. Pagan and Mongoven managed to draw the MTF away from the boycott, and into dialogue with the company. The UMC's choice not to support the boycott damaged the INFACT coalition, and this – as intended – eroded support for the campaign against Nestlé.

Consolidation?

In January 1984, an agreement to end the seven-year boycott was signed after a long process of decision making of all groups involved in the campaign. Boycott leaders and Nestlé officials symbolically marked the occasion at a joint news conference by unwrapping Nestlé Crunch bars, one of the items hardest hit by the boycott, and tapping them together as if clinking wineglasses in a toast (Marquez, 1984). Pagan and Nestlé claimed victory, but this was somewhat premature. The widely reported end of the boycott would later prove to be just a suspension of campaigning. After the agreement was ratified in October 1984, Nestlé's marketing initially improved – very slowly. However, once the boycott was over and the spotlight on the company dimmed, Nestlé returned to business as usual (Salmon, 1989: 44).

The fourth phase, following the official end of the boycott, was aimed at consolidation and the implementation of a stable corporate social environment and public policy (Pagan, 1986: 16). However, this failed completely. Within a year, Nestlé officially dismantled Pagan's NCCN, claiming that the new realities did not justify maintaining a satellite organization in the US with direct links to the head office in Switzerland. Pagan and Mongoven declined senior positions in the Nestlé hierarchy and decided to start their own firm, Pagan International. Financial claims were settled in kind. The firm was allowed to stay in the old NCCN offices rent-free and to keep the (expensive) furniture and equipment free of charge (Sethi, 1994: 236).

Ten years later Sethi concluded that Nestlé had not learned any lessons in handling the controversy. For example, a wholly owned subsidiary of Nestlé entered the market for infant formula in the USA for the first time in 1988. By directly advertising to the consumer, the company raised a storm of criticism: 'It is as if the company had never heard of the WHO code or was insensitive to the concerns of the health and medical community about infant formula marketing practices' (ibid.: 241). Indeed, many of Nestlé's foreign subsidiaries were not persuaded that Nestlé had any problem at all. They did not see any adverse affects of the US controversy in their regions. Sethi outlined the unchanged position of the Nestlé management, sketching the opposition against the Muskie Audit Commission. An inward-looking corporate culture made Nestlé reluctant to embrace the idea of transparency in its governance procedures. The company felt that, given the pervasive anti-business and anti-Nestlé climate of public opinion, the cost of such an action might far outweigh any potential benefits. The internal opposition was intensified by the fact that there was no guarantee, or even reasonable certainty, that the Audit Commission would successfully re-establish Nestlé's credibility (ibid.: 266).

When a renewed boycott to force Nestlé to keep its promises was announced in October 1988, Nestlé hired Ogilvy & Mather, a renowned advertising and public relations firm, to devise an international operation to deal with this boycott. The plan subsequently leaked to the media in April 1989 was called *Proactive Neutralisation: Nestlé Recommendations Regarding the Infant Formula Boycott*. The O&M plan echoed Pagan's ideas by proposing 'interest group assessment and monitoring' and an 'early warning system' that would alert Nestlé to decisions of local church groups on whether to join the boycott. The programme also embraced the divide and rule strategy, as it was

> built around the idea of neutralising or defusing the issue by quietly working with key interest groups [and argued that] activities should be implemented as soon as possible in order to most effectively pre-empt boycott activities. (cited in Mokhiber, 1989)

The document did not explain the meaning of 'neutralising', the *Multinational Monitor* noted. After the leak, a spokesperson claimed that Nestlé had rejected the recommendations, but remained an Ogilvy client (Mokhiber, ibid.).

Although the boycott of Nestlé resumed in 1989, Muskie's Audit Commission was disbanded in 1991. Through the years, the Commission had widened the scope of their mandate with fact-finding missions in developing countries. When Muskie concluded that Nestlé had violated the provisions against free supplies of infant formula in Mexico, this experiment with auditing and transparency was terminated (Margen et al., 1991).

Today, the company continues to ignore criticism while attempting to undermine campaigning groups. In June 2008, the Swiss investigative television programme *Temps Présent* revealed that Nestlé had infiltrated Attac Switzerland for more than a year (Losa and Ceppi, 2008). The food multinational paid Securitas, one of Switzerland's largest security firms, to plant a woman in the protest group from the summer of 2003 until 2004. Using a false name, the infiltrator participated in Attac meetings and preparation sessions around the time of the 2003 G8 summit in Evian in June. After the summer members of the group started editing a book about the Nestlé empire. As a co-author, she had complete access to the group's documentation and strategy plans, she visited the homes of fellow activists, and is suspected of having made secret recordings of internal discussions. Through the computer network, she also had access to Attac's email contacts all around the world, and the correspondence with them. This included information on union members in Colombia fighting for workers' rights in Nestlé plants. Such information is potentially dangerous in the wrong hands; as detailed earlier in this book, a Colombian union man was killed after filing a complaint against the company (see Bussey, 2006).

The infiltrator wrote regular reports about the group's meetings for Securitas, and was also introduced to Nestlé's head of security to clarify her findings. The surveillance reports were subsequently passed on to the federal police to be used according to their needs.

Nestlé refused to comment on camera and issued a written statement instead, aimed at downplaying the affair. The company's response to the accusations, *Temps Présent* reported, was limited to saying it took a series of 'appropriate measures' to boost the security of its staff and buildings at the time of the G8 summit five years ago (the additional year of working on the book was conveniently omitted). The company added that it took these measures in close cooperation with Securitas and the Vaud cantonal police, while strictly respecting the law.

Around the same time, in 2004, the International Baby Food Action Network (IBFAN) published a report documenting violations of the WHO Code and Resolutions gathered in 69 countries. The publication, *Breaking the Rules, Stretching the Rules*, explained why Nestlé is singled out for boycott action: 'As in past monitoring exercises, Nestlé was found to be the source of more violations than any other company' (Kean and Allain, 2004: 2). In 2005, a campaign to challenge Nestlé's public relation policies began. The boycott coordinators called for a public tribunal to evaluate who is telling the truth. Nestlé rejected the proposal (Baby Milk Action, 2005).

The Nestlé case offers a clear example of the two sides of PR. On the one hand, there is a public strategy to create an image of a company with a sound policy of corporate social responsibility, while on the other hand the company engages in covert strategy to undermine its critics. The examples discussed here show that this dual strategy has been applied consistently from the 1970s up to the present day.

THE NEPTUNE STRATEGY

After the settlement in the Nestlé case, Pagan and his associates founded Pagan International (PI) as an independent company in 1985 (*Business Wire*, 1985). Among its first clients was Shell Oil. The company needed help in dealing with the growing support for the anti-apartheid boycott in 1986. The plan Pagan developed to address this issue, the *Neptune Strategy*, aimed to neutralize the boycott in three years. The *Neptune Strategy* was anonymously sent to the ICCR, the large coalition of church groups that played a key role in coordinating the Shell boycott – as it had in the Nestlé boycott. Ideas and strategies developed while working for Nestlé reappear, often in a more elaborate form and structure. Some of the key people Pagan encountered when working for Nestlé had now been added to his team, and important figures within the church groups were targeted once again. The overall strategy was to divert public attention from the boycott and disinvestment efforts, by concentrating on South Africa in a post-apartheid context. The *Neptune Strategy* includes proposals for comprehensive information-gathering operations, dialogue with moderate groups and attempts to entice church groups into working with Shell. The document also outlines sophisticated schemes to drive a wedge between black organizations. Pagan set up a front group of black professionals to argue that disinvestment would harm the black population of South Africa. To provide what Pagan called 'a balanced view' of the apartheid issue, he proposed a proactive strategy aimed at 'the phase of the forming of ideas' (University Strategy, 1986: 4). The *Strategy* was a three-year plan leaked to the press in September 1987 – a year into its implementation. Shell acknowledged the origins of the document, but tried to downplay the reach and effects of the operation, as we will see at the end of this chapter.

Background

In the 1980s, Shell and other corporations that continued to do business in South Africa came under fire from protesters who pressured them to disinvest. Shell was targeted for not observing the oil embargo. In the United States, Shell's problems were exacerbated when the United Mine Workers of America (UMW) called for a consumer boycott in solidarity with South African trade unionists. A labour conflict ignited the controversy in early 1985. The South African National Union of Mineworkers (NUM) demanded the re-hiring of 90 workers fired after a strike in the Rietspruit mine that had been broken with brutal force. Soon other large unions and labour federations in the United States joined the boycott. Anti-apartheid groups and American church groups became part of the coalition too (Walker, 1986). It was not until the launch of the consumer boycott in January 1986 that Shell realized it could no longer hope to avoid or ignore the anti-apartheid campaign (Van Dieren, 1986). After the 1979 OPEC oil embargo Shell had become the main supplier of oil to South Africa, profiting from the premium price it could demand. Shell South Africa, along with other resident oil companies, fuelled the apartheid regime and more specifically military operations in the townships and in Namibia, Angola and other neighbouring black states (Pratt, 1997: 244; also see Hengeveld and Rodenburg, 1995). Pagan advised Shell at this time, when the company policy involved denying any responsibility and refusing to discuss disinvesting or putting pressure on the apartheid regime.

The Plan

The *Neptune Strategy* was a 256-page three-year plan to neutralize the boycott and to divert the attention away from the apartheid issue. Shell South Africa was urged to emphasize what it did locally to address the situation, and internationally Shell focused on future post-apartheid scenarios. A key message was that sanctions and boycotts were not the solution.

The *Neptune Strategy* contains four sections:

1. Intelligence assessment, a summary of the state of the art on several fronts: USA activity against Shell, European activity and a collection of source material to support these findings.
2. Several chapters focusing on how to deal with the various target groups, in which religious groups and the universities accorded the most detailed treatment. Further strategies involved educators, the union, the news media, civil right groups, professional organizations, government relations, employees and international organizations.
3. Strategy evaluation, methodology, and an assessment of cost effectiveness.
4. Timelines indicating the planned implementation of a detailed list of elements of the strategy and a project leader for every subsequent targeted group (the references in this case study

cite the chapters and the corresponding page numbers, as the document does not have an overall page numbering system).

Intelligence Gathering

The report's chapter on intelligence assessment details the information-gathering exercise that was to provide an in-depth understanding of the individuals, groups and networks targeting – or likely to target – Shell on the South African issue. To prepare intelligence reports the analysts could use 'background data already existing in PI's [Pagan International's] computerised data base and hard copy files and publicly available sources' (Intelligence Assessment, App. VIII, 1986: 1). An experienced full-time analyst (called R. Bell) was assigned to use less conventional ways of gathering information too, such as:

- Establishing personal contacts either in the boycotting organizations or with access to such organizations who [sic] can provide information not available to the public;
- Using accepted investigative journalism techniques and personal interviews with key members of the boycott coalition as a reporter for the *International Barometer*; and
- When possible, attending meetings, conferences or direct-action events sponsored by critic groups. (ibid.: 2)

This shows that the company used informers as well as spies – at least one of them is known to have posed as a journalist (as detailed below). Pagan International claimed to have 'a network of correspondents' (ibid.). To evaluate the tactics of the various anti-Shell groups, analyse their political background and assess their influence, PI 'also activated an experienced associate in Europe' (ibid.: 1). In May 1986, several Dutch groups were questioned at length about their work, funding, opinions and networks. They were interviewed by Alan Fuehrer, who claimed to be a freelance journalist working for the *International Barometer*, a newsletter aimed at bridging the gap between activist groups and business (Runderkamp and Salverda, 1987). Fuehrer did not mention the fact that the magazine was founded by Pagan in 1986 as a platform to disseminate his views to his clients and other interested parties. Traced in Brussels by two Dutch investigative journalists after the exposure of the *Neptune Strategy*, Fuehrer denied being a correspondent for the *International Barometer*. Confronted with the business card he had used to introduce himself in the Netherlands, he said: 'Look, this was just a way of showing people I was authorised to track information for them.' While Fuehrer sought to downplay his role as intelligence functionary, he gave away further details about Pagan's practices: 'All I did was send the tapes to Pagan. He knew my name from a list of former US foreign services officers. Pagan solicited a whole list of people like that' (cited in Runderkamp and Salverda, 1987).

Nestlé Strategy Revisited

The *Neptune Strategy* explored the problems with various target groups. On several fronts, the possible solutions resonated with the lessons learned from the Nestlé controversy.

The chapter on union strategy, for instance. emphasized the difficulties of talking to trade unionists, who – unlike the religious leaders – had already made up their minds. 'The primary objective of the union strategy is to prevent labour boycott efforts from expanding to new unions, and to bring about an inactive or almost inactive boycott' (Union Strategy, 1986: 3). In order to reach this goal '[o]bjective discussions will be initiated [...] every effort will be made to ensure that these discussions are seen not as negotiations (as is common in the labour milieu) but as an exchange of ideas' (ibid.). However, it becomes clear that this initial meeting was actually an 'information-gathering session and would establish the baseline from which other steps could be formulated' (ibid.: 5).

Pagan advised Shell to try to convince union leaders that the role of the company in South Africa had been misrepresented in boycott rhetoric. Pagan looked for an equivalent of the Muskie Audit Commission and suggested appointing a 'senior, respected, well-known public figure as an ombudsman between Shell and organised labour'. The aim of these 'informational meetings' was 'calming the rhetoric used by the unions and seeking points of mutuality' (ibid.: 6). This clearly echoes the plan to 'stop the shouting match' between Nestlé and its opponents. Labour was not the only target.

The strategy proposed for local classroom teachers included 'community building' and the creation of citizen committees that in some respects resembled those set up to break strikes early in the twentieth century (see Chapter 2). Teachers were to develop a better general understanding of the apartheid issue and 'an atmosphere which will foster sympathetic understanding of the plight of the local

Shell dealer unfairly targeted by the boycott' (Educators Strategy, 1986: 2). Local teachers had to be convinced that apart from the hardship for the dealers, 'the boycott represents a disservice to the community' (ibid.). This part of the strategy echoes the citizen's committees discussed in the last chapter. Leading members of educational organizations not completely supportive to the boycott were to be identified and subsequently targeted with 'individualised information packages' in order to change their position. Third-party contacts potentially sympathetic to Shell – such as the National Congress of Parents and Teachers – were singled out to work with teachers in order to influence them (ibid.: 3). Likewise, the employee strategy described Shell's 35,000 employees as 'one of the company's most effective communication tools' and the company's large pool of loyal retirees as 'a valuable resource in communities around the country'. Together they had to be turned into 'Shell Ambassadors' to 'defend the company on the grassroots level in their churches, local business and women's clubs, unions and other local organisations' (Employee Strategy, 1986: 1).

For Nestlé, announcing support of the WHO code on marketing of infant formula had been a 'breakthrough' moment. Pagan suggested that Shell South Africa should be encouraged to review its policies and practices in terms of the Sullivan Principles. The Sullivan Signatory Group was an initiative of corporations that supported change in South Africa, but did not want to disinvest and leave the country. A private audit could estimate the 'grade' the company would get. A good grade could be 'publicly announced with some fanfare' and make it more difficult to single out Shell US for a boycott (Civil Rights Groups, 1986: 3). The content of the Sullivan Principles was of no real interest to Pagan:

> It does not matter whether the Sullivan guidelines are correct or whether the audit programme is perceived at some levels to be flawed. They are the only standing criteria, which the average person knows anything about. (ibid.)

What counted for Pagan was the PR exercise, and the possible positive effects for the reputation of the client company. What is today called CSR was used as a policy for PR reasons only.

Divide and Rule

One of the plans fully implemented by the time Shell's strategies were revealed was the creation of a front group set up to divide black constituencies. The Coalition on Southern Africa (COSA) was launched by several prominent black clergymen on 10 September 1987 – just days before the exposure of the *Neptune Strategy*. Supposedly, COSA was an independent organization preparing South African blacks for leadership in a post-apartheid society. In fact, Pagan organized this new religious coalition to oppose corporate disinvestment from South Africa. The key to this plan was to give religious and black groups 'sufficient reasons not to join the boycott' (Religious Groups Strategy, 1986: 1). The proposal was a double-edged sword.

> One of the most politically effective and legitimate reasons for a continued multinational business presence in South Africa is the need to train Black South Africans to create wealth and jobs, and to participate at the highest levels of government in a multiracial, democratic society. (Breakthrough Elements, 1986: 1)

So, in addition to Shell South Africa training people in technical and managerial skills, within the corporate structure, the company could do more. 'The Shell Company could create or contribute to programmes that recruit talented young Blacks for training in public administration and management in institutions located in the United States and Europe' (ibid.: 2). Pagan singled out key black activists and church leaders to help develop 'post-apartheid plans' that would 'ensure the continuation and growth of the Shell companies in the United States and South Africa' (Religious Groups Strategy, 1986:1; also see Breakthrough Elements, 1986: 1–3). Mongoven confirmed that Pagan International had provided free office space and use of telephones to COSA, and had paid for travel by COSA's staff. Mobil Oil, Johnson & Johnson and several other companies with interests in South Africa, provided the start-up capital, $765,000 (Anderson, 1987; Runderkamp and Salverda, 1987).

Companies with South African operations immediately began to point to COSA to show that not all US church groups backed disinvestment. Donna Katzin, a leader in the Shell boycott, claimed executives of Mobil Oil, Caltex, and Colgate-Palmolive cited COSA during board meetings at which shareholders raised questions concerning these companies' South African operation (Sparks, 1987). However, the effect was short-lived. Although Pagan stepped down as a paid adviser of COSA after the exposure of Shell's involvement, the organization was branded a front group for business interests (*Katholiek Nieuwsblad*, 1987).

Sacrificing Trust

A large part of the plan focused on cultivating relations with religious organizations in a move to 'deflect their attention away from boycotts and disinvestment efforts'. Drawing from his experiences with the Nestlé controversy, Pagan emphasized: 'Mobilised members of religious communions provide a "critical mass" of public opinion and economic leverage that should not be taken lightly' (Religious Groups Strategy, 1986: 1).

James (Jim) Armstrong was responsible for the outreach programme to organized religion. He was introduced to Shell as a former bishop and former president of the National Council of Churches with a unique knowledge of the church community and its inner workings. His biographical note in the Neptune report failed to mention his key role in Pagan's strategy to break the Nestlé boycott, and the fact that he had joined Pagan International and had been promoted to CEO in 1985 (nor did it bring up the fact that Armstrong had been forced to resign as head of the National Council of Churches in 1983 after he confessed to infidelity to his wife. See Hyer, 1984; Herron, 1990).

The *Neptune Strategy* identified 17 church targets with more than 50 individuals to be contacted. Most of these people were singled out because of their position, their networks and their influence in the community. Among those scheduled to be contacted were the Rev. Emilio Castro, president of the World Council of Churches; the Rev. Arie Brouwer, general secretary of the National Council of Churches, Bishop David Preus of the American Lutheran Church and the Rev. Avery Post, president of the United Church of Christ and co-chair of the Churches Emergency Committee on South Africa (Religious Groups Strategy, 1986: 3–13). The help of Bishop Desmond Tutu and Dr Alan Boesak would be sought in finding a constructive role for companies like Shell in changing South African society. Both influential leaders were 'known as aggressive moderates'. Pagan realized that Tutu was a strong anti-apartheid fighter, so 'securing his help will not be easy' (ibid.: 7), but if successful they could be *utilised* in developing a strategy to deal with present realities and post-apartheid prospects' (ibid.: 12; emphasis added). An appendix chart outlined when the meetings were to take place, who was to make contact and then rated the degree of probable 'success'. ICCR, the organization that exposed the *Neptune Strategy*, did some follow-up research and confirmed that many of these meetings had taken place as planned. 'Many of those targeted said they had met with Armstrong and or others but said the meetings were unsuccessful in undermining support for the boycott' (Anderson, 1987).

In the Netherlands, Shell's secrets meetings with delegates of the Roman Catholic bishops' conference caused considerable disarray. After consultation in 1985, the Dutch Council of Churches had decided to support disinvestment from South Africa. Dialogues with the oil company over 20 years had proved fruitless. The Council also agreed to a coordinated approach in dealing with Shell. In spite of this agreement, Catholic bishops had accepted Shell's invitation without consulting other members of the Council. Pax Christi thought this was a major mistake. The secretary of the Dutch Council of Churches, Wim van der Zee, concluded that Shell was trying to split the churches (*Volkskrant*, 1987).

The publication of the Pagan report strengthened distrust of Shell, particularly among religious groups. A Dutch magazine discussing Christian-democratic issues published a remarkably critical analysis of the *Neptune Strategy* written by the scientific office of the Christian Democratic Party. Most worrying from their perspective, was that the report allowed no dialogue:

> The Neptune Report aims to let the financial and economical reasoning prevail over social and moral virtues. That is against any of our beliefs especially when this is disguised as an ethical motivation. This involves pure deception! (*Christen Demoncratische Verkenningen*, 1988)

The magazine refused to print a response from Shell's Dutch public affairs director Van Rooijen, indicating the extent of Shell's isolation at that time. Van Rooijen was a well-respected member of the Christian Democratic Party and a former state secretary (Van der Bergh, 1995: 317–8). His appointment as director of public affairs in 1987 was retrospectively viewed as part of the strategy, according to Jan van der Laak, secretary of Pax Christi in the Netherlands: 'A Christian Democrat with an ecumenical background sure helps to give the company a human face' (cited in Obbink, 1987).

In the UK, similar issues arose. In his strategy plan, Pagan had advised Shell that Anglican support for the boycott could have 'serious repercussions' for its influence on Anglican communities elsewhere in the world (Religious Groups Strategy, 1986: 7). Shell should approach appropriate leaders of the Church of England, perhaps even to the Archbishop of Canterbury, to seek their assistance in working with their own church and the churches of South Africa, to reduce conflict and to engender co-operation with Shell South Africa and others who are committed to a just society in South Africa in which business could be a positive force. (ibid.)

The Church of England accused Shell of dishonesty after the *Neptune Strategy* was exposed in October 1987. John Gladwin, secretary of the Church of England Synod's Board for Social Responsibility, had met with Pagan in December 1986. Gladwin said: 'He never told me that he was working for Shell, and I feel we were deceived' (*Newsletter on the Oil Embargo against South Africa*, 1987).

For the organization that received the leaked *Neptune Strategy*, the revelations were particularly damaging. In the press release exposing Pagan's report, Tim Smith of the Council of Churches' ICCR explained:

Jim Armstrong and Ray Pagan have vigorously argued on numerous occasions to the press and the public that Pagan International was not involved in defending Shell from the boycott, gathering intelligence for Shell on the campaign, or giving Shell guidance on how to counteract the boycott. (Smith and Katzin, 1987)

The *Neptune Strategy* revealed that Pagan and Armstrong were doing just that: defending Shell from the boycott, by gathering *intelligence* on *activists* and advising on *covert corporate counter-strategies*. Smith and the ICCR were specifically targeted by Pagan's strategists. Because the ICCR played such a significant role in the resolution of the Nestlé boycott, they were to be approached for assistance in the resolution of the Shell US boycott (Religious Groups Strategy, 1986: 5). 'Building on a previously established relationship of mutual trust, PI will attempt to enlist and include Smith in the development of win/win strategies' (ibid.: 6). The church organization felt betrayed. The press release concluded:

In fact, these public assurances were part of a calculated, duplicitous plan, outlined in the *Neptune Strategy* document, to rechannel energy from the boycott. Shell's goal, as implemented by Jim Armstrong and other Pagan International staff, was to obscure the ways in which Shell concretely supports white minority rule and apartheid by diverting the debate to 'post-apartheid South Africa'. (Smith and Katzin, 1987)

Denial is a common response in the face of exposure of covert activity (as will be seen in other case studies below). However, in this instance the deception was even more pronounced. After the experiences with Nestlé, the ICCR and specifically its coordinator Tim Smith had reasons to be suspicious when Pagan tried to involve them in resolving yet another boycott. Other targets of the religious groups strategy felt equally deceived. The fact that Pagan and Armstrong strongly denied any suggestion of acting for Shell is a clear example of how companies under pressure may deal with dialogue and how they tend to treat their opponents. The *Neptune Strategy* places a premium on engagement with critics, but only as a means to secure corporate interests and a licence to operate. Since the late 1980s, such dialogues have increased in number – but critics rightly question what this form of engagement actually delivers (see, for instance, Gray and Bebbington, 2007; Hess and Dunfee, 2007; Doane, 2005a, 2005b; Owen, Swift and Hunt, 2001; Gray, 2001). The issue is how to evaluate the efficacy of dialogue. This case study shows why misgivings about CSR may be well founded.

Engineering Consent

There are two reasons why the university strategy was one of the main features in the plan. The first was the importance of campus politics, as mobilized students provided a strong base for support of the boycott. A greater focus on US corporate activity in South Africa by campaigning students could also imply recruitment problems for Shell. Second, Pagan argued that corporate management generally becomes aware of threats and new ideas when it is too late, often after they have become part of the political agenda and are on the way to becoming a public issue. Pagan placed great emphasis on changing this. His solution to both problems was 'to involve Shell US at earlier stages of idea creation to increase the impact of the corporate viewpoint on South Africa' (University Strategy, 1986: 6). Anti-apartheid positions on campuses were well defined, Pagan argued:

The campus environment is beset by heightened emotional and political activity and anti-corporate sentiments. Most student groups are either controlled or strongly influenced by student leaders who have a radical or left-of-center orientation. In such an environment, even moderate leaders may be reluctant to associate directly with corporate representatives. (ibid.: 8)

Shell US could expect considerable opposition across college campuses. 'However, any activities to stem this hostility must be carefully undertaken so as to avoid being portrayed by radical students as an example of corporate efforts to mislead and manipulate students' (ibid.). The basic strategy is to 'deflect attention from company-specific actions to broader questions of disinvestment, operating in a police state, and developments pertaining to a democratic post-apartheid South Africa' (ibid.). To channel campus unrest, Pagan intended to persuade teachers to provide 'a balanced view' of the problems and 'a knowledgeable treatment of the South African issue' (ibid.: 4). Pagan suggested that Shell 'create greater infusion of South Africa-related materials in emulator teaching and writing in a manner considered legitimate and enriching' (ibid.). 'Credibility and balance' were key elements in the strategy (ibid.).

CONFLICTING INTERESTS

For the proactive strategy to influence campus debate and 'the forming of ideas' (ibid.: 4) the academic community was important. The *Neptune Strategy* listed Professor S. Prakash Sethi as 'Project Manager' for the university strategy. At the time, Sethi was professor at the Center for Management, Baruch College, City University of New York. When confronted by the Interfaith Center on Corporate Responsibility, Sethi said he had been a paid consultant in 1986, hired to advise Pagan and Shell on how to reach out to the academic world. He denied that he had been paid to do hands-on staff work, describing his role as advisory (Smith and Katzin, 1987). However, the Timeline Chart dated 10 June 1986 for the university strategy assigned ten out of the 29 planned projects to Sethi, while the other projects had no one listed as responsible (yet). Sethi's tasks included: identify South African scholars for the PI database, develop the student association debate kit, arrange exchanges with young scholars in South Africa, plan academic association sessions, plan regional post-apartheid seminars, ties with student associations and academic sessions on South Africa (Timeline University Strategy, 1986). The focus, however, was on planning international and regional post-apartheid seminars, described in detail in the Tactics

Section of the university strategy aimed at 'Intellectual Elites and Thought Leaders' (University Strategy, 1986: 9). And a lot of those actually took place.

Sethi organized the 'International Conference on South Africa in Transition: The Process and Prospects of Creating a Non-racial, Democratic Nation of South Africa', held at White Plains, New York, from 29 September to 20 October 1987. The conference mirrored the goal of the *Neptune Strategy*. This was reflected in the objectives, focusing on South Africa after apartheid, the implementation, the delegates, as well as the support and funding. As outlined in the *Neptune Strategy*, the speakers represented 'the top leadership of political, business/labour, academic and religious groups' from the United States and South Africa. The Strategy proposed 'to enlist cooperation of the US and South African business community' (ibid.). The steering committee of the conference included Rafael Pagan and Sal Marzullo, chair of the US Industry Group of the Sullivan Principles Signatory Companies, and an executive of Mobil Oil. While Shell reportedly did not fund this conference, the Sullivan Signatory Group did provide a grant (Smith and Katzin, 1987) – just as the *Neptune Strategy* had suggested (University Strategy, 1986). Furthermore, James Armstrong convinced Bishop David Preus of the American Lutheran Church (ALC) to offer a $6,000 grant for the conference (Anderson, 1987). After the *Neptune Strategy* was exposed, several church leaders involved in the conference cancelled their participation and financial support (Smith and Katzin,1987). Although Shell denied it had anything to do with the event, the ALC grant was withdrawn. 'What poisoned it for me', said the Rev. Ralston Deffenbagh of Lutheran World Ministries, who was originally on the planning committee for the conference, 'is that it seemed aimed at helping Shell break the boycott' (Anderson, 1987).

The papers produced in this seminar were placed in 'respected academic/professional journals' just as the *Neptune Strategy* had proposed 'to give them wider currency and be used as source material for the media' (University Strategy, 1986: 10). Both the Spring and Summer issues of *Business and Society Review* were dedicated to the conference in 1986 (Sethi, 1987: xiii). The proceedings of the conference were published in book form 'to be made available to libraries and students [and to be] used as classroom texts' (University Strategy, 1986). The book appeared as *The South Africa Quagmire: In Search Of a Peaceful Path to Democratic Pluralism*, edited by S. Prakash Sethi (1987). In the preface, Sethi acknowledged the help of James Armstrong in encouraging religious leaders and other public figures to write for *Business and Society Review*, and Sal Marzullo from Mobil Oil for his efforts in the business community. He does not, however, refer to the White Plains conference that preceded the book. The quarterly *Foreign Affairs* dedicated a short and critical review to the book, pointing at its biased premise:

> Trying to close the barn door after the horses have fled, this collection of essays musters some cogent economic and political arguments against sanctions, and a number of essays amount in effect to a defence of inaction by outside parties. The editor himself advocates a visionary scheme for aid to South Africa coupled with precisely targeted sanctions, and a few advocates of international pressure, including Archbishop Tutu and Congressman Howard Wolpe, are given a platform alongside more than 30 opponents, mostly Americans and white South African moderates. Notably missing, apart from Tutu, are any voices of the authentic black opposition. (Whitaker, 1988: 891)

Sethi not only advised Pagan on the university strategy, but was also engaged in putting it into practice. As a result, his academic work on business ethics intertwined with developing strategies for companies. A few years earlier, in a discussion on 'Corporate Money and Co-opted Scholars' in *Business & Society Review*, Sethi took the position that most academics would see through 'cheap attempts to influence the direction of research findings' (Sethi, 1981). However, Sethi wrote that he was not against corporations funding 'research in areas of particular interest to them' or funding 'research scholars whose policy views may be more in line with those advocated by the corporation'. Sethi thought of these approaches as 'quite honourable and legitimate' (ibid.). In the post-apartheid conference volume, Sethi acknowledges the support and cooperation of the Research Program in Business and Public Policy, Center for Management Development and Organization Research, Baruch College, City University of New York. He also mentioned that 'the Research Program received partial financial support (with no strings attached) from the business community to conduct studies on different aspects of business and public policy' (Sethi, 1987: xvi). The Center's resources made available his time as well as other logistical support (ibid.).

Others in the academic world were not so happy about Sethi's involvement with Pagan. The Faculty Senate of the University of Notre Dame had an 'extensive discussion' about the *Neptune Strategy*.

Professor Kathleen Biddick 'sought clarification of the University's involvement in the attempt by bishop James Amstrong and Prof. S. Prakash Sethi of New York to circumvent or compromise the university's policy on South Africa and its reputation'. The president of the University, Rev. Edward A. Malloy, remarked: 'The University is not thinking of any participation in any effort associated with Rafael Pagan, who seems to believe he has some intimacy with people at Notre Dame.' The President referred to sections in the *Neptune Strategy*, citing his university as 'a unique opportunity for creating an institution for the study of post-apartheid problems' as well as the alleged 'close ties' of some of the senior people with the South African business community (the sections he was referring to were probably Breakthrough Elements, 1986: 4; Religious Groups Strategy, 1986: 9–10). 'The president concluded that apologies to Notre Dame and several of its people are in order from Armstrong, Sethi and Pagan' (University of Notre Dame, 1988). The minutes of the Faculty Senate of the University of Notre Dame do not mention receiving apologies or further clarifications.

The fact that Sethi was working for Pagan on the boycott of Shell while – at the same time – he was doing research on Pagan and the boycott of Nestlé, has never been addressed before. Notwithstanding the value of the insights delivered in his book *Multinational Corporations and the Impact of Public Advocacy on Corporate Strategy*, the position of academics supporting corporate strategies aimed at undermining such public advocacy needs to be part of the debate on secret manoeuvres in countries referring to themselves as democracies.

DAMAGE CONTROL AND DENIAL

After the exposure of the *Neptune Strategy*, the company tried to control the damage by downplaying the reach and effects of the operation. Shell officials admitted that the company commissioned the plan, but claimed that little had been adopted as policy (Barrett, 1987). According to Shell official Tom Stewart, however, Pagan International was still retained by the time the *Neptune Strategy* was exposed 'for advice on anti-apartheid criticism and boycotts' (ibid.). Shell spokesperson Norman Altstedder confirmed that the plan existed, but denied that it was secret (Anderson, 1987).

Pagan himself, however, was furious about the leak. In a letter to Emilio Castro, General Secretary of the World Council of Churches, he wrote:

Most regrettable of all is that the stolen document has also been placed in the hands of Dutch activists that have a sorry track record for violent behaviour. If violence and personal injury result from this ill-gotten and carelessly shared information, the responsibility will have to rest with those who sent it. (Pagan to Castro, letter dated 5 October 1987, cited in van Drimmelen to Pagan, 1987)

While Shell tried to control the situation after the exposure by downplaying the damage, Pagan's anger is one indication of the importance of the strategy. Moreover, Shell's claim that not much had been implemented was misleading. Close reading of the report indicated that some of the strategies *had* commenced as planned. The *Neptune Strategy* was prepared in 1986, and became public in September 1987. Pagan had developed specified strategies for different target groups, as detailed below. The report included timelines pointing out the implementation of the various aspects for every subsequent group strategy. The religious groups strategy and the university strategy had been prioritized, because churches and students represented a crucial threat in terms of widening support for the boycott. The timelines also identified a project leader for the union strategy, Paul Jensen, a partner in the consulting firm Public Strategies (Timeline Union Strategy: 1). Together with Robert Strauss, former Democratic Party chairman, he had started making calls on Shell's behalf to approach union leaders (*Labour Notes*, 1988). Judging by the parts that evidently *had* been implemented, it is fair to say that Shell appreciated the intention of the *Neptune Strategy* and were following Pagan's counsel.

Another feature of the strategy that dealt with the exposure consisted of a policy of 'plausible denial'. When operations go wrong in the world of intelligence, authorities higher up in the hierarchy often try to distance themselves from the people involved in the actual operation. The goal is evasion of responsibility and accountability.

As a response to the exposure of the *Neptune Strategy*, Royal Dutch Shell took the position that the strategy was purely a Shell US affair. However, the subtitle told a different story. Officially, the report was called *Shell US South Africa Strategy. Prepared For: The Shell Oil Company*. The subtitle indicated the purpose of the strategy: *For use in the US and for the development of global coordination within the Royal Dutch Shell Group*. Furthermore, unity of approach by Royal Dutch Shell companies when dealing with their critics was an essential part of the plan. The *Neptune Strategy* involved a coordinated worldwide campaign, because '[t]he Shell US boycott cannot be neutralised or ended through action in North America only'. Pagan warned Shell it would be confronted with 'a well coordinated international effort, the pressures applied on Shell US will be strongly supplemented with political/economical/ violence pressures and through *intellectual terrorism* against Shell's affiliates' (Structure and Organisation, 1986: 5, emphasis added). The plan included detailed analyses of the anti-apartheid movements in the Netherlands, the UK and several other countries (Intelligence Assessment, 1986: 14–20). The accounts of anti-Shell activists in those countries related above suggest the implementation of an international plan.

A defensive argument repeatedly used by Shell was the claim that every company in the Shell Group was supposed to act independently.[7] At a shareholders' meeting of Shell Canada held on 27 April 1988, chair J.M. MacLeod assured the public that he personally abhorred apartheid, but that Shell Canada had no influence outside of Canada. L.C. van Wachem – managing director of the Royal Dutch Petroleum Company, Shell Canada's majority shareholder (71.4 per cent) and one of its directors also present at the meeting – underlined that position by cutting short the discussion with the shareholders. He 'affirmed that each national company was autonomous and none should try to influence the other' (Pratt, 1997: 247). A Dutch television documentary later revealed that Van Wachem – officially in his capacity of chair of the board of Shell US – had met Pagan in the summer of 1986 in Houston, Texas to discuss his work for the company (Runderkamp and Salverda, 1987; Obbink, 1987).

In the Netherlands, Shell claimed it first heard of the report after it was exposed. The Dutch director of public affairs, Martin van Rooijen, tried to disassociate the Dutch operation completely from the *Neptune Strategy*: 'A report like that is something Shell Netherlands can do without,' he told a Dutch weekly. 'Our actions are open and above board' (Obbink, 1987). A statement that unintentionally qualified the operations of the American sister company Shell Oil, the author of the article remarked (ibid.). However, Van Rooijen did coordinate a series of secret meetings with Dutch church leaders to set up a dialogue – which followed the *Neptune Strategy* to the letter (Religious Strategy, 1986: 9).

Misleading shareholders, activists and the press were essential elements of both the covert corporate strategy and operational damage control. These were part of the broader plan to influence public opinion and to engineer consent in order to minimize the effects of the boycott.

COMPANY AND PEOPLE, PAGAN AND MONGOVEN

Pagan wrote a clear outline of his strategy in the early days of his work for Nestlé in a speech delivered to the Public Affairs Council in 1982. He argues that any company's primary goal is survival. To do so a company must separate the 'fanatic' activist leaders from those who are 'decent concerned people'. In particular, 'strip the activists of the moral authority they receive from their alliances with religious organisations' (Pagan, 1982: 3–4). In order to reach these goals, a company under fire would need to establish a strategic capability, an issue management unit. This unit should set up a well-focused information-gathering operation and include an analysis function. For Nestlé, Pagan developed a database of more than 700 organizations that had endorsed the boycott and a distant early-warning system to monitor any issue or trend as it passed from the initial forum to scholarly journals to church bulletins to political broadsheets and local magazines to the general media. As a result, he claimed, a company would have at least two years' notice that the issue was growing, enough time to resolve the problem early on (ibid.).

The focus on strategies such as divide and rule, and the emphasis on gathering intelligence resemble a military approach to issue management. This is reflected in their methods, but also in the way both Pagan and Mongoven understood and articulated their work. 'The boycott movement is guerrilla warfare. It is an international war; its roots are ideological and political and we are being used as a means to a political end,' Pagan wrote to Nestlé (Sethi, 1987: 223). 'It was like planning for a major combat mission,' Mongoven, his partner, recalled of preparing the Nestlé action plan, 'It included an assessment of field conditions, strengths and weaknesses of our opponents, characteristics of their leaders, our own strengths and weaknesses and how they matched with those of our adversaries' (ibid.: 225).

Pagan had a military career before he became a company strategist. His father left an executive position to be an Episcopal priest in a village in Puerto Rico when Rafael Jr. was nine years old. Remaining in the village until after high school, Pagan graduated from the University of Puerto Rico and joined the US Army in 1951 (O'Dwyers, 1990). He was awarded a Bronze Star when he was wounded after parachuting behind enemy lines in the Korean War. He stayed with the army as an intelligence officer assigned to the General and Joint Staffs of the Office of the Secretary of Defence. He briefed Presidents Kennedy and Johnson on the Soviet bloc's military and economic capabilities[8] (*Washington Times,* 1993). His career path is common for many propagandists and lobbyists. He retired as a colonel after 20 years' service in 1970 to become Director of International Affairs at the International Nickel Company. Then, in 1975, he joined Castle & Cooke, Inc. as Vice President for Government and Industry Affairs (Denig and van der Meiden, 1985: 488). This was a large multinational agribusiness corporation with a reputation for aggression towards activists. Here Pagan first encountered the churches' corporate responsibility office, ICCR (*INFACT Update*, 1991, cited in Sethi, 1994: 222).

Mongoven did not have a military background. He had been a journalist, worked as an organizer for the Republican Party, and in the communications office of the Nixon and Ford administration. He did however study military strategy in his own time and reportedly introduced the 'nine principles' of German military strategist Carl von Clausewitz at a Nestlé strategy meeting. Pagan and Mongoven also turned to Sun Tzu's classic theoretical work The *Art of War* for inspiration (Stauber and Rampton, 1995: 51–2).

The director of Pagan's intelligence department was Arion N. Pattakos, a former US army intelligence officer (*Labour Notes*, 1988). As a colonel in the army, in 1978, Pattakos prepared memoranda for the 'director defence communication agency' and signed for the Joint Chief of Staffs, as a recently declassified but still heavily censored document shows (Pattakos, 1978). He worked for Nestlé, Pagan International and later Mongoven, Biscoe and Dutchin.[9] A 2006 biographical note adds that he is also a 'principal instructor/ facilitator' for the CIA course in analytical risk management, and a founding member and former president of the Operations Security Professionals Society (Pattakos, 2006).

Pagan International became an independent company in May 1985. The company reportedly offered advice to defence contractors as well as the chemicals, pharmaceuticals and food industries. The client list included Union Carbide, Chevron, Campbell and the government of Puerto Rico (*O'Dwyers PR Services Report*, 1990). After a couple of years of successful expansion, however, Pagan International fell on hard times. Pagan's success with Nestlé made him quite attractive to some companies, but others considered him too controversial (Sethi, 1987: 236). The new firm also had problems matching the terms and conditions which the executives had become accustomed to while working for Nestlé. After a fall-out between the partners, Mongoven and two other senior PI executives left and formed Mongoven, Biscoe & Dutchin, Inc. – a public affairs consulting company with offices in Washington DC. Lawsuits followed, with MBD 'complaining that Pagan owed them money, and Pagan accusing them of deliberately undermining the firm by leaking the *Neptune Strategy* to the press' (Stauber and Rampton, 1995: 53). The lawsuits revealed that Shell, according to PI, had a written contract to pay Pagan $50,000 monthly until June 1989. Pagan told the respected PR trade magazine *O'Dwyer's* that 'the firm started having trouble when the *Neptune Strategy* leaked to the press even before the company had a chance to see it' (*O'Dwyers*, 1990). Pagan International went bankrupt and was eventually dissolved (Pagan died of pneumonia in 1993, aged 67).

Pagan International had failed to capitalize on its strength – issue resolution in the public policy arena, where it had built a unique niche for itself, according to Sethi (ibid., 236). Mongoven, Biscoe & Duchin did manage to take PI's work to a higher level, by fine-tuning the divide and rule strategy – prompting Pagan to sue the company for stealing 'trade secrets' (*O'Dwyers*, 1990).

Ron Duchin, the third partner in the firm, graduated from the US Army War College and worked for the Department of Defense and as director of public affairs for the Veterans of Foreign Wars before joining Pagan International and then MBD. In 1991, Duchin, speaking at a conference of the National Cattlemen's Association, outlined MBD's strategy to divide and conquer activist movements (Duchin, 1991). Duchin's speech was extensively quoted by Montague (1993) and Bleifuss (1993), and by Carter (2002) in her sharp analysis of how MBD destroyed tobacco control from the inside.

> Duchin explained that activists fall into four categories: radicals, opportunists, idealists and realists, and a three-step strategy was needed to bring them down. First, you isolate the radicals: those who want to change the system and promote social justice. Second, you carefully 'cultivate' the idealists: those who are altruistic, don't stand to gain from their activism, and are not as extreme in their methods and objectives as the radicals. You do this by gently persuading them that their advocacy has negative consequences for some groups, thus transforming them into realists. Finally,

you co-opt the realists (the pragmatic incrementalists willing to work within the system) into compromise.

The realists should always receive the highest priority in any strategy dealing with a public policy issue [...] If your industry can successfully bring about these relationships, the credibility of the radicals will be lost and opportunists can be counted on to share in the final policy solution.

Opportunists, those who are motivated by power, success, or a sense of their own celebrity, will be satisfied merely by a sense of partial victory. (Duchin, cited in Carter, 2002: 112)

Confidential MBD memos found their way into the public domain in the 1990s, often published by PRwatch.org, the American NGO monitoring the PR industry. Military terminology recurred throughout MBD's 1994 reports for the Chlorine Chemistry Council, which warned that activist groups were preparing for 'protracted battle [...] recruiting and training activists in an anti-chlorine campaign [...] initially targeting the pulp and paper industry'. MBD's memo's showed that the industry was aware of the risks of dioxin and did not attempt to refute the US Environmental Protection Agency's 1994 reassessment of dioxin. This EPA report 'indicated that there is no safe level of dioxin exposure and that any dose no matter how low can result in health damage' (Stauber and Rampton, 1996). Rather than show concern for these 'complex and severe effects', however, MBD was worried about defending the chlorine industry's image. An example of this is the 1996 advice prepared for the chemical industry on 'how best to counter [...] activists' claims of the evils associated with dioxin as a weapon against chlorine chemistry' (ibid.).

MBD have created their own form of scaremongering, Stauber and Rampton (2001: 151) argued, where the industry is an 'innocent giant under attack from radicals', mobilizing grand narratives of modernisation, technology and western values against the 'threats' of community concern and the developing world. MBD are specifically unconcerned about the impact they have on disempowered others (Carter, 2002: 117).

CONCLUSION

Pagan's work for Shell and Nestlé is a perfect example of activist intelligence and covert corporate strategy, encompassing the defining elements of intelligence: surveillance, power, knowledge and secrecy.

It includes many examples showing the tangled relationship between the gathering of intelligence and subsequent covert action.

Although for reasons of comprehension, at first sight it might seem useful to distinguish between corporate tactics and strategy, the reality is more complex. The Pagan case study illustrates that dialogue between a company and its critics is a vital element of the corporate counterstrategy and needs to be understood as a tactical information-gathering exercise too. Any contact between a company and its opponents is as much an information-gathering exercise as anything else. In the long term, the dialogue served to seize the moral initiative from the 'confrontationalists' and to encourage conflicts between groups in order to destabilise the boycott coalition. Likewise, the creating of an audit commission in the Nestlé infant formula controversy served a multitude of purposes. Its official task was to ensure compliance with the WHO code and provide a complaint procedure. Compliance helped restore the company's credibility to the outside world and bridge the gap between management and leaders of the boycott, while at the same time the audit commission took over responsibility for dealing with the issue from the company. Strategically, the commission also worked as damage control and containment policy: it diverted the media focus away from activists, and caused disarray amongst boycott groups, which together eroded the rationale for the boycott.

Secrecy is an essential element in Pagan's work. It is crucial in securing the credibility of the PR work on what we now call corporate social responsibility. Many of the moves Nestlé made were meant to weaken the support for the boycott more than effectively changing corporate policies.

Battlefield strategy acquired in former careers in the military was reflected in subsequent work for big business. In Pagan's words, any company's primary goal is survival, to continue business as usual. This case study shows that activist intelligence is essential to that survival, and is part of the corporate exercise of power. Pagan's strategy includes various examples of the engineering of consent such as his advice to have Shell focus on the post-apartheid area and to influence 'the phase of the forming of ideas' at universities and elsewhere in education. It also shows in his attempts to erode the rationale for the boycott by trying to convince union leaders that the role of the company had been misrepresented by boycott rhetoric. Furthermore, his proactive work on various campuses was intended to hamper the recruitment of activists. Moreover, where

Pagan persuaded church leaders to work with Shell and Nestlé, he effectively neutered their leading role in the boycott.

Pagan's strategies and tactics belong to a repertoire of misleading and deceptive manipulation of sentiment and opinion. He is part of a long tradition of corporate propagandists that also includes Edward Bernays, Ivy Lee, Nick Nichols, Eric Dezenhall, John Hill and Donald Knowlton (see Chapter 2).

The Pagan case study provided examples of the overall strategies developed to undermine corporate critics, thanks to the unique nature of the source material. The other case studies will highlight more specific elements of covert corporate strategy. The next one focuses on the effects of infiltration for the targeted group, and explores the collusion between corporate spies and Special Branch.

4
McSpy: Case Study

Fast-food company McDonald's hired at least seven private detectives to identify who was responsible for London Greenpeace's leaflet *What's Wrong With McDonald's?* which had been distributed outside many McDonald's outlets in the UK since the mid-1980s (London Greenpeace, 1986a,1986b). The surveillance operation was exposed after McDonald's sued the activist group for libel. Under cross-examination, the company was forced to provide many details of its extensive surveillance operation on London Greenpeace. Agents infiltrated London Greenpeace for varying lengths of time between October 1989 and early summer 1991. The court transcripts and notes made by the investigators reveal the lengths McDonald's went to in procuring information about this small activist group.

London Greenpeace had been campaigning on a variety of environmental and social justice issues since the early 1970s. The group was formed several years before the more famous Greenpeace International and is entirely unrelated to it. In the mid-1980s, it began a campaign against McDonald's as a high-profile organization symbolizing everything it considered wrong with big business. In 1985, it launched the International Day of Action Against McDonald's, which has been held annually on 16 October ever since. In 1986, London Greenpeace produced a six-page leaflet, *What's Wrong with McDonald's? Everything they don't want you to know*, criticizing many aspects of the corporation's business. It accused the burger chain of seducing children through advertising, promoting an unhealthy diet, exploiting its staff and contributing to environmental damage and the mistreatment of animals.

In 1990, having ignored London Greenpeace for many years, McDonald's decided to take action: it sued for libel. McDonald's is extremely sensitive about its reputation. It has fought legal battles across the world to stop people using its name, symbols and slogans (Armstrong, 2002). McDonald's claimed that the leaflet was libellous and defamatory. Its libel writ identified five campaigners and required them either to retract the allegations made in the leaflet and apologise, or go to court (McDonald's Corporation, 1990). Unlike anyone McDonald's had sued for libel before, two of the campaigners accepted the challenge. Local postman Dave Morris and gardener Helen Steel went to trial representing themselves, with only very limited legal help from sympathetic lawyers and a growing support group. The actual proceedings started in June 1994 and concluded in December 1996 after a marathon court hearing, recorded at the time as the longest trial in British history.

This case study documents a range of methods employed in the intelligence operation against London Greenpeace, and considers the close cooperation between McDonald's, its private investigators, and Special Branch of the London Metropolitan Police. This chapter describes how McDonald's' surveillance was organized, how instructions were given to agents and how they infiltrated the group. The scale of the penetration raises questions about how infiltrators affected London Greenpeace's activities. The various intelligence tactics are mapped by using trial evidence and interviews with defendants. The activities of the agents are reconstructed from their own notes and their statements at the trial, complemented by the experiences of London Greenpeace members.

The prime reason for hiring the investigators was to identify the organizers of the anti McDonald's campaign, responsible for the production and distribution of the disputed leaflet. However, careful analysis of the available documents suggests that there may have been other goals, including establishing if there were connections between the group and more radical animal rights activists. The latter appears to have been undertaken in cooperation with the police and Special Branch. The recent exposure of Bob Lambert, who admitted to having infiltrated London Greenpeace for Special Branch in the 1980s, confirms the theory of such cooperation outlined in the last section of this chapter.

BACKGROUND

Gathering data from court hearings requires endurance and patience. In this case, the data became public due to the efforts and the persistence of the two defendants, Helen Steel and David Morris. Their personal experience, having been the target of surveillance and invasion of their private space, motivated the investigation. Practical issues complicated the gathering of data. First, it is important to know that the infiltration operation was not one of the key topics at the hearings. The case was built around the content of the London Greenpeace leaflet. McDonald's had to prove that the defendants were personally responsible for publication of the pamphlet, and it was for this aspect of the case that the private investigators were called as witnesses. The extent of the spying operation became known little by little, towards the end of the trial. The hearings about the surveillance took only about ten of the 314 court days. It was not the ideal timing to explore an entirely new issue in any further depth, and the situation did not represent the best circumstances for investigating a case of infiltration. There were yet other hurdles to overcome.

McDonald's and their agents tried to withhold evidence of their intrusive practices. Originally, McDonald's applied for the four identified agents to remain anonymous. The investigating agents would make notes as soon as they left the meetings – recording many details about the group, their office, their members and activities. McDonald's resisted making these notes available to the defendants. When the judge eventually decided to disclose the original notes, McDonald's failed to deliver the complete set. (The court procedings show that not all notes of all investigators were included, and not all meetings spied on between the start of the operation in October 1989 and the delivery of the writs by the end of September 1990 were covered.) In addition, the initially released documents often had pages missing or sections blanked out. McDonald's claimed the reports were censored in order to protect the privacy of the agents, and claimed that it had only blanked out sections that were not relevant to the court case. Comparison of successive releases of less censored versions indicates that this was not necessarily true. For this book the 'least censored' versions have been used (with thanks to Helen Steel for sharing her McLibel archive).

Although the evidence gathered in this court case offers a rare opportunity for research, and the extensive reporting at McSpotlight. org website certainly helped (see, for instance, McLibel Support Campaign, 1999), several other limitations need to be mentioned. When examined in court, the investigators necessarily relied on their notes rather than on memory or recollection, since six years had passed since the infiltration took place. They were sometimes reluctant to reveal details or to disclose any further evidence. Every so often, they evaded questions or gave different answers to the same line of questioning on different days. Judge Justice Bell (1997) eventually ruled it unsafe to rely upon the evidence of Allan Clare, one of the agents, when other reliable evidence did not support it.

This case study maps the various intelligence tactics and strategies used by McDonald's agents by comparing what was asserted in testimony to what was actually done. The mapping started with uncovering the discrepancies between the reports of the spies and the experiences as the activists recalled them. As members of London Greenpeace targeted at the time, the defendants, Dave Morris and Helen Steel, were in the unique position to investigate the surveillance of their own group. And just before *Secret Manoeuvres* went to press, they did it again, in October 2011. At an anti-racist conference at the Trades Union Congress HQ in Central London, they confronted Robert (Bob) Lambert about his past infiltrating London Greenpeace in the 1980s, and supervising the operation of other undercovers since. Now an academic involved in countering and preventing the radicalization of Muslim jihadis in the UK, Lambert worked continuously as a Special Branch specialist counter-terrorist and counter-extremist intelligence officer from 1980 until 2007 (London Greenpeace, 2011). He has publicly acknowledged his involvement and apologized for it. Details of his involvement published since his exposure help to flesh out a better picture of the cooperation between police and corporate spies.

The references in this chapter link to the court transcripts and documents available at McSpotlight.org[10] and the investigators' notes from Steel's trial archive.

SECRET ALLIANCES AND STRATEGIES

The London Greenpeace leaflet came to McDonald's security chief Sidney Nicholson's attention in 1987 when it was sent to him by the Economic League, an organization that he described as aiming 'to defend the interests of multinationals'[11] (Nicholson, Day 249: 46). The infiltration of London Greenpeace, however, was initiated through close contacts between McDonald's Security Department and Special Branch, the intelligence department of London's Metropolitan Police.

Nicholson (ibid.: 36) told the court he had 'quite a lot of experience with Special Branch'. He had been meeting with intelligence officers since 1984 to discuss animal rights activities. In 1987, Special Branch founded a dedicated desk to monitor animal rights activists and supply intelligence information to forces across the UK. This department was called the Animal Rights National Index (ARNI). Nicholson's contacts originated from his long career with the police. Prior to working for McDonald's, he had spent 31 years policing, first in South Africa and then in London. He reached the rank of chief superintendent in charge of Brixton police station, a multi-ethnic neighbourhood in the British capital. Carroll, his second in command at McDonald's since 1984, had served under Nicholson in Brixton before becoming a chief superintendent himself elsewhere in London. Nicholson explained in court that 'all the [members of the] security department have many, many contacts in the police service; they are all ex-policemen; I would not ask them who their contacts were'. If Nicholson wanted information about a protester, he could 'make contact with the local crimes beat officer, the local CID officer, the local collator […] and officers I used to work with, certainly' (ibid.: 38).

McDonald's initially identified those involved in the London Greenpeace campaign through these contacts. The collaboration was one of mutual benefit. ARNI Special Branch officers called Nicholson in September 1989 to warn him of a planned demonstration outside McDonald's' offices. '[T]hey indicated that they were interested in the organization [London Greenpeace] and did I have a perch they could use, and a perch is police parlance for an observation post' (ibid.: 32–3). Nicholson was glad to help and allowed them to make use of any facilities they wished. In return, one of the Special Branch officers stood with him during the demonstration and passed on information about certain protesters. At least two of those identified subsequently received libel writs from the burger chain (ibid.; also see McDonald's Corporation et al., 1990).

So the initial identification of several members of London Greenpeace was assisted by Special Branch officers from ARNI. However, Nicholson knew it would be impossible for McDonald's to use information obtained in this manner. The identification could not be used as evidence because the police are not authorised to disclose information on the Police National Computer to third parties. This explains why Nicholson was discreet about his contacts with these Special Branch officers. He had not wanted anyone at McDonald's to know he was talking to ARNI. He said he did not even bring his immediate junior, Carroll, into the operation until a year after the decision to infiltrate was taken (Nicholson, Day 249: 52).

In court, Nicholson also tried to downplay his relations with Special Branch. He wanted the court to believe that the 1989 collaboration had been his only contact with ARNI about London Greenpeace, but evidence suggests the liaison had continued (ibid.: 38–41).

First, the Court discussed an internal memo dated 27 September 1990 about the London Greenpeace day of action 1990. This was after the writs had been served. The memo about an upcoming demonstration had a note at the top addressed to Nicholson in Carroll's handwriting saying: 'I will get on to Special Branch, to get an assessment' (Nicholson, Day 250: 7). Although normally Special Branch worked just within the police service, according to Nicholson they gave McDonald's the available information about upcoming events on request, 'the numbers, the people, and groups likely to be involved' (ibid.).

Second, an internal memo dated 22 September 1994 indicates that the company remained in close touch with ARNI during the McLibel trial. Steel found a memo in the trial documents stating: 'From the desk of Terry Carroll. I had a meeting with ARNI from Scotland Yard today who gave me the enclosed literature. Some of it we have, other bits are new. For your information' (Nicholson, Day 249: 40).

Nicholson also insisted he had 'never approached any police officers at any time about any person concerned in this operation'. When he was subsequently asked about the identification of members of London Greenpeace, he insisted he had not asked for that: 'they volunteered that information to me' (ibid.: 38–9). Because this collaboration between the company and the police was illegal, the information about London Greenpeace could not be used as evidence and when the company wanted to sue London Greenpeace for libel, it could only do so against named individuals. McDonald's therefore needed independent sources to identify the members of the group.

Double-Check

McDonald's instructed two private investigation firms to infiltrate London Greenpeace without telling either about the other. In effect, each agency would unknowingly be checking on the other. The decision to hire private investigators was taken by Nicholson, in June 1989. This was soon after McDonald's UK CEO Paul Preston had asked Nicholson whether it was possible to mount an operation to end the distribution of the leaflet. Nicholson approached McDonald's solicitors, Barlow Lyde & Gilbert. He told them he wanted 'at least two teams to work independently of one another, and unknown to one another, with a view to obtaining our objective, which was to stop the distribution of the leaflet' (ibid.: 59). Kings

Investigation Bureau, one of the oldest security firms in Britain, was hired on 29 September 1989 (ibid.). The other firm, Robert Bishop Ltd (part of Westhall Services), was retained a week later. Richard Rampton, QC, McDonald's solicitor, explained the arrangement to the court:

> Both were instructed to infiltrate London Greenpeace to ascertain as much information as possible about the organisers of the group and, in particular, the people responsible for writing, distributing, publishing, and printing defamatory information about McDonald's. (Rampton, Day 262: 50)

Both agencies hired agents to infiltrate London Greenpeace. The investigators told the court they were given a rather general brief to attend meetings and report anything relevant. Some agents were tasked to concentrate on gathering data about what was said in relation to McDonald's, while others claimed they had not been told what the case was about. In general, the aim of varying assignments in this manner is to get multiple perspectives on the targeted group. In this case however, their statements in court contradicted the notes the infiltrators made at the time. The notes show that, instead of having started the operation with an open mind, the private investigators had specific knowledge of what the case was about, and who to look for.

Jack Russell claimed there was no mention of McDonald's in his instructions (Russell, Day 263: 59). Brian Bishop was not told that the inquiry was about McDonald's either, but considered that normal practice for freelance investigators. Kings' managing director, Gerald Hartley, had explained 'that this group is populated by some animal rights supporters, and it is necessary to find out what is being said at their meetings' (Bishop, Day 260: 7). Bishop recalled how he always referred to this assignment as *the animal rights case* (ibid.). Allan Clare, who worked for the second agency, testified: 'I was asked to attempt to become accepted as a group member and to, in that role, identify those involved with the group and primarily those involved with the anti-McDonald's campaign' (Clare, Day 265: 45). Frances Tiller worked at Kings' office as the personal assistant to the director. When the agency ran short of prospective agents, she was asked to take this assignment. She received a very open briefing:

Just go along, attend the meeting, notice as much as you can, write it all down afterwards and take a special note of anything mentioned in relation to McDonald's. [...] [A]nd if you find any leaflets that relate to McDonald's then grab some, take them. (Tiller, 1997)

Antony Pocklington told the court he was instructed to attend specific meetings and was asked to report on what occurred. He claimed not to have been told, but had become aware early on, that McDonald's issues were of key interest (Pocklington, Day 261: 46). This statement contradicted his written notes. He had already referred to McDonald's as the client company in his first reports on the public meetings of London Greenpeace (Pocklington, investigator's notes on 26 Oct. 1989 and on 2 Nov 1989).

In order to identify the organizers of the campaign, Nicholson provided the agencies with photographs of a picket line held in front of a McDonald's store on an annual International Day of Action against McDonald's. Although he already knew the identity of some people in the pictures (from Special Branch), Nicholson claimed not to have shared those names with the private detectives. Asked if there was a reason not to, he answered: 'Absolutely. It was their job to find out. I wanted their information' (Nicholson, Day 249: 61).

The investigators' notes indicate that this is untrue. After the first London Greenpeace meeting Pocklington attended at Caledonian Road (early November 1989), he reported: 'Helen Steel fits the description of Helen Steel described by Client Company in the letter accompanying the photographs' (Pocklington, investigator's notes on 2 Nov. 1989). Russell also testified that the managing director of Kings had shown him 'half a dozen or so photographs' of particular people to look out for – Morris and Steel among others (Russell, Day 263: 50–53).

Overkill

It became evident from the statements and notes of the private investigators that the activist group was in fact quite small. During the surveillance period, attendance at London Greenpeace meetings varied between five to ten people, and sometimes it was even less. With at least seven spies infiltrating the group, each over a period of time, their presence – absolute and relative – was fairly large.

Entry into the group was gained simply by attending public meetings. These meetings were held on the last Thursday of every month at Endsleigh Street, while group meetings took place every week on the remaining Thursdays at the London Greenpeace office on Caledonian Road. The public meetings were organized around a special theme and usually attracted 20 to 30 people. At the group's meetings, organizational topics were discussed, including the incoming mail, financial affairs and upcoming events. The turnout at these meetings was significantly lower.

A breakdown of the attendance at the various London Greenpeace meetings shows a heavy presence of infiltrators, both in absolute figures and in relation to presence of genuine campaigners. The overview, based on the minutes of the meetings and the notes of the spies, reveals a high frequency of investigators visiting meetings. Pocklington attended 26 London Greenpeace meetings and events between October 1989 and June 1990. Clare attended 19 meetings in four months through 1990, half of which overlapped with Pocklington's. Bishop attended at least twelve meetings in four months through 1990, and he started before Clare disappeared from the scene. Tiller attended six meetings over three months' time, while Hooker went to four meetings in the first four weeks after she was introduced. Between them, the agents of McDonald's attended a total of 68 meetings and events until the end of September 1990 (and an estimated 90 until the last spy left the group, as calculated by the defendants).

The sequence of meetings the investigators attended made them regulars in the group. On a number of occasions, meetings were made up of as many spies as campaigners. The investigators' notes show that at two separate meetings (1 March and 10 May 1990), the four people attending included one spy from each bureau (Clare, Day 267: 40 and Day 265: 41). On five different occasions, there were five people, two of whom were spies; five further meetings included two spies and four or five others. Half a dozen meetings had one spy and four, five or six activists. Tiller mentioned a meeting with at least three investigators in the room, and perhaps only a maximum of seven or eight people altogether (Tiller, 1997). Such a ratio of activists to spies apparently happened twice. In May, three spies reported the presence of three activists plus someone not fully attending the meeting (Pocklington, investigator's notes, 24 May 1990). Four months later Bishop reported four activists present, one of whom left early, plus both Hooker and Tiller (Bishop, Investigator's note on 20 Sep. 1990).

Nicholson received weekly reports from each agency, and had a progress briefing every month at Barlow solicitors' office. Nicholson said he never issued any instruction regarding the numbers of agents that should attend or not. The agencies could use as many agents as they wanted. However, he claimed he had no idea an agency would put in more than one agent on any night. 'The reports on occasions did refer to agent "A" or agent "B" or agent "C", but generally it was just a report of what an agent had seen – no identification, no numbers, nothing' (Nicholson, Day 250: 31). The reports from the separate agencies were received at different times. The calculations about which agent had been where, and when, were not made until much later (ibid.). The number of spies infiltrating the group and their disproportionate presence at meetings had various implications for the operation, as detailed below.

Partners in Crime

In order to be accepted as a full member of the group, agents needed to act the part. When cross-examined in court, each stated in one way or another that they believed it would be good to appear willing and to help out where they could. Subsequently, they all ended up distributing the contentious leaflet!

The first investigator, Pocklington (Day 261: 38), told the court how he volunteered to help answering letters. On one occasion, he spent eight hours in the London Greenpeace office writing replies, many of which were sent out accompanied by the leaflet at the centre of the trial. Pocklington (Day 263: 46) testified that he never heard anything from his supervisors to suggest he was doing something wrong. Clare also helped to answer letters. Bishop admitted to having staffed a booth where the anti-McDonald's leaflet was available to the public, some of the time on his own, at a well-attended public event. Michelle Hooker had been caught on video distributing anti-McDonald's leaflets in the street. She was identified from photographs by Tiller (Day 270: 4–5) and by Clare (Day 265: 25). Steel testified how Hooker attended pickets of McDonald's outlets on a regular basis, every month, throughout late 1990 and some of 1991 (Steel, Day 249: 69). Hooker helped organize the annual London Greenpeace Fayre, held in October 1990, including compering from the stage during the day. She was coordinating events, something Steel and Morris had been brought to trial for (ibid.). Tiller volunteered to organize the crèche at the Fayre (Tiller, Day 270: 18). Clare too was involved in organizing the Fayre, and had taken minutes at meetings of London Greenpeace. Pocklington was identified in court by another spy as the 'Antony' who took the minutes of the meeting on 24 May 1990 (Bishop, Day 260: 14). Steel recalled both Pocklington and Clare taking the minutes of London Greenpeace meetings on more than one occasion (Steel, Day 276: 39). Taking minutes was held against the defendants Morris and Steel as proof of being seriously involved in the group (ibid., Day 250: 18).

The spies' activities raised an important legal point. The McLibel Two formally argued that because McDonald's investigators had been actively involved in the group and had helped circulate the disputed fact sheet, McDonald's had consented to its publication. Morris and Steel applied to include three of the spies in the action as 'third parties' – effectively making them co-defendants and thus liable to contribute to any damages awarded (Steel and Morris, 1996). Justice Bell ruled that the appropriate time for such action would be after he issued his verdict. However, after the trial McDonald's abandoned all legal action, including pursuit of damages, and the McLibel Two decided to take no further steps.

Agenda-Setting

Identifying those behind the campaign was difficult, because McDonald's was not very high on the London Greenpeace agenda. However, adding items to the agenda proved fairly easy, as did influencing the direction of the group's activities. The input of newcomers was a welcome reinforcement for a group of fluctuating membership.

Some investigators were given the impression that London Greenpeace was set up to campaign against McDonald's. But according to Tiller, it was obvious that this was not the case. 'My impression was that it had been maybe an important issue in the past but it did not figure very highly, it came quite low down on the agenda' (Tiller, 1997). Her observations were supported by other infiltrator reports. One month into the operation, Pocklington noted 'McDonald's as a project they [London Greenpeace] felt was now self-perpetuating in that it was being carried on by so many other groups worldwide' (Pocklington, investigator's notes on 9 Nov. 1989). In addition, in February 1990, Clare noted that the group's involvement in the anti-McDonald's Fayre would die down, observing: 'They will still help with distribution etc but they are/ want to try to get other groups to organize their own antiMcD campaigns' (Clare, investigator's notes on 8 Feb. 1990). Shortly before the writs were served, Bishop added a longer personal comment to his observation report:

> While London Greenpeace certainly initiated the idea and supplied the drive for the anti-McDonald's concept, now it has been taken over by other groups such as the Hackney Solidarity Group, the Haringey and Islington Direct Action movements, and most certainly the various Animal Rights groups throughout the country. (Bishop, Day 261: 3)

Many remarks throughout the investigators' notes support these observations – for example, 'Nothing else of relevance was discussed' and 'No mention was made of Client company, either in the meeting or afterwards in the pub. Nor was any mention made of any other subject relevant to this case.' Where McDonald's was discussed, it was usually in the context of letters referring to the company written by members of the public, rather than planning activities.

Before the meeting started, a sheet of paper would go round and everybody could suggest points to discuss. Brian Bishop's account of the first meeting he attended illustrates how easy it was to influence the course of affairs. He suggested a title for the next public meeting: 'Anarchism versus socialism: is there a difference?' To his surprise, although nobody knew who he was, this idea was accepted. Bishop wrote in his notes: 'It was of interest to discover that this is the actual title used' (Bishop, Day 260: 17–18). The intervention of infiltrators shaped some activities. As nobody else had volunteered, Tiller's offer to set up a crèche helped the Fayre get off the ground. Tiller said: 'My impression was that it was proving very difficult to get the thing together. [...] There was not a lot of inspiration' (Tiller, Day 270: 18).

Against the relatively low attendance of the meetings by members of the group and the recurring problem of staffing a stall, the assistance offered by the spies did make a difference. Steel told the court that Pocklington, Bishop, Clare and Hooker were considered to be among the regulars at meetings; all four expressed interest in anti-McDonald's campaigning, asking questions about the campaign (Steel, Day 276: 39).

Actually, the attendance of the investigators gave the real members the feel that the group was doing well again. Steel told the court that in January 1990 London Greenpeace held a meeting about the future of the group. Attendance had tailed off to such an extent that people were concerned that the group might not carry on. 'So, obviously, when the private investigators were coming and they expressed interest in the group and the anti-McDonald's campaign and [...] they basically kept the numbers up and kept the group going' (Steel quoted by Justice Bell, Verdict: 81–2).

The number of agents could easily affect the decision-making process, and permit the focus of the meeting to return to McDonald's. The newcomers, the frequency of their attendance and their willingness to participate effectively reinforced the anti-McDonald's campaign. The questions they asked were perceived as showing a genuine interest in and commitment to the campaign, Steel explained (interview with the author, October 2006).

Creating Suspicion

The infiltration operation did not pass entirely unnoticed. There were moments when members of London Greenpeace felt there was something amiss within the group. The infiltration operation created an atmosphere of suspicion, with spies spying on spies, and activists trying to find out if they were infiltrated.

Since McDonald's had not told either agency about the other and not all investigators of the same bureau necessarily knew one another, the spies were also spying on each other. This sometimes showed in their notes. Clare for instance wrote about Tony: 'Antony never has much to say' and: 'Antony is not as radical as others. No leadership. Not involved with organization of McDonald's' (Clare, Day 265: 41). Some of the investigators were aware of the fact that appearances could create suspicion, and they were worried about the risks of blowing their cover. Tiller had to introduce Michelle Hooker to London Greenpeace. In an interview for the documentary about the McLibel Trial, Tiller explained their different approaches to presumed dress codes. The two would drive to the London Greenpeace office in Hooker's black BMW, parking a few streets away. Tiller:

> I sort of dressed down, wearing sandals and hippie-type clothes, but she came along with quite flashy jewellery and long, tapered, and painted fingernails and makeup. I thought that people would have suspected that she was not one of them, but in fact she got involved quite deeply afterwards. (Tiller, 1997)

When Michelle Hooker was introduced, Bishop made a note about her appearance, 'she was about 5 ft. 6 in. tall and aged around

19–22 years. She had full, light brown hair. She was of medium build and had a fresh complexion, devoid of makeup. She was attractive in both face and figure' (Bishop, Day 259: 86). He felt there was something suspicious about this new woman. Her grey stonewashed jeans 'did not appear to be at all old' and the rips in the knees looked like they'd been 'administered rather than worn in place'. He had his doubts, he told the court: 'I reported on her as being a member of the group that I was a bit suspicious about. She was a bit too keen' (ibid.).

When Clare 'managed to borrow' some photographs from the group, the pictures went missing. Steel recalled there was a big row about whose fault this was, with several people accusing each other. In this discussion, Pocklington claimed that Clare was the last one seen with the photographs (Clare, Day 267: 42).

Sometimes the investigators followed people home from meetings to discover or verify addresses, Pocklington confirmed in cross-examination. In his notes about a meeting in 1990, Pocklington wrote: 'As arranged, I left the building talking to Helen Steel.' When asked in court about the reason for this arrangement, he said: 'I can only assume it would have been to aid any surveillance that might have occurred or any identification' (Pocklington, Day 262: 29). In another set up to find out Morris' home address, Pocklington offered to drop off a parcel of baby clothes for Morris's newborn son (ibid., Day 263: 42). (Morris was disgusted by the idea that his son could have been wearing clothes sent by a McDonald's agent. In terms of the personal effect it had on him, this was one of the worst things he had heard in this case; cited in Vidal, 1997: 196.)

In turn, suspicious members of London Greenpeace were observing the spies. 'As the group was only involved in legal activities such as leafleting, picketing and demonstrations we had no real reason to suspect that it might be infiltrated,' says Steel (interview with the author, October 2006). But every now and then, some got the feeling that something was wrong. Suspicions were discussed outside of the meetings. Bishop once reported having been subject to counter-investigation in the pub after a meeting. 'I stayed in the public house for around one hour, during which time I was gently questioned by Helen as to my age, occupation, and present domicile etc. [...] On several occasions during this period I saw Helen looking at me' (Bishop, investigator's notes, 27 May 1990).

The campaigners eventually followed some of the suspected agents after a meeting, but discovered nothing that proved they were spies. With nothing solid to go on, not much could be done,

Steel explained. 'That is partly because we only thought about the risk of being infiltrated by the police or intelligence services. We never considered that they might be working for a company rather than the state' (interview with the author, October 2006).

Creating suspicion is a known side effect of infiltration and it can be an effective way to derail any group of people working together (see, for instance, More and Viehmann, 2004; Marx, 1974). Suspecting new volunteers can hinder recruitment and deter people from joining and participating. Worries about whether people are to be trusted undermines organizational and outreach activities.

Steel was effectively concerned about the air of distrust building up in the group. 'We have tried to be aware of this, as McDonald's, other companies and the state would be very happy if groups become less active and effective because we all distrusted each other' (interview with the author, October 2006).

Breaking the Law

As much as the agents pretended to behave as full members of the group, they remained private investigators. Apart from surveillance, they confessed to having been involved in acts of searching, stealing, and breaking and entering.

One night Clare searched the office for additional information. On 8 February 1990, Clare wrote in his notes: 'Before the bulk of the group arrived I had the opportunity to go through certain documents on the desk. I managed to find in a drawer bank statements for London Greenpeace'. He wrote down the name of the bank and the account number (Clare, Day 267: 28). In his notes, Clare mentions 'borrowing' letters several times. When he was asked in court: 'When you say "borrow it," you do not say you said to the meeting: "Do you mind if I take it away for a little while. I will bring it back?"' Clare's answer was 'No, I do not' (ibid.: 43). On 13 September 1990, Bishop reported that a letter concerning McDonald's had been discussed at the meeting. 'I managed to purloin this letter and have enclosed it with this report' (Bishop, Day 260: 61). He showed no doubts when he was cross-examined about taking letters. Bishop stated: 'An inquiry agent would be required to obtain written evidence if it were possible to do so, yes' (ibid.: 65).

The agents testified that they never received any specific instruction to steal letters. Nor were they told *not* to take them. Absolutely not, Bishop confirmed – nothing was ruled out (Bishop,

260: 8, 65). When the agents handed the letters to their principals, they were photocopied and returned. The agents were never given instructions to stop passing letters and the ethics of taking letters was not discussed. They were given a free hand (Clare, Day 265: 46). The letters were not always returned though. In the pre-trial proceedings, Steel asked McDonald's lawyers for copies of the stolen correspondence: 15 *original* letters were returned. The letter from the lawyer's office did not explain whether these were all the letters the spies had taken, or just Clare's share of 'borrowed' letters (Steel, Day 250: 21–2).

Nicholson said he had not approved the theft of letters. He claimed he could remember only one occasion where he received a letter obtained by an investigator attached to a report from the agency. Nicholson was certain he ordered his lawyers to tell the managing director of Kings that this was contrary to his instructions. 'It was not to happen again' (Nicholson, Day 249: 62). However, this order apparently never reached the agents in the field. In his defence, Nicholson insisted he had instructed the agencies to do 'nothing illegal and nothing improper' when he hired them, but also admitted to not issuing specific instructions beyond that. He claimed to have been concerned about the reliability of agents: 'people do make mistakes' (ibid., Day 250: 23–4). The agents felt free to obtain documentary evidence and to testify about it in court, although Justice Bell cautioned these witnesses not to put themselves at risk of being proceeded against for a criminal offence (Bishop, Day 260: 65).

There is further evidence of investigators breaking the law. After his first meeting, on 17 May 1990, Bishop wrote a report containing a detailed description of the London Greenpeace office. He noted that one window 'had no security locks on the frame and opened out to the outside,' adding that the office next door was occupied 24 hours a day (Bishop, Day 261: 21). Questioned as to the relevance of such information, Bishop denied it was to advise anyone who might wish to break into the office (ibid.). However, Clare admitted gaining entry to the group's office a few months before Bishop (on 6 March 1990), accompanied by a manager from his firm. He obtained access to the building using the entryphone system of the office next door. He denied that it was a break-in, despite admitting that he had used a phone card to force open the office door. Clare told the court 'the door lock on the office to London Greenpeace was basically not very strong and it was decided by me and my principals that entry to it would not be a problem' (Clare,

Day 265: 33). He took photographs that were later used during the trial. In cross-examination, Steel put to him that she did not believe he went to the office and risked being caught just to take a few pictures (ibid., Day 267:52). Clare answered that the photos were taken to describe the venue clearly, to show the extent of the McDonald's campaign; photos were better than his description only: '[s]omething that can be seen by others' (ibid.). Steel suspected Clare of planting bugs, but he denied this, saying: 'throughout all of my investigative experience I have never placed a bug' (ibid.).

The agents worked with the consent of their supervisors. The ethics of taking letters were never discussed. Neither McDonald's nor their lawyers seemed to worry about abiding by the law. None of the parties involved appeared to have any problem with the use of unlawfully collected evidence.

Mission Accomplished?

McDonald's claimed that the infiltration operation ended once the writs were served, on 20 September 1990. However, the evidence given in court shows the investigation continued for several months beyond that date. There were various reasons for some spies to linger. Nicholson wanted to retain at least one operator to monitor reactions to the writs. He claimed that he was concerned for the safety of McDonald's premises and staff. The managing director of Kings Detectives had other worries. He feared for his agents if they were all removed at once. Kings had three or four agents operating at that moment. In order to facilitate the withdrawal without suspicion, McDonald's and the agencies agreed a phased exit. According to Nicholson, the contract ended in January 1991 because he received no further reports, but there is no formal written evidence to confirm this (Nicholson, Day 249: 63), while statements he made about the reporting arrangements of Michelle Hooker contradict it.

The assignment of Hooker was significant. She started going to meetings at the end of August 1990, less than a month before writs were served. While McDonald's claimed to have hired the investigators to identify the people responsible for the pamphlet, one could argue it made no sense to bring in a new investigator while the writs to named subjects were being prepared, Steel argued (interview with the author, October 2006). After the decision to go to court was taken and strategies to phase out spying were being discussed, Hooker was brought in the field. She stayed undercover for nine months and attended meetings until May 1991. Furthermore, she became intimately involved with Charlie Brooke, one of the more active members of the group. When Hooker was introduced to London Greenpeace, Brian Bishop – as noted above – found her suspicious and a bit too keen. She, in turn, immediately noted a 'quietly spoken' young man called Charlie. 'He is 5ft 10in in height, slim to medium build, collar-length light brown wispy hair with a fringe, and he was wearing black trousers with holes in the knees and a tatty T-shirt,' she wrote in one of her first reports (Hooker, investigator's notes on 13 Sep 1990). Her relationship with Brooke proved fortunate, as it allayed the group's suspicions. The *Observer* quoted someone from London Greenpeace close to the couple who said: 'At the time we were concerned that the group may have been infiltrated, but she was beyond suspicion because she was going out with Charlie' (Calvert and Connett, 1997). Friends told the paper her relationship with Mr Brooke flourished. The couple spent Christmas 1990 together and exchanged gifts. Michelle Hooker 'helped in the health food shop where he worked and she even went to visit his mother in West Yorkshire. Mr Brooke, in contrast, was never introduced to any of her friends nor did he ever go to her rented bed-sit' (ibid.). The relationship cooled towards the end of her assignment. Hooker began saying that she could no longer spend weekends at his flat because of work commitments. The *Observer* heard that Brooke never saw her again after he ended the relationship. The newspaper report concluded: 'Only one memento of the strange affair remains: the tabby cat Ms X left at his flat and never collected, a physical reminder of how the detective for McDonald's had touched his private life' (ibid.). Charlie Brooke discovered her spying role when her name was released during the McLibel case in 1996.

ANIMAL RIGHTS

Michele Hooker was a relative latecomer to the London Greenpeace operation. She became intimately involved with one of the activists. Seducing someone in order to procure inside information is a stereotypical tactic in espionage. If it was not an unprofessional step – a *faux pas* – it may have been a tactic to gain access to circles of people supporting animal rights activism and to gather intelligence on them. (Out of seven police infiltrators exposed in 2011, at least five had intimate relationships with activists in the movement they monitored (Lewis and Evans, 2011b).)

There are some details to support the notion that Hooker was on a special assignment. First, she was determined to get in touch with animal rights activists from the moment she entered the London Greenpeace milieu. Her relationship with one of the activists not only allayed suspicion, it facilitated access to the circles she was interested in, as explained below. Second, Hooker had different reporting arrangements from the other infiltrators. Third, a closer reading of the court transcripts points at further involvement of Special Branch's Animal Rights specialists (ARNI) in encouraging the infiltration operation.

The exposure of Bob Lambert as an infiltrator supports this line of thought. Using the name Bob Robinson, he infiltrated London Greenpeace meetings and events for about five years up to 1988; this was before the McDonald's operation started in October 1989. He went on to supervise other agents who continued with infiltration of groups such as London Greenpeace and Reclaim the Streets, along with anti-fascist protests and actions against genetically modified crops (London Greenpeace, 2011). Challenged by SpinWatch (2011) in an open letter, Lambert replied that his undercover role in the 1980s was part of a secret infiltration of the Animal Liberation Front, which he said was involved in a violent campaign against targets in the vivisection, meat and fur trades at the time.

> As part of my cover story, so as to gain the necessary credibility to become involved in serious crime, I first built a reputation as a committed member of London Greenpeace, a peaceful campaigning group. (Lambert, 2011)

The Animal Liberation Front operated through a tight network of small cells of activists, making it difficult for spies to get among them. In the *Guardian*, Lambert claimed that it was *his* information that put Andrew Clarke and Geoff Shepherd behind bars in the summer of 1987. His intelligence was so precise that the police caught the two activists red-handed in a flat in Tottenham. The prosecution told the court that they were sitting at a table covered with dismantled alarm clocks, bulbs and electrical equipment for making firebombs. Shepherd, then 31, was jailed for four years and four months, and Clarke, then 25, for more than three years. Still according to the *Guardian*, 'Lambert had skilfully disguised that he was the source of the tip-off, managing to throw the suspicions on to others within the small ring of activists who knew about the attacks'. He even went to visit one of the accused in jail while they were awaiting the trial, his former girlfriend remembered (Lewis and Evans, 2011c).

The fact that Lambert had managed to get close enough to the two activists to know what they were up to raises a new set of questions about his own involvement. According to London Greenpeace (2011), Lambert was very active in the animal rights movement himself. He was prosecuted at Camberwell Green Magistrates Court for distributing 'insulting' leaflets outside a butcher's shop. At the request of Scotland Yard, the Independent Police Complaints Commission opened an inquiry into Lambert and an undercover officer acting under his supervision called Jim Boyling, who disclosed in the *Guardian* that he had given evidence under oath concealing his real identity in court (Evans and Lewis, 2011). The inquiry was still under way at the time of writing. Unfortunately, none of the present set of official inquiries into police infiltration of the activist movement in the UK addresses the issue of provocation, of undercover officers recruiting activists, changing agendas and inciting violence. The McLibel case shows that the role of corporate infiltrators and their cooperation with the police needs to be put on the agenda as well. Lambert's past with Special Branch helps to confirm that more recently exposed police spies (such as Mark Kennedy detailed in the Introduction) were not 'rogue officers'. They were part of a pattern of infiltration of environmental and other activist groups, which seems to have been condoned at the highest level.

This section of the McSpy chapter summarizes the evidence pointing towards close collaboration between the McDonald's private investigators and Special Branch, closer than has been recognized so far.

Getting Through

Hooker used her new contacts at London Greenpeace to get in touch with activists who were more radical. After the second meeting she attended, Hooker talked to two members of London Greenpeace and immediately brought up the topic of animal rights. The talk in the pub went fine, she reported. 'I appeared to get on well with both of them and felt that they spoke openly and freely with me' (Hooker, investigator's note on 30 Aug. 1990). When Hooker indicated she was interested in animal rights, she was referred to someone (not a member of London Greenpeace) associated 'with the activists who were responsible for breaking into several laboratories and releasing animals' (ibid.).

Hooker misheard the name of his group but understood that it was associated with the Animal Liberation Front. It was her impression that this group was a radical organization, prepared to actively back up its views. Hooker also managed to get the diary of events for September 1990 issued by the Hackney and Islington Animal Rights Campaign – a group she would subsequently infiltrate as well (ibid.).

Hooker became an active member of London Greenpeace. As already noted, she was one of the organizers of the Fayre, compering on stage and handing out leaflets. She regularly attended actions throughout her assignment. Through her relationship with Brooke, Hooker met many other activists who were of interest to the animal rights officers at Special Branch. Brooke worked with London Greenpeace only part time and was more involved with Hackney and Islington Animal Rights. One of this group's members was Paul Gravett, who – according to the *Observer* (Calvert and Connett, 1997) – the authorities considered a lynchpin in both the animal rights group and the anti-McDonald's campaign of London Greenpeace. Another member, Geoffrey Shephard, had been convicted for setting off sprinkler systems and destroying fur stocks at three Debenhams department stores in the mid-1980s. Hooker – the *Observer* reported – hosted dinner parties for both of them at Brooke's north London flat. She also became very active in the animal rights group, joining pickets and handing out leaflets.

Hooker's trajectory mirrors the route Lambert took to get access into animal right groups. Taking London Greenpeace as a starting point was only one of the similarities. To enhance his credibility Lambert also used the tactic of pursuing a long-term intimate relationship. Admitting that this was just a part of his alter ego's cover story, in his reply to SpinWatch Lambert apologised unreservedly for forming false friendships. The woman, who asked to withhold her name, discovered his true identity more than 20 years after they first met. She told the *Guardian* that the discovery left her feeling that Lambert had deceived her about the bedrock of any relationship – his identity. 'I was cruelly tricked and it has made me very angry. I feel violated,' she said (Evans and Lewis, 2011).

Another detail linking Special Branch to the McDonald's operation is the fact that Hooker set out to become close to Shephard, one of the activists Lambert claims to have put away a few years before that. Meanwhile, Lambert was promoted to a position in which he controlled a network of spies – a position he held at the time Hooker started her undercover operation.

Reporting Arrangements

At the very end of the trial, Morris and Steel tried to force McDonald's to disclose the names of *all* agents hired to infiltrate London Greenpeace (as opposed to the six already identified). The aim was to gain access to the investigators' notes dated after the writs were served, and to get a full overview of who worked on this operation and for how long. Although this appeal was not granted, the legal battle revealed some information about Hooker.

Rampton, solicitor to McDonald's, disclosed that Hooker's assignment and reporting arrangements were different from those of the rest of the agents. He told the court that when there was only one inquiry agent still in the group (i.e. Hooker), a number of the reports were sent to Nicholson instead of directly to the lawyers' office. Rampton revealed the existence of these reports in order to protect them from disclosure:

> Those, if the question should arise, are plainly covered by litigation privilege, but my primary submission about those is that, in any event, they are completely irrelevant, since they do not bear on any question arising in this action – interesting though, because they are personal contact[s]. (Rampton, Day 262: 52)

With this, Rampton also revealed the existence of personal contact between Nicholson and Hooker. It also contradicts Nicholson's claim (Day 250: 12) that he did not know any of the hired agents – except from meeting Clare once.

Encouraging Infiltration

Both Nicholson and Preston made statements in court confirming that concern about animal rights action was a factor in deciding to infiltrate London Greenpeace.

Nicholson had since 1984 been discussing animal rights issues with Special Branch officers; they were, he stated, 'of much more concern to me at that time'. He claimed that London Greenpeace had come to his attention in that context (Nicholson: 249: 10). In 1984, Lambert started to infiltrate London Greenpeace as an undercover agent for Special Branch. (This puts him in the group as an active member at the moment the disputed pamphlet was written as well – according to Helen Steel, he was in fact part of the sub-group that produced the leaflet.) In early summer 1989, McDonald's suffered several arson attacks on their outlets; these were claimed by animal liberation activists. Nicholson argued that the attacks justified the infiltration operation (ibid.). The McDonald's UK president, Paul Preston, also stated that 'he was told' London Greenpeace had something to do with the fires. He could not remember who told him: '[i]t had had to be either internally or by someone from the police' (Preston, Day 248: 29). Steel and Morris were infuriated by this attempt to connect London Greenpeace to the arson attacks. There was no proof of any connection (Steel, Day 248: 32–3). In a subsequent attempt to convince Morris and Steel that no harm was meant, Nicholson disclosed ARNI's underlying intentions:

> They told me they were not particularly interested in London Greenpeace. They regarded you as a small organisation of very little importance. What they were interested in was the possible connections with the animal liberation groups, and they did not indicate either of you two were involved in that. [...] They said there were associations between the group and Animal Liberation. (Nicholson, Day 249: 34)

In the context of the McLibel trial, these statements from Nicholson and Preston are nothing more than efforts to justify the infiltration operation in court. Furthermore, they indicate that Special Branch played some role in prompting the London Greenpeace inquiry. ARNI suggested links between the group and firebomb attacks, and these alleged links persuaded McDonald's to take steps.

But these statements also point to Special Branch's special interest in gathering intelligence about animal liberation activists. And, reading back once more, the infiltrating agents were focused on the topic too. Bishop was initially told that some animal rights supporters populated the group, and he needed to find out what they talked about. He had always referred to this case as 'the animal rights case' (Bishop, Day 260: 7), and his notes indicate that for him this was part of the assignment. For instance, Bishop reported how two members of London Greenpeace 'had been involved with an all-night vigil outside an animal research centre in Mill Hill. Not a great deal of activity had apparently taken place during this event' (Bishop, investigator's note on 17 May 1990). Referring to the group's 'annual mail out' he reported: 'Without exception, all the addresses I saw were of animal rights groups; spread through the country' (Bishop, investigator's notes, 20 Sep. 1990). Pocklington told the court: 'The initial request I received was to attend a meeting in Blackstock Road, which I think was a Hackney and Islington Animal Rights group meeting, and to report on what happened at that meeting' (Pocklington, Day 261: 28). Further references to the Hackney and Islington Animal Rights group can be found throughout the private investigators' notes. There are several announcements of pickets by this group, and allegations about which of the London Greenpeace people were supposed to have a strong involvement with animal rights groups (see for instance Pocklington, investigator's notes on 22 Feb. 1990 and 1 March 1990; Clare, investigator's notes, 4 Jan. 1990).

What was the aim of the infiltration operation? Was it to reveal London Greenpeace's involvement in leafleting McDonald's, or was it to get closer to animal rights activists? Who was in charge of the operation? The available pieces of the puzzle do not allow a full view of the picture yet. What we know is that Special Branch was involved in the operation to infiltrate London Greenpeace. ARNI's interest in animal rights activists had a role in prompting the McDonald's infiltration operation. Special Branch unlawfully exchanged personal details about London Greenpeace activists with McDonald's, and with at least one of the private investigators hired by the burger giant. Michelle Hooker used the infiltration operation to get to (alleged) animal rights activists. She had a special assignment and different reporting arrangements – for a period of time she sent her files directly to McDonald's security. Morris and Steel tried to locate Hooker for the trial, but failed to find her.

With the recent exposure of Bob Lambert and the long-term involvement of Special Branch with London Greenpeace thus confirmed, the questions about the private investigators hired by McDonald's, their role and the extent of their involvement, only become more pressing.

Unfortunately, various attempts to find out more about the cooperation between the McDonald's hired spies and Special Branch detectives ended in deadlock.

After the McLibel trial finished, in September 1998, Morris and Steel started proceedings against the London Metropolitan Police. Apart from the exchange of information between McDonald's, its private spies and Special Branch discussed at the trial, there was more proof of illegal cooperation – as Helen Steel found out. Clare, one of the spies, had at least one meeting with police officers in June 1990: the meeting Clare had was with Sergeant Valentine, a detective working on the poll tax protests.[12] In court, Clare admitted he went to a demonstration following the anti-poll tax riots. He claimed that this had nothing to do with McDonald's (Clare, Day 265: 38). Clare's notebook, however, told a different story. 'The notes of Clare show that he identified London Greenpeace activists in photographs that the police had taken at the huge anti-Poll Tax demonstration in 1990,' Steel explained (interview with the author, October 2006). Furthermore, the notebook confirmed that the police had told him where Steel and Morris lived. Clare was also given other confidential details, some of which were misleading and incorrect. Information collected by the private spies likewise found its way to the police and Special Branch, according to Steel.

Morris and Steel claimed damages for malfeasance in public office, breach of confidence, and breach of their right to privacy (McLibel Support Campaign, 1998). In July 2000, almost two years after the start of the proceedings, the police announced that they preferred an out-of-court settlement. In order to avoid what the police called 'a difficult and lengthy trial', they agreed to pay the McLibel Two £10,000 plus legal costs. Detective Sergeant Valentine even apologized for distress caused by the disclosure of claimants' personal details to the private investigators (McLibel Support Campaign, 2000). The settlement also required the London police commissioner to remind all officers of their responsibility not to disclose information. Although, *de facto*, the police admitted to the unlawful exchange of information, they successfully evaded the disclosure of more details about the collusion between them, McDonald's and the private investigators.

Several requests under the UK Freedom of Information Act did not disclose any new evidence either. The first requests, asking for information about several named groups involved in animal rights activities, were considered too broad. A narrowed-down request asked for the release of 'any records held in any form by the Special Branch of the Metropolitan Police which relate to groups and people that had (alleged) affiliations with London Greenpeace between 1985 and 2005' (Lubbers, 2006). The police information manager, Julie Harknett (2006) confirmed that such information is held by the London Metropolitan Police. And although it 'would contribute to the quality and accuracy of public debate' because '[t]he public could express concerns regarding accountability, public spending and public safety', she decided against disclosure. Harknett explained: 'The Public Interest is not what interests the public, but what will be of greater good if released to the community as a whole.' And for the Met, disclosure was not in the public interest 'as it may endanger the health and safety of our officers' or 'undermine their goodwill and confidence in the Metropolitan Police and could result in a lack of engagement with the MPS' (ibid.). The Freedom of Information Act only goes so far. The police are not willing to discuss their intelligence operations.

CONCLUSION

Of the five case studies, this one essentially focused on how infiltration affects the targeted group. Furthermore, it points at a specific effect of intelligence gathering via infiltration. Intended or not, the steady influx of 'new blood' with a proclaimed interest in the anti-McDonald's campaign put the issue back on the agenda for London Greenpeace. The McDonald's investigators all ended up circulating the contentious leaflet. At the same time, stealing letters caused irritation among members of the group, while the sudden influx of active newcomers raised concerns for other activists. The infiltration operation also created an atmosphere of suspicion, with private investigators at work, spies spying on spies, and activists trying to find out if they had been infiltrated. Creating suspicion is an inherent element of infiltration – either as an unintended by-effect or as part of the strategy – and can lead to a paralysis that undermines the spirit and the endurance of any group.

The story in this chapter shows that intelligence gathering and covert strategy cannot be considered separate procedures. If the collection is by human means it is often impossible to determine where collection ends and some form of (covert) action begins (Gill, 2008). The influx of newcomers changed the agenda of the group, and raised issues of trust. Secrecy made it impossible effectively to investigate feelings of doubt about certain newcomers. Furthermore, McDonald's and its lawyers did not worry about abiding by the law and – bringing it to Court – had no problem with the use of unlawfully collected evidence. This story also shows that even after infiltration is exposed in court, it is hard to hold to account the agents and those responsible for their practices.

The operation described in the last part of this case study opens up all kinds of questions about cooperation between Special Branch, private detectives and corporate security departments. Was the infiltration operation some kind of joint project? Exactly how it was organized remains difficult to reconstruct. There are several possible forms for state–private cooperation on intelligence matters; however, the day-to-day affairs have most probably been a mix of the most convenient options. The cooperation could have been unplanned, with McDonald's infiltrating London Greenpeace solely to sue it over the leaflet, and Special Branch taking advantage of the opportunity while it was there. Or ARNI could have become more interested as the infiltration proceeded. Maybe the operation started with the mutual worry about animal rights activists. The police may have used McDonald's private investigators as a stepping-stone to get information about people Special Branch was specifically interested in. In that case, a police intelligence squad used private investigative agents to do its dirty work. Another possibility would be a further form of cooperation, with the police using the openings the private agents created, to bring in their own infiltrators.

The special operation described here underscores the increasing informal links between corporate spies and government intelligence. It is an example of 'incestuous relationships' as the Tofflers (1990: 313) call it, or of 'grey intelligence' as Hoogenboom (2006: 373) puts it. The cooperation was informal, and lacked accountability.

This unwillingness to discuss secret operations in the wider interest of the public good illustrates the difficulties in the discovery of secret documents, and more specifically the limited opportunities legal frameworks offer for research into intelligence and covert operations, particularly those that have a political dimension. To substantiate the theory that the activists were infiltrated by Special Branch assisted by corporate spies, other means of disclosure have to be found.

In 2006, the Metropolitan Police confirmed the existence of Special Branch files on London Greenpeace but stated that it was not in the public interest to release them. Today, the situation is changing. The pressure for a public inquiry is growing. In October 2011, Lord Macdonald, the former director of public prosecutions in the UK, called for one overarching proper public inquiry into undercover police operations. Pete Black, another former undercover officer, argued for a full inquiry reminiscent of the Church Committee in the US in the 1970s, which uncovered the illegal activities of the FBI, CIA and other American intelligence agencies, as detailed in Chapter 8.

Furthermore, civil claims against Special Branch and their successors in the covert units of the Metropolitan Police and the Association of Chief Police Officers (ACPO) provide opportunities to unearth further evidence as well as openings to underline the demand accountability.

5
Cybersurveillance and Online Covert Strategy: Case Study

The internet was adopted early and effectively by anti-corporate campaigners. Their ability to exploit the global reach of the web and by-pass other mass media is a levelling factor in the battle for public opinion between activists and powerful companies (Verhille, 1998). The PR industry recognized this over a decade ago. The internet was said to reduce the advantage that corporate budgets once provided (Hamilton, 1997). Meanwhile, corporations have learned to use the internet as well, and not just to sell their goods and services, to present their business, or to promote their latest corporate social responsibility achievements. Companies under fire today hire cybersurveillance services to monitor their brand position online. Some of these agencies claim to be much more than a simple digital clippings service. Preparing briefings on what is happening online and how campaigning organizations are linked is just the beginning. A sophisticated communication plan not only maps sentiments in the blogosphere and scans for future issues, but may also include strategies to undermine the campaigns of online activists, the activities of disgruntled employees or the criticism of experts.

This case study profiles three different agencies specializing in online intelligence services – Infonic, eWatch and Bivings – each with an example of a controversy in which they featured. In 2000, Infonic, a London-based agency, promoted use of the internet for enabling corporations to get closer to their stakeholders. However, when asked to advise the IT industry on how to deal with a campaign demanding regulation for waste from electronic goods, their advice included counterstrategies such as approaching the funders of the campaigning groups to undermine their financial stability. Also in 2000, the American agency eWatch explicitly promoted its 'CyberSleuth' services. It offered to 'neutralize news' and to identify and 'eliminate' online activists (eWatch, 2000c). This second example explores the potentially far-reaching consequences of being labelled a 'perpetrator' by eWatch or other monitoring agencies. The third and last profile investigates internet communications firm the Bivings Group, hired by the largest developer and producer of genetically modified (GM) seeds, Monsanto. Together they manipulated online discussions and attacked critics of genetically engineered maize. The companies had created online identities exclusively for this purpose. Monsanto used these so-called independent third parties as a covert strategy in an attempt to influence the debate on genetic engineering. As far as is known, this was the first time that the use of (fake) electronic personae had been convincingly proved.

The controversies discussed in this chapter took place between 2000 and 2002. The period is significant, as it represents a loss of innocence regarding virtual communities and networks. Today, TNCs have become more aware of online risks – and as a result, online counterstrategies are more difficult to detect. While the importance of online communication and virtual networks is still growing (Castells, 2003; Pickerill, 2002, 2006), the monitoring industry had kept pace (*The Economist*, 2009). Recent exposures of sophisticated online intrusion – including the French electricity company building nuclear plants accessing the hard disks of Greenpeace campaigners – indicate a continued market for inside information on the work of campaigners provided by consultancies that specialize in cybersurveillance (Campbell and Gourlay, 2009; Mamou, 2009).

BACKGROUND

Shell was one of the first companies exposed to a new-media battle. The company was taken by surprise in 1995 when a Greenpeace campaign to stop the sinking of the redundant Brent Spar oil platform succeeded. Shell was forced to shift ground, surrendering a position it had held to fiercely. The company had done too little too late to defend itself, refraining from publicly explaining why dumping was the best solution, according to Eric Faulds, head of the Brent Spar Decommissioning Project (TU Delta, 1996). This only reinforced the image of Shell as arrogant in the eyes of campaigners and members of the public. Brent Spar has since become a celebrated case study in poor issue management (see, for instance, Lietz, 1997; Van Tulder and Van der Zwart, 2003) and crisis PR (see Kitchen, 1997; Seymour and Moore, 2000; Sriramesh and Verčič, 2003). Even the use of language in the Brent Spar case has been analysed in *Eco-Identity as Discursive Struggle* (Livesey, 2001).

After the crisis, the company got involved in setting up a private intelligence company with former staff of MI6 to keep track of potential opponents – as we will see in the next chapter. Shell also appointed its first internet manager, Simon May. I first met him at a PR conference called 'Putting the Pressure on: The Rise of Pressure Activism in Europe', held in Brussels in 1998. He was refreshingly open about what Shell was going through and about his work for the company, both in his talk at the time, and in our extended email correspondence afterwards. May added a new perspective to the many analyses of the Brent Spar affair. Shell had been wrong about its own influence on the media, and had completely overlooked the new media. A few months later, after the execution of Ken Saro-Wiwa and eight other Ogoni opposition leaders, the company was again in the spotlight, now for its intimate links with Nigeria's military regime. This also prompted what May called 'a massive online bombardment of criticism' (May, 1998). A third PR disaster could not be allowed to happen.

Shell International's online strategy after Brent Spar was an example quickly followed by other companies under fire. The strategy required constant monitoring of what was said about the company in cyberspace. The company hired specialist, external services to trawl the web daily, listing all the places the company was mentioned, and in which contexts. May insisted: 'You need to keep track of your audience all the time, since you may learn a lot from it' (interview by email, 19 June 1998). May believed that the online community could not be ignored. 'There are pressure groups that exist only on the internet. They are difficult to monitor and to control. You can't easily enrol as a member of these closed groups' (May, 1998). The agencies Shell hired to conduct this monitoring were Infonic and eWatch, both of which are profiled in this chapter.[13] How well this monitoring worked, I was soon to find out. A day after I first published an article about the Brussels conference, I got an email from Infonic's director expressing his interest in explaining more about his work and his views – an offer I gladly accepted. eWatch, however, was less pleased by my awareness of their activities hunting down critics of companies, as detailed below.

Another industry that quickly discovered the power of the internet was the biotech industry, producers of GM seeds and food. Monsanto made a huge error of judgement in underestimating the resistance against the introduction of GM food in Europe, which included Prince Charles speaking out against what the tabloids called 'Frankenstein food' (Windsor, 1999; 2000). In 1999, the company nearly collapsed because of the disaster on the European market. For help with their internet strategy, Monsanto turned to Bivings.

The examples presented here cover a wide range of countering critics online and involve monitoring, spying, targeting and the use of fake identities to manipulate public debates. Bivings called covert methods to influence discussions *viral marketing*, and described it as using word-of-mouth strategy to disseminate clients' views online.

INFONIC

In the early days of the internet, Infonic claimed to exist 'to help companies understand and engage with the growing living space that is the internet' (Bunting and Lipski, 2000). In an interview by email (10 November 2000), Infonic founder Roy Lipski suggested that the internet redefine relationships between companies and their stakeholders. 'It is not that the internet has an anti-corporate culture; it is people who have that culture. What internet has allowed us to do is simply to see the scale of that anti-corporate culture.' The agency believed it was better positioned to advise its clients on the most appropriate course of action, because 'Infonic thinks from and for the point of view of the online communities that we are in touch with'. However, when a leaked document suggested that Infonic was undermining those online communities, Lipski changed his tone and denied any involvement.

NGO Strategy

In the late 1990s, environmentalists were pushing for regulations to make electronics manufacturers responsible for their own toxic waste. These efforts culminated in what is known as the European Commission Directive on Waste from Electrical and Electronic Equipment (or WEEE). The proposed law would force producers of electronic products and electrical equipment to take financial responsibility for managing their products throughout their lifecycle, and for their disposal (Knight, 2000). As might be expected, the industry was not amused. Organized in the European Information and Communication Technology Industry Association (EICTA), the industry set out to undermine the environmental campaign pushing for the regulation. Since renamed DIGITALEUROPE, this trade association is based in Brussels and according to its mission statement (EICTA, 2009a), it is 'dedicated to improving the business environment' for the IT industry; in other words, it is a lobbying organization. Among its 61 digital technology company members from 28 European countries are large IT companies such as HP, Nokia, Dell and IBM, as well as smaller corporations (EICTA, 2009b).

In the summer of 2000, EICTA had a plan. Andrew Baynes from Sony explained the details at a meeting of the organization, but his PowerPoint presentation was subsequently leaked to the independent news agency Inter Press Service (IPS) and *Inside EAP Weekly Report*. The *NGO Strategy* outlined an 'action plan for counteracting the efforts of several domestic and international environmental groups' (Baynes, 2000 – the following quotes are from the original document). The IT industry was advised to set up a 'detailed monitoring and contact network [on] NGOs'. Infonic was the 'web intelligence agency' recommended for this task. Initial work had been conducted. The first section of the *NGO Strategy* called *NGO Overview* disclosed names and contact information for groups that allegedly posed a threat to the IT industry. The report described Greenpeace, Friends of the Earth and the small California based Silicon Valley Toxics Coalition as 'highly active, well-organised' with a successful 'global reach' in their efforts to expose human health hazards. The EICTA members were advised to 'look into partnership support with reliable NGOs' and the accompanying availability of 'tax rebates in some Member states' for doing so. Future legislation could be pre-empted by working with NGOs on localized recycling campaigns. While some of the recommendations showed great similarity to Infonic's mantra of getting closer to stakeholders, other strategies proposed were aimed at undermining the work of the campaigners. The section entitled *Action Strategy-Proposal* urged a 'unified action strategy' to deal with the environmental groups: 'Don't wait!!' The companies were advised to confront the waste campaign allegations from a high level within the company, and to prepare industry template responses in order to avoid individual fragmented responses. The electronics industry was also encouraged to try to curtail the funding of the campaigning groups: 'Early pre-funding intervention could be beneficial,' it said in the leaked document. According to the *Inside EAP Weekly Report* this

> likely refers to a growing movement in the business community to take industry problems with activists' agendas directly to

donors, charitable foundations and companies that sponsor the environmental organizations, in an effort to stall the campaigns before they even commence. (*Inside EPA Weekly Report*, 2000)

Together the recommendations outlined a basic set of counter-strategies to deal effectively with an activist campaign. To have these details reported in the press is damaging for the online intelligence agency, and its potential clients and targets.

Denial

When the strategy leaked and attracted widespread criticism, Sony and Infonic went to great lengths to deny any involvement in preparing the strategy plan (Wazir, 2000; Gruner, 2001). EICTA also kept a low profile.

Roy Lipski did not like his company being portrayed as spying on activists. He insisted that Infonic had nothing to do with the action plan beyond providing a standard information pack: 'One representative within Sony had misinterpreted what we do and had presented ourselves in a manner which suited their own objectives, without our knowledge or consent, and which did not reflect what we do or believe' (Lipski, interview by email, 5 February 2001). Sony too attempted to distance itself from the *NGO Strategy*. A spokesperson told the *Wall Street Journal* that it was *not* a Sony document although the company's name was on the document and one of its employees had written it. It was not Sony's, because it had been created on behalf of EICTA (Gruner, interview by email, 29 January 2001). A few months after the exposure, on 30 October 2000, Sony met with a delegation of the activist groups targeted in the document. Iza Kruszewska of ANPED, the Northern Alliance for Sustainability, was at the meeting, where Sony denied it had hired Infonic, and claimed it had merely mentioned the company as an example of a service others might want to use (Kruszewska, interview by email, 2 February 2001).

The content of the *NGO Strategy*, and the subsequent damage control operation, show that there is a demand for such plans as well as a desire to keep such strategies secret. Furthermore, Infonic was monitoring Greenpeace closely in the months prior to the presentation of the *NGO Strategy*. In those days, Greenpeace's web statistics were available on its website (Greenpeace, 1999/2000). The statistics show that Infonic was among the ten most frequent visitors for six months in a row, with an average of 300 to 450 hits a week. Infonic alone entered the Greenpeace site more often than all the users via Google or Alta Vista combined. This intensive monitoring started in December 1999 and – coincidently or not – ended in the week the Sony presentation was held.[14]

Additionally, in the first media reports about the NGO *Strategy* Sony freely acknowledged that the company was tracking environmental groups. Before ranks closed the company's vice-president of environmental, health and safety issues, Mark Small, said: 'We are obviously concerned about our image. [...] If Greenpeace is pushing something, we want to be on top of it.' He also admitted that the NGO *Strategy* had not been put together in the 'most tasteful' way, but said the presentation had not been meant for public release (Knight, 2000).

The plans presented to the IT industry show the apparent need for a set of counterstrategies to deal with an environmental campaign on responsible disposal of toxic waste. The NGO *Strategy* reflects the connection between gathering intelligence and developing counterstrategies. Detailed monitoring of NGOs, their contact network and their online activities provided the intelligence needed for strategic action. A part of the plan implied covert measures to undermine critical NGOs such as an attempt to challenge the funding of NGO campaigns and to drive a wedge between groups in a coalition by seeking cooperation with the more moderate ones. The NGO *Strategy* has parallels with Pagan's strategy (Chapter 3) to separate 'realist' activists from 'radical' groups, and deal with them in different ways. The general idea is to be proactive, to deal with the activists before problems have become a major issue on the public agenda. The efforts of the companies involved to disassociate themselves from the leaked documents indicates that secrecy is an inherent part of such corporate strategy.

EWATCH

The business philosophy of eWatch appealed to the bunker mentality many multinationals adopt when first faced with online activism. The terminology used to promote the spying services to help companies 'neutralise news' or identify and 'eliminate' online activists (eWatch, 2000c) echoed Cold War paranoia and hostility.

eWatch pioneered internet monitoring in 1995, scanning online publications, discussion forums, bulletin boards and electronic mailing lists on behalf of clients. By the end of 2001, it claimed to be continuously screening more than 4,700 online publications and 66,000+ Usenet groups, bulletin boards and mailing lists. A growing number of large corporations – more than 900 by late 2000 – used this virtual clippings service. These statistics remain largely unchanged over the years (eWatch, 2000b; 2009).

Early in 1999 eWatch launched a service called CyberSleuth, targeted at counteracting online anti-corporate activism. The promotional website was unambiguous about the services for sale. First, if a corporation wished to know who was behind a given screen name, the service would provide a complete dossier in seven to ten days. The price for targeting individual users was $4,995 per name. 'Identifying these perpetrators is done using a variety of methods such as following leads found in postings and websites, working ISPs, involving law enforcement, conducting virtual stings, among other tactics' (eWatch, 2000c). Depending on the 'seriousness of the offence', CyberSleuth promised to take appropriate counter-measures. 'These may include everything from simply exposing the individual online, all the way to arrest. In some cases, the perpetrator is an employee of, or contractor to, the targeted company. In these cases, termination of employment is customary' (ibid.). And CyberSleuth would make sure no further damage was done: 'We can neutralise the information appearing online, identifying the perpetrators behind uncomplimentary postings and rogue websites' (ibid.). 'Info-cleansing' was an essential part of eWatch's containment policy. 'This may mean something as simple as removing a posting from a Web message board on Yahoo! to the shuttering [*sic*] of a terrorist website' (ibid.). CyberSleuth claimed a success rate of more than 80 per cent in rooting out online offenders (Green, 2000).

Cybersleuth

CyberSleuth was advertised on the eWatch website from February 1999 until mid-July 2000.[15] An article in *Business Week* made eWatch understand the downside of being so explicit about its intentions, methods and techniques. The magazine reproduced the website's promotional text and quoted eWatch's product manager Ted Skinner on a recent success story. Early in 2000, CyberSleuth had helped Northwest Airlines (NWA) track down the alleged organizers of an employee 'sickout' that had nearly halted flights over the Christmas holidays. The airline had fired the alleged organizers, and eWatch claimed a court had upheld the legality of the action. Northwest had since continued to use CyberSleuth, according to Skinner, to 'help it target – for re-education – the most teed-off of its fed up fliers' (Stepanek, 2000).

This was one of the first times that people discussing labour conditions on a public website had been the target of a far-reaching virtual and real investigation. What are the possible consequences of being labelled a 'perpetrator' by eWatch – or a similar service?

The target of this online surveillance was a chat room on a flight attendants' website where Northwest employees discussed work-related issues. This included a long-running dispute between the airline and its 11,000 flight attendants, dating back to 1993, when Northwest employees accepted pay cuts to help keep the airline solvent. They had been working without a contract since 1997. Their pay therefore lagged dramatically behind the industry standard. Northwest Airlines and the flight attendants' union, Teamsters Local 2000, entered contract negotiations in late 1998, but reached a stalemate on 7 December that year. The postings on the flight attendants' website voiced a wide range of opinions, from employees advocating sickouts and strikes, to others opposing such actions (Digital Discovery team of Harvard Law School students, 2000).

After the sickout, Northwest filed a federal lawsuit in Minnesota. District Judge Donovan Frank granted NWA a temporary injunction prohibiting the union from encouraging its members to participate in a sickout or other illegal activity (ibid.). This in itself is a far-reaching decision. Then, the company obtained a court order requiring 43 named defendants to turn over their office and home computer equipment. Instead of going to the authorities, the machines were handed to the accounting company Ernst & Young. They copied information and communications before returning the computers. After the E&Y enquiry, Northwest Airlines fired more than a dozen employees for having participated in a sickout. The union filed grievances claiming that none of the employee's sick calls were false (ibid.). Eventually, however, all lawsuits were dropped as part of a collective bargaining agreement to improve working conditions.[16]

This case raised questions among defenders of civil liberties in the United States. Harvard Law scholars at the Berkman Institute of Internet and Society queried whether an employee who expresses support for a sickout or strike on a publicly accessible website should properly become the target of further investigation. Jim Dempsey of the Washington-based Center for Democracy and Technology warned that such searches mark a departure from normal evidence-gathering procedures. Usually, parties that have to produce evidence in a civil law case are permitted to do their own review and then turn over relevant material. In this case, Northwest confiscated the computers. Dempsey pointed out that they should have given the evidence to the union's attorneys first. 'This arrangement is setting more intrusive rules for digital evidence than we have for paper evidence' (Catlin, 2000).

The effect on employees' use of the website forums has been marked. Posts critical of Northwest dwindled, and some worried that more messages since have been posted anonymously (Digital Discovery team of Harvard Law School students, 2000).

This case marks an important shift towards private justice. The airline used an online monitoring agency to track down employees who expressed support for a strike from their office and home computers, and an accounting company reviewed the evidence. The discovery and investigation were never judged, the accusations never proved, the employees never tried in a court of law. But they were clearly punished: they lost their jobs.

Furthermore, this case touches fundamental issues such as the freedom of association and the freedom of expression (Hamelink, 1994; 2000). It brings back elements of blacklisting, as practised by the Economic League in the UK for decades (see Chapter 2). To participate in online discussions about working conditions was sufficient to become suspect in the eyes of employers, and perhaps adversely affected career progression and job security.

Research on monitoring employee email and web use confirmed that these forms of surveillance have increased enormously since the beginning of this century. Such monitoring is taking place for a wide variety of reasons, and is considered a benefit in terms of efficiency on the work floor and 'proactive intervention' with 'potential behavioural risks' (Hansen, 2007: 164; also see Ball and Webster, 2003; Hier and Greenberg, 2007). In 2007, Walmart was involved in a widening spying scandal. It was revealed that the company employed a 20-strong in-house team called the Threat Research and Analysis Group to monitor email and internet activity by suppliers and consultants working for Walmart. In trying to find out the source of leaks to the company's critics, the team tapped phone calls and pager messages between Walmart employees and a *New York Times* reporter. The company also infiltrated the consumer campaign group Up Against The Wall, to see if they were planning protests at the company's annual shareholder meeting (Foley, 2007).

The economic downturn has increased spending on security software. Research by IT consultants Gartner found that the market for systems used to mine emails for keywords and security breaches grew by 50 per cent in 2008. The fastest-growing area is network forensic software, recording exactly what happens on employees' computer screens (cited in *The Economist*, 2009). Advances in technology have increased opportunities to monitor employees who are not trusted, and anyone else critical of the company.

Denial

Privacy activists had been circulating details about CyberSleuth at the time, but Stepanek's *BusinessWeek* article caused quite a stir online. eWatch had been purchased by *PR Newswire* earlier that year and the new owner was not amused. *PR Newswire* is one of the two wire services that traditionally dominated the public relations scene (*Business Wire* is the other). In addition to disseminating news releases to thousands of newspapers and other media outlets, they distribute quarterly financial reports and other corporate information. Journalists have come to depend on the credibility of *PR Newswire*; the company has a reputation to maintain (Rampton, 2002). (In recent years, more wire services, such as *US Newswire* and *Newsbytes*, have entered the commercial news distribution market on the internet.)

The damage control operation that followed, however, was itself an example of poor reputation management, involving obvious attempts to spin different versions of what had happened, including a straight denial that CyberSleuth had ever existed.

Initially, *PR Newswire* asked *BusinessWeek* to publish a correction. The magazine refused, stating that Stepanek, their Technology Strategies editor, had her facts straight. Further claims about 'errors' and 'misquotes' were easily countered with printouts and screen grabs of the CyberSleuth website. When *PR Newswire* subsequently disavowed the eWatch product manager's quotes, Stepanek produced notes by Skinner himself, she explained in an email on 14 November 2000.

PR Newswire decided to change strategy and subsequently tracked down journalists and net activists who had quoted the article online or in print. Spokesperson Renu Aldrich made it her personal quest to convince the audience that eWatch was nothing but a clippings service (see, for instance, Koch, 2000; Cox, 2000). She claimed the company had never undertaken any of the activities described in the *BusinessWeek* article. 'We do not remove postings for them or take any other measures' (Cox, 2000).

Five weeks after the exposure, *PR Newswire* disassociated itself – formally – from the CyberSleuth service. On 15 August 2000, eWatch officially announced a partnership with the Internet Crimes Group. The move officially to separate the practice of 'info-cleansing' from eWatch and *PR Newswire* was presented as a new service. The announcement ran under the headline: 'Online monitoring goes beyond anonymous postings, Investigative Service to Uncover Identities of Malicious Attackers' (eWatch, 2000d). In fact, *PR Newswire* created a separate umbrella to continue the CyberSleuth service under another name. The announcement included a special offer: in addition to ICG's service, there was a complimentary 30-day subscription to all eWatch monitoring services (ibid.).

The Internet Crimes Group (ICG) was founded in January 2000 as a subsidiary of International Business Research, a company dedicated to web investigation. The former's managing director Cameron H. Graig (retired FBI), became president of the new company.

ICG's founders and directors proudly identified themselves as a former British intelligence officer and a retired FBI agent. According to interviews in the press, ICG did not shy away from using the full range of investigative tricks, from lurking in newsgroup discussions to creating hoax identities – attractive females if necessary – to seduce culprits into traceable statements or actions (Buckman, 1999; Daragahi, 2001). Their ideas, too, matched the early CyberSleuth rhetoric and showed little respect for freedom of speech. Discussing constitutional rights with a reporter from the online publication *WebWatch*, one ICG director said bluntly, 'Anonymity does for the internet poster what the white robe does for the KKK' (Daragahi, 2001). ICG chose not to reply to my repeated questions.

My inquiries into CyberSleuth a few months after the *BusinessWeek* article still touched a nerve. According to *PR Newswire* spokesperson Renu Aldrich, the article consisted of 'lies and misinformation'. She said the website promoting CyberSleuth – *BusinessWeek*'s prime source of information – had never existed. However, the content of the website had been widely circulated on the web, after Internet rights activist Dr James Love posted it on his mail server late June 2000 (Love, 2000). I had reported about it online myself (see Lubbers, 2000a, 2000b). Further research revealed that immediately after the *BusinessWeek* article was published, eWatch swiftly disconnected the link to CyberSleuth from its main page (on 18 July 2000, according to Netscape's Page Info feature, checked in November 2000).[17] However, eWatch failed to remove the disputed content as such.

So, at the very moment Aldrich was trying to convince me that the CyberSleuth site did not exist and had never existed (interview by email, 10 November 2000), the site was still online and available – one just had to know the exact URL. Within 24 hours of informing *PR Newswire* about this, the page was completely removed from the eWatch website (It is, however, still accessible through the internet archive, eWatch, 2000a.) Now, before answering any further questions, Aldrich insisted on issuing a statement (interview by email, 11 November 2000):

> eWatch has never done more than provide monitoring reports or refer people to ICG. eWatch has never nor will it call an ISP or otherwise to try to alter or delete posts or websites for its clients.

Aldrich also claimed that eWatch no longer offered the CyberSleuth product. Companies wishing to investigate anonymous screen names were now referred to ICG. Asked about this sudden need for licensed detectives, Aldrich said: 'We wanted a partner who would be beneficial to our clients and do proper investigations legally and above board as well as successfully.' Asked if eWatch had ever gotten into trouble with the law, Aldrich did not answer with a clear 'no' but said: 'Not that I am aware of; certainly nothing untoward has occurred since *PR Newswire* has owned eWatch' (interview by email, 14 November 2000). Nancy Sells, vice-president of eWatch services, had a similar explanation as to why eWatch did not provide strategic analysis for its clients any more: 'We deliver the information to the customer. It is up to them to do what they see fit. We do not take a stance, intervene or do anything else [...]. Our customers don't want us to do that for them' (Sells, cited in Mayfield, 2001).

For an agency offering reputation management services to other companies, the sudden need for public relations advice for itself is somewhat ironic. But this case touches upon fundamental issues of the information society, fundamental rights and privatization. This example marks the growing importance of the internet as a useful tool to discuss work-related problems and to organize collective action.

The cases involve issues of freedom of expression, freedom of organization and modern forms of blacklisting. For Americans this refers to the First Amendment to the Constitution, freedom of speech, but also to the Fourth, and possibly the Sixth Amendment. The Fourth ensures the right of people to be secure in their persons, houses, papers and effects, against unreasonable searches and seizures. Writing something on a public forum, DeWitt (2000) argued, would still constitute 'papers or effects'. Even if someone posted a message anonymously, it seems that 'ferreting out the human behind the screen name would be a search without probable cause' (ibid.). The Sixth Amendment guarantees a speedy and public trial in all criminal prosecutions, which is a basic right in most if not all democratic states. When users are banned from public forums, their messages removed, their content destroyed by an ISP threatened by a corporate lawyer, their rights to fair trial are being violated. 'They've often had no opportunity to find counsel because the corporations were able to take action secretly and without notice' (ibid.). In Orwell's *1984*, the oppression was government based, DeWitt writes. 'In real-life 2000, newspeak and oppression are carried out by corporations with tacit government approval.' The possible danger of a cease-and-desist order could evoke self censorship.

Finally, the eWatch example shows several levels of 'plausible denial:' responsible authorities – such as spokesperson Aldrich – sought to create as much distance as possible from the exposed malpractices. Often tactics involved lies and threats to prevent the scandal from spreading.

These cases illustrate the variety of ways that corporations sought to gather intelligence to use it. The intelligence is connected to concrete action. An unfounded accusation led to a privatized search of the content of home computers and far-reaching consequences for those involved. In this case, it may not have been 'covert action' in the strictest sense, but it was not accountable or controlled by a court or a judge.

BIVINGS

TNCs have become increasingly sophisticated in their use of the web. This section explores the wide-ranging attempts of Monsanto and its online PR consultant Bivings to shape discourse and opinion. It involves the use of fake identities, exclusively existing on the internet, to influence and manipulate online discussions critical of genetic engineering.

The Bivings Group specializes in online PR. The company's slogan used to be: 'Wired engagement. Global reach. Lasting impact.' Until mid-2006 the more compact version 'wired.global.impact' was part of the company's logo (Bivings Group, 2006). The company was founded in 1993, and was originally known as Bivings-Woodell Inc. It has developed internet advocacy campaigns for corporate America since 1996 and serves a number of Fortune 100 clients in the biotechnology, chemical, financial, food, consumer products and telecommunications industries. Among the notable clients are Dow Chemicals, Kraft Foods, Phillip Morris, BP Amoco, the Chlorine Chemistry Council and Crop Life International (Bivings Group, 2009). Many of those clients have been targeted by campaigners for their environmental, labour and consumer records.

The biotechnology industry was a particularly visible target. As a response to marketing and regulatory problems in the late 1990s, Monsanto hired Bivings to develop a wide-ranging internet strategy. In 2002, Bivings had more than a dozen Monsanto companies as clients and it ran the main Monsanto website, as well as some of their European sites. Bivings also designed several sophisticated campaigns for the company to influence the debate on the risks of GM (Rowell, 2003: 158, fn. 42).

Bivings' work for Monsanto was widely praised for its transparency. The company received the Advocacy Award from the *New Statesman*, which described its work as: '[o]penness in the face of controversy' (*Holmes Report*, 1999). According to a PR industry's trade report '[t]he sites provide a wealth of information on GM foods and engage the company's critics in a non-confrontational discussion of the issues' (ibid.).

The PR professionals' magazine *Inside PR* praised Bivings' work for Monsanto for 'addressing consumer concerns about genetically modified foods in a calm and rational way, even providing access to opposing viewpoints so that consumers can be better informed' (*Inside PR*, 1999). Open, calm and rational were the buzz-words, but the following case shows that Bivings and Monsanto had other ways of dealing with life science industry critics.

The Mexican Maize Controversy

The strategy Bivings and Monsanto developed to influence discussion on the safety of genetically manipulated (GM) crops became evident from examining their role in what has become known as the Mexican maize controversy. This started when two researchers from the University of California in Berkeley published a paper in the journal *Nature* (Quist and Chapela, 2001). The authors claimed that native maize in Mexico had been contaminated, across vast distances, by GM pollen. Cross-pollination was then an important argument against GM crops. This issue involved much more than reputational risk for the GM industry, because verified cases would lead to renewed regulatory action based on the precautionary principle. The principle implies that there is a responsibility to intervene and protect the public from exposure to harm where scientific investigation discovers a plausible risk.

> Recourse to the precautionary principle presupposes that potentially dangerous effects deriving from a phenomenon, product or process have been identified, and that scientific evaluation does not allow the risk to be determined with sufficient certainty. (European Commission, 2000)

The *Nature* paper was a disaster for the biotech companies seeking to persuade Mexico, Brazil and the European Union to lift their embargos on GM crops. Even before publication, the researchers knew their work was sensitive. One of the authors, Ignacio Chapela, had been talking to Mexican government officials even though it was preliminary research. At one meeting, the aide to the Biosafety Commissioner, Fernando Ortiz Monasterio, privately told Chapela that he was creating a really serious problem and he was going to pay for it. Monasterio said Chapela could be part of the solution:

> He proceeded to invite me to be part of a secret scientific team [with two scientists from Monsanto and two from DuPont] that was going to show the world what the reality of GM was all about. (Chapela, cited in Rowell, 2003: 152)

When Chapela refused, Monasterio told him he knew where to find his children (ibid.). Monasterio acknowledged meeting Chapela, but denied threatening him in any way (BBC Radio 4, 2003; see also Rowell, 2003: 153).

To minimize the impact of the paper in *Nature*, Monsanto and Bivings tried to influence its discussion amongst scientists. Together they created fake identities purposely for a covert counterstrategy to discredit the authors of the paper. The forum of choice to interfere in the discussion was the biotechnology list server AgBioView. It was discovered that two regular posters, called 'Mary Murphy' and 'Andura Smetacek', did not exist. Jonathan Matthews and Andy Rowell revealed how the two 'women' acted as allegedly independent third parties actively engaging in the discussion on the Mexican maize paper. On the day *Nature* published the paper, messages questioning the authors' credibility started to appear on AgBioView. The first message, opening the issue of the *Newsletter* that day, was signed by 'Mary Murphy'. Because Chapela was on the board of directors of the Pesticide Action Network, she wrote, he is 'not exactly what you'd call an unbiased writer' (Murphy, 2001). Subsequently, 'Andura Smetacek' claimed that Chapela's paper had not been peer-reviewed. This was untrue. She also wrote that he was 'first and foremost an activist', and that the research had been published in collusion with environmentalists (Smetacek, 2001a). The next day, another email from 'Smetacek' implied the Berkeley scientist was on the activists' pay list: 'how much money does Chapela take in speaking fees, travel reimbursements and other donations [...] for his help in misleading fear-based marketing campaigns?' (Smetacek, 2001b).

Together Smetacek and Murphy posted around 60 messages, which stimulated hundreds of others, some of which repeated the accusations they had made. Several biotechnologists called for Chapela to be sacked from Berkeley – see for instance the posting from Trewavas (2002) of the Institute of Cell and Molecular Biology, University of Edinburgh. For other postings, see the Mexican Maize Resource Library at the AgBioWorld website (AgBioWorld, 2009d) and the AgBioView Archives from 2001 and onwards (AgBioWorld, 2009b); also see Monbiot (2002a).

Nature eventually gave in to the pressure and retracted the article – an unprecedented decision in its 133-year history. *Nature* (2002) wrote: 'Because of several criticisms of the paper, *Nature* has concluded that the evidence available is not sufficient to justify the publication of the original paper.' Just a few days before crucial negotiations at the UN Convention on Biological Diversity held in The Hague from 7 to 19 April 2002, the *Nature* climb-down was an important trump card for the GM lobby.[18] However, at the conference, Jorge Soberon, the executive secretary of Mexico's National Commission on Biodiversity, confirmed that according to research by the Mexican government the level of contamination was far worse than initially reported (Brown, 2002; Clover, 2002).

Fake Persuaders

who were 'Mary Murphy' and 'Andura Smetacek'? Campaigner Jonathan Matthews (2002, 2003) has been monitoring the GM expert community for a long time and noticed these new names on the discussion forum and the ferocity of their messages.

'Mary Murphy' used a hotmail account for posting messages to AgBioWorld: mrph@hotmail.com. Anyone can create a hotmail account, with any given name. However, this specific hotmail address had a history. In July 2000, a Mary Murphy posted a fake *Associated Press* article satirizing the opponents of biotech (Murphy, 2000). It was posted on the message board of foxbghsuit. com, a website dedicated to a legal case connected to Monsanto's genetically engineered cattle drug rBGH. The hotmail reply address was identical, but the message board showed additional identifying details in the headers: 'Posted by Mary Murphy (bw6.bivwood. com)' (ibid.). Bivwood.com is the property of Bivings Woodell, the previous name of the Bivings Group (Networksolutions.com, 2009a). This meant that 'Mary Murphy's' hotmail emails were sent from a Bivings computer.[19] The last mail signed by Murphy was posted to AgBioWorld on 8 April 2002, and after that, she completely disappeared from the internet. Rowell (2002a: 158) suggested that the impending exposure inspired the sudden disappearance.

'Andura Smetacek' was harder to trace. Her name appeared only on AgBioWorld and a few related list servers, but nowhere else on the internet. Issues concerning her alleged residency eventually provided some clues. Smetacek refused to verify a land address or to provide an employer, despite numerous requests by the *Ecologist*, nor did she respond to emails from other journalists in the UK and the US (Rowell, 2003: 157; Monbiot, 2002a; Platoni, 2002). In her emails, she claimed to live in London and in New York. Matthews checked every available public record, but found no person of that name in either city. Further research revealed that 'Smetacek' was indeed connected to Monsanto. In her first email to the AgBioView list, she presented herself as a concerned observer of the GM debate writing from London (Smetacek, 2000). However, this email (and two of her earlier emails to the list) arrived with the internet protocol address 199.89.234.124.[20] This was – and still is – the address assigned to the server gatekeeper2.monsanto.com, belonging to the Monsanto headquarters in St Louis, in the United States (Networksolutions.com, 2009b). So, from her email address, it seems that Andura Smetacek writing from London never actually existed: '"she" was a virtual person whose role was to direct debates on the web and denigrate the opposition' (Rowell, 2003: 159). Smetacek also disappeared just before exposure (also see PowerBase, 2009a).

The third key-player in this affair was Dr C.S. Prakash, the founder and moderator of the AgBioView mailing list, where the fake emails were posted. With several associates, Prakash established the AgBioWorld Foundation in January 2000 as a 501(c)(3) non-profit organization. AgBioWorld presents itself as a mainstream science campaign 'that has emerged from academic roots and values'. Prakash claimed he received no funding or assistance for the Foundation and denied working with any PR company (Rowell, 2003: 158). However, a connection to Bivings was established when an error message appeared while searching the AgBioView online archives: 'can't connect to MySQL server on *apollo.bivings.com*'[21] (PowerBase, 2009b, 2009c; also see Monbiot, 2002a). The error message revealed that the AgBioView archives were stored on a Bivings' computer. *Apollo.bivings.com* was – and still is – one of the three servers of the Bivings Group (Networksolutions.com, 2009c).

Although the foundation carefully eschewed corporate support, it was set up in close cooperation with the Competitive Enterprise Institute (CEI), a conservative lobby group with a multimillion dollar budget. Its sponsors include Monsanto, Philip Morris and Dow Chemicals. The cooperation is most evident through the involvement of Gregory Conko, one of the original founders of AgBioWorld in 2000, who has since become vice-president of the Foundation and a member of the Board of Directors (CEI, 2009). At the time, Conko was Director of Food Safety Policy at CEI, and in 2009 he became a senior fellow at the Institute. The book he co-authored, *The Frankenfood Myth: How Protest and Politics Threaten the Biotech Revolution* (Miller and Conko, 2004), reflected his particular interest 'in the debate over the safety of biotechnology and bioengineered foods, as well as the application of the Precautionary Principle to domestic and international environmental and safety regulations' (CEI, 2009).

Further collaboration was marked by the launch of the so-called *Declaration of Scientists in Support of Agricultural Biotechnology.* CEI was proud to take an active part in the fight against what they call 'death by regulation' – regulatory policies that threaten people's health and safety. The battle over biotechnology was foremost in this fight, according to the CEI *Annual Report 2000*. The Institute 'played a key role in the creation of the *Declaration*', the president and founder of the Institute Fred L. Smith claimed in his foreword (in CEI, 2001: 1). Yet the Declaration was hosted on the AgBioWorld website, and Prakash presented it as an initiative of his organization (AgBioWorld, 2000) and one of his own achievements (AgBioWorld, 2009c).

Although Conko and Prakash were the two founders, the involvement of CEI was not mentioned on the AgBioWorld website at the time of the Mexican maize controversy. It was not until a few years later, in 2005, that Greg Conko was first introduced at the AgBioWorld website as its vice-president. Archive.org documents the first appearance on 17 August 2005 (AgBioWorld, 2005). The web page offering his biography provided an exact copy of his information at the CEI site (CEI, 2009).

Denial

Rowell (2002a) and Matthews (2002) published their findings in the *Big Issue* and in the *Ecologist* respectively. Subsequently, George Monbiot devoted two columns in the *Guardian* to the research (Monbiot, 2002a; 2002b). Bivings and Monsanto chose a strategy of straight denial. The PR company issued a statement on the *Ecologist* story, saying:

> This author and publication have a long history of making these types of baseless claims. The claims made in the *Ecologist* story, and the subsequent story that appeared in the *Guardian*, are false. From our perspective, this piece merits no further discussion. (Bivings Group, 2002a)

Monbiot's articles received a carefully worded response from the company's president, Gary F. Bivings. The allegations made against the Bivings Group were completely untrue, he said. The 'fake persuaders' mentioned were 'not employees or contractors· or aliases of contractors of the Bivings Group'. In fact, he claimed, the Bivings Group had 'no knowledge of either Mary Murphy or Andura Smetacek' (Bivings, 2002a).

However, before Bivings' letter to the editor was printed, the company's head of online PR, Todd Zeigler, appeared on the BBC current affairs programme *Newsnight*. In the interview, Zeigler admitted that 'at least one of the emails' came from someone 'working for Bivings' or 'clients using our services' (Newsnight, 2002; see also Monbiot, 2002c). Gary Bivings later tried to disavow the words of his head of PR. He said the company had 'never made any statements to this effect', and claimed that *Newsnight* had been 'wrong' about the origin of the emails (Bivings, 2002b).

Bivings' categorical denials backfired completely when it transpired that he had sent his letter to the *Guardian* by email. The technical properties revealed that the director's message came from bw6.bivwood.com, the same computer server that 'Mary Murphy' had used (Monbiot, 2002b).

Industry Influence

In his dissertation 'Pathways of scientific dissent in agricultural biotechnology', Jason Delborne explored several controversies surrounding agricultural biotechnology. One of the case studies analysed was the Mexican maize controversy. He notes:

> Regardless of the degree of coordination of the campaign, the discourse emerging online to discredit Chapela and the discovery of the questionable identities of two of the key contributors to that conversation [Murphy and Smetacek] suggest an important pattern of resistance with central themes of credibility and power. (Delborne, 2005: 229)

The attack on Chapela and Quist relied upon an attack on the *character* of the scientists rather than on the scientific research. 'The accusations of being an "activist" and associating closely with activist groups implied that such character qualities and affiliations polluted their scientific claims' (ibid.). Apparently the association with activists diminishes a scientist's credibility.

The AgBioWorld forum allowed false rumours (for instance that the Quist and Chapela article was not peer-reviewed) and speculation (that Chapela had coordinated his research with activist NGOs) to circulate. Delborne concludes that the mailing list served as an incubator for an intense campaign, with enough momentum eventually to develop into a stronger and more technical critique that could reach and influence a wider audience. The fact that AgBioWorld allowed this to happen is less surprising given that the forum itself is part of a larger strategy to promote the interests of the GM industry.

In hindsight, the Mexican maize controversy brought together several, interlinked issues of major importance in one heated debate. First, the possibility of cross-pollination, which at that time was seen as closely related to the safety and thereby the future of genetically engineered food production and its regulation was disputed. Second, the influence of large corporations at universities was called into question. Chapela was an outspoken critic of the long-running multimillion-dollar collaborative research agreements between Berkeley and the Swiss pharmaceutical and biotech company Novartis (now Syngenta) (see, for instance, *California Monthly*, 2002). This placed Chapela in the arena of political debates on genetic engineering, and made it relatively easy to link his critical position to the question of academic integrity in general. Or, as Prakash put it: 'since the dogged and relentless pursuit of truth is the ultimate goal of science, should Quist and Chapela have been allowed to publish such obviously flawed findings?' (AgBioWorld, 2009d).

This question is closely related to the third and final major issue, the value of peer reviewing in general, and the quality of publications in *Nature*. The reputation of the highly respected journal was at stake as its scientific independence was brought into question. The apparent flaws in the Mexican maize research – flaws that could have been corrected had the researchers been given the chance – had escaped the eye of the reviewers. Chapela and Quist were allowed to provide further data on their research; however, the details were published in the same issue of *Nature* that retracted their original paper. The question was raised whether the decision to retract was based purely on issues with the peer review system, or whether it was influenced by the pressure of the GM industry. Or, in other words, was it 'due process or double standard'? (Salleh, 2002). *Nature*'s editor Philip Campbell (2002) insisted that the journal's turnaround had nothing to do with the fact that the paper was about genetic modification. 'It must have been Murphy's law that ensured that our technical oversight, embarrassing in itself, was in relation to a paper about one of the most hotly debated technologies of our time.'

Untangling these still ongoing debates is almost impossible. However, the role of the GM industry and their PR advisers in influencing these debates usually remains under-exposed.

Viral Marketing

The Bivings Group (then Bivings Woodell) started developing covert strategy long before the Mexican maize controversy, and even before 1999, the year that Monsanto nearly collapsed as a result of the failure to introduce GM food on the European market. Reflecting on the PR debacle, Monsanto's communications director Philip Angell told the *Wall Street Journal*: 'Maybe we were not aggressive enough [...] When you fight a forest fire, sometimes you have to light another fire' (Kilmann and Cooper, 1999).

In October 1999, the *New York Times* highlighted the emerging industry among consultants specializing in spinning online discussions on behalf of clients. Bivings was among the firms admitting to adopting pseudonyms and participating in online discussions on behalf of some clients.[22] 'If participated in properly,' Matthew Benson, senior director at Bivings, told the paper, 'these can be vehicles for shaping emerging issues'. Moreover, some firms 'recruit scientists and other experts to voice clients' perspectives in on-line discussions' (Raney, 1999).

To understand a group or an issue requires long-term monitoring, as online researchers 'have to develop a cultural memory for the issues they're following' (ibid.). Benson and other consultants claimed to approach online forums cautiously:

> When deciding whether to intervene in a discussion, Mr Benson said, they weigh a number of factors: How serious a forum is it? Do influential people frequent the discussion? How much reach does the forum have outside its own boundaries? Are the critics considered influential by the group, or are they merely considered annoying? (ibid.)

For instance, the site of the Organic Consumers Association, dedicated to informing the public about food safety, organic farming and genetic engineering, did not attract enough visitors to be seen as a real threat. Monsanto's director of internet outreach, Jay Byrne, used the Organic Consumers site as an example when explaining in the *Monthly Newsletter for Web Professionals* about his job in 2000. Instead, he preferred to spend 'his time and effort participating in even-handed online discussions about the industry' (Ragan Interactive Public Relations, 2000). To illustrate this, Byrne singled out the AgBioWorld website run by Professor C.S. Prakash. As a list providing information to scientists, policy-makers, journalists and the general public on how agricultural biotechnology can help sustain development, AgBioWorld fitted Bivings' above-cited criteria for intervention. 'Byrne subscribes and offers advice and information when relevant and ensures his company gets proper play' (ibid.). At least that is what he told the *Monthly Newsletter for Web Professionals*. The archives of the AgBioView list, however, show no entry signed by him under his own name. Moreover, as detailed above, Bivings is closely connected to this list.

Byrne is fond of telling professional peers: 'Think of the internet as a weapon on the table. Either you pick it up or your competitor does

– but somebody is going to get killed' (Byrne, 2001, 2002, 2003; see also PowerBase, 2009d). Byrne (2001) attributed the quote to Michael S. Dell, founder and CEO of Dell Computer Corporation.

Bivings calls covert methods to influence online discussions *viral marketing*: using word-of-mouth strategy to disseminate clients' views online. Andrew Dimock, head of online marketing and promotions, explained the concept of viral marketing on the Bivings website. The original version was published in November 2001 as *Thebivingsreport.com* (Dimock, 2002a). However, following the Mexican maize controversy, Dimock's piece was amended to eliminate the following quotation:

> There are some campaigns where it would be undesirable or even disastrous to let the audience know that your organization is directly involved [...] it simply is not an intelligent PR move. In cases such as this, it is important to first 'listen' to what is being said online [...] Once you are plugged into this world, it is possible to make postings to these outlets that present your position as an uninvolved third party. [...] Perhaps the greatest advantage of viral marketing is that your message is placed into a context where it is more likely to be considered seriously. (ibid.)

The current version now online advises just the opposite: 'Once you are plugged into this world, it is possible to make relevant postings to these outlets that *openly present your identity and position*' (Dimock, 2002b, emphasis added). And the word 'anonymously' has been strategically removed from this sentence: 'Message boards, chat rooms, and listservs are a great way to *anonymously* monitor what is being said' (ibid.). Bivings had obviously learned a lesson, as the following warning was added: 'You should be as transparent in your efforts as possible – even innocuous promotions can anger people if they somehow feel that they are being misled' (ibid.).

The covert corporate strategy using Murphy and Smetacek as 'fake persuaders' reveals a particular relationship between credibility and power. Delborne emphasizes that it 'suggested the potential for enormous disconnect between the face of resistance (personal emails) and the sources of power that support those faces (PR and biotech firms)' (Delborne, 2005: 229). The hidden and coordinated support behind people acting as independent individuals makes them harder to oppose. Simultaneously, powerful interests can also participate through covert representation in controversy. Such covert campaigns and the lack of transparency render the business interests extremely difficult to counter (unless they are uncovered) (ibid.).

CONCLUSION

The issues profiled in this chapter illustrate the variety of opportunities the internet offers to gather intelligence and to carry out counterstrategy. Online monitoring agencies provided client companies with practical advice in countering the campaign groups under surveillance. The IT industry received advice to curtail funding of campaigning groups, which is an example of restricting a movement's resources and limiting its facilities. Specialist technical knowledge allowed Bivings and Monsanto to introduce virtual identities aimed specifically at manipulating online discussions about genetic engineering. The digital identities encouraged a mudslinging campaign against two scientists critical of GE techniques that can be understood as a serious attempt of character assassination. The affair caused lasting work-related problems for the scientists. The eWatch case showed how people were fired because of their alleged role in industrial action, an example of counterstrategy imperilling employment (Marx, 1979). The stories indicate that on the internet too, monitoring what is said and done is only part of the story. The information was processed, analysed and used to develop covert corporate strategy to counter critics. In short, the cases in this chapter contain the essential elements that fit with ideas of theory of intelligence according to Gill (2009: 85): surveillance, power, knowledge, secrecy and resistance. The chapter illustrates the flipside to the idealized accounts of the internet such as that of Castells (2003).

Furthermore, these experiences show that the shift towards privatized intelligence instigates similar shifts on the internet. Corporations hire private firms to manage critics and opponents online. The risks to the privacy of citizens and the fundamental rights of activists, workers and other people should not be underestimated, and urgently need to be incorporated in future research agendas. Like the other companies investigated for this book, the online intelligence agencies had taken measures to prevent disclosure of their activities. Bivings created digital personalities to discredit scientists critical of biotechnology, trusting that they would be next to impossible to trace on the internet. Even in the face of incontrovertible evidence, denial was used in attempts at damage control. Infonic, eWatch and Biving refused to admit their involvement in covert operations undermining activists. The spokesperson of eWatch tried both straight denial and blaming the messenger, while at the same time distancing the company from the Cybersleuth service it provided. The founder of Infonic chose a softer focus and used reasonable arguments and persuasion. As its director, Biving himself wrote several letters to editors to deny the claims made against his company. These attempts to cover up are part of a wider culture of secrecy. Covert corporate strategy online undermines the space for open debate, accountability and transparency – in short, it endangers universal rights to communicate (Hamelink, 1994).

The online strategies, like the strategies in most other case studies in this book, were made visible through research by dedicated activists and investigative journalists. Research on the internet, however, requires specific technical skills to identify the origin of emails, to recover links that have been removed, and to interpret web statistics. Technologies have progressed rapidly and the possibilities of acting anonymously on the internet have increased, which may add to the temptation to choose this as a covert strategy. At the same time, such strategies are implemented by people, and people make mistakes or might be willing to talk, or to leak. In other words, these increased possibilities on the internet might also offer an avenue of opportunities for research and investigation.

The cases underscore the need for research on the field of cyber-surveillance, the political economy of agencies specializing in online monitoring and strategy as well as investigations into the specific techniques used in covert operations.

6
Hakluyt and the Jobbing Spy: Case Study

This case study first examines how a private intelligence firm linked closely to the British foreign intelligence service spied on environmental campaign groups to collect information for oil companies. The intelligence firm is called Hakluyt, and it attracted attention when an allegedly left-wing film-maker was exposed for spying in Germany, Switzerland and elsewhere in Western Europe. Manfred Schlickenrieder's cover was blown after a Swiss activist group published confidential files that proved he was on Hakluyt's payroll. The Schlickenrieder documents provide examples of covert corporate strategies developed for Shell and BP. Confronted with this material, Hakluyt reluctantly admitted having employed the spy. After the British press published the story, both Shell and BP acknowledged hiring the firm.

The second part of this story concentrates on Manfred Schlickenrieder's activities. The documents show that his spying experience had been built up during years of working for Germany's domestic and foreign intelligence services. In this context his work focused on revolutionary groups such as the Rote Armee Fraction (Red Army Faction, RAF), their supporting network and their connections with similar groups in Germany and elsewhere in Europe.

For more than 20 years, Schlickenrieder's secret work was paid for by private intelligence agencies as well as state services. He received assignments from both, alternately or simultaneously. Schlickenrieder's existence as a freelance spy is a personification of what Hoogenboom (2005, 2006) calls 'grey intelligence' and as such, this chapter maps the blurring boundaries between public and private intelligence and espionage.

BACKGROUND

The case is primarily based on research by an activist group in Switzerland, Revolutionäre Aufbau.[23] Schlickenrieder was uncovered as an infiltrator of this group because he was no longer trusted in his private and his public life. Strong suspicions by other members of the Aufbau group proved to be well-founded, as it was discovered that he held an archive of intelligence files. One of the members of the informal investigation group had access to his office, discovered the spy files, and took them (Eine Deutsche Genossin, 2001).

My involvement with this case started when the Aufbau group went public with the findings of their comprehensive internal investigation. They published the outcome of their research on the internet, illustrated by a selection of the discovered documents. Several German and Swiss papers reported the exposure of the spy and his intelligence files. I met with several people from the Aufbau group to share some of the Jansen & Janssen expertise, and subsequently investigated some links leading to people whom Schlickenrieder had approached in the Netherlands. As a freelance investigative journalist, I covered the case in the Dutch press (Lubbers, 2001a–d).

After our two-day meeting, the Aufbau group trusted me with a more complete set of the discovered documents on a CDrom, given to me for research purposes only. In addition to the many talks we had, the group also provided reports of their research, not all of which had been published in full. It included, for instance, the rough recordings (90 minutes) of an interview with a business journalist who had investigated the corporate assignments of the freelance spy. To complete the analysis of the material I have subsequently interviewed members of some of the targeted groups, such a Greenpeace Germany and various Dutch groups.

Although the discovery and initial verification of the secret documents happened before my involvement with the Aufbau group, this case brings up the issue of using deception as a method to gather information. Because the field of activist intelligence and covert corporate strategy may sometimes need unconventional research tactics, it is important to discuss the issue here.

A well-known example of the use of 'deceptive' methods is that of the German journalist Gunter Wallraff (1985a, 1985b, 1987), who exposed the horrific working conditions of migrant workers in German industry in the early 1980s and the misleading and deceitful practices of German's leading tabloid, *Bild*. In order to expose those practices, he went undercover and lived the life of a migrant worker and a tabloid reporter respectively. He had to do the trade and be part of it, in order to expose social abuse.

The use of deception can be problematic for both investigative journalists and social scientists for a variety of reasons, including 'important ethical issues such as lying, invasions of privacy, manipulation, and involving subjects without their consent'. Or, as Gary T. Marx (1984: 97) puts it:

> In getting at the dirt, one may get dirty oneself. Seeking data on illegal actions may draw the researcher into illegal activities, and he or she may face temptations not usually considered in graduate methodology classes.

Unconventional methods are thus tactics of the last resort and should be restricted to a narrow range of issues, for example discrimination in housing, employment, or law enforcement. In such cases, the researcher may present him or herself as a client, patient, stooge or ally, to see if the expected behaviour is, or appears to be, forthcoming. For reasons of resources and ethics, Marx says, there are limits. The researcher should not 'take this to a point where actual damage is done, or the law is violated, as with unnecessary surgery, actually paying a bribe, or purchasing contraband' (ibid.: 98). However, Marx is prepared to stretch the rules when it comes to dealing with cases of surveillance, infiltration and other covert operations and summons sociologists to go further and be more imaginative:

> [P]erhaps different standards with respect to deception, privacy, informed consent, and avoiding harm to research subjects ought to apply when the subjects themselves are engaged in deceitful, coercive, and illegal activities, and/or where one is dealing with an institution which is publicly accountable. (ibid.: 108)

In the absence of a clear and agreed upon moral framework, Marx proposes a kind of reverse golden rule: 'persons who violate the public trust are appropriate subjects for investigative tactics that would otherwise be inappropriate' (ibid.: 108, fn. 25). There is one remaining question. Who is to decide, and by what criteria is it appropriate to conclude that a research subject may be deceived?

> The great Catch-22 comes with the (large?) number of cases for which it is not possible to know beforehand that violations are occurring. To exempt such persons from deceptive tactics until probable cause appears makes it unlikely that the wrongdoing will be discovered. (ibid.)

The weakness of this rule is in its character, its 'eye for an eye' approach. Infiltration and spying essentially involve issues of trust and betrayal. The public interest would be a better justification for the use of unconventional methods of discovery. Sometimes exposure of secret information is necessary to raise issues of importance that threaten democracy, as demonstated by the case studies in this book.

The Files

The documents found at his office indicated that Manfred Schlickenrieder worked as a freelance spy for state intelligence agencies, as well as for corporate clients. The files can be categorized accordingly. The first category concerns his work for Hakluyt, the second relates to his work for state intelligence services, and the third is a database of left-wing activists and campaigners of interest to his clients, held partly on printed index cards and partly in electronic format.

The Hakluyt file contains comprehensive reports on meetings, correspondence and bills. Among the documents are detailed email exchanges between Schlickenrieder and Hakluyt (MS docs: 45–47). The second category of files is partly comparable but concerns his work for various state intelligence services. It contains invoices and claims for expenses such as travel costs, phone costs including the use of a mobile phone (which was an expensive luxury in the 1990s), administrative help and the rent of the office (MS docs: 18, 19).[24] But this file also holds various kinds of official documents that appear to originate from intelligence services. Some of the documents come from Italian agencies (MS docs: 31–42); others are prepared by German agencies in close cooperation with the French and the Belgian police and state secret services (MS docs: 24–30). These documents summarize the whereabouts of people involved in support work for political prisoners and detail the movements of people believed to be involved building international networks between groups like the Belgian Cellules Communist Combattantes, CCC (Communist Combatant Cells), the French Action Directe (Direct Action) and the Italian Brigate Rosse (Red Brigades) (MS docs: 24–30). There are official intelligence reports containing overviews of '*Besuchs-beispielsweise Postkontakte*' ('visits or contacts by mail') of several people detained for membership of the Rote Armee Fraktion, detailing the frequency of contacts. The period in the column 'Datum Erstkontakt' ('date of first contact') ranges from 1986 until 1998 (MS docs: 22, 23). There are two telex messages (in capitals) about the – alleged – resurrection of the Red Brigades and their anti-imperialist struggle. They read as an alert by the Italian national secret service SISDE updating fellow agencies about a campaign called 'Primavera Rossa' ('Red Spring') targeting NATO during the military interventions in Serbia, in 1999 (MS docs: 32, 33).

The third set of files is a database compiled of people Schlickenrieder had met, interviewed or filmed. The Swiss researchers discovered a detailed archive of the members of their own group, Revolutionäre Aufbau (MS docs: 11–16). Each record contained two photographs of the 'subject': one full-face and one in profile. According to the appended references most were video stills taken from the films Schlickenrieder made while posing as a documentary-maker. The files record personal details such as special features and nicknames, addresses and telephone numbers, but also the subject's main activities and his or her contacts with other groups, at home or abroad. There is a dossier on people active in Italy (MS docs: 34–42). The filing method, the sequence of the codes used, the numbering of the individual items, indicate that the Aufbau and Italian archive was just a small part of a larger documentation system.

The expert who attested to the authenticity of those documents attributed to state intelligence agencies was Otto Diederichs. Working at the Berlin Institute Bürgerrechte & Öffentliche Sicherheit (Institute for Civil Rights and Public Security) and publisher of the institute's quarterly magazine *CILIP*, he has been studying police and intelligence services since 1990. The problem with intelligence files is the lack of letter headings and signatures, he explained. Therefore, they need to be identified by the specific language, codes and abbreviations used. Diederichs (2001) writes: 'My contacts at the domestic intelligence service the *Bundesambt für Verfassungsschutz*[25] and at the *Bundeskriminalamt*[26] have seen the Aufbau website, and they confirmed these documents could indeed be originating from their respective services.' None of the German agencies or other intelligence services involved publicly acknowledged that Schlickenrieder had been working for them. However, Diederichs understood the general feeling about the agent's exposure was that of '*eine peinliche Panne*' for the German intelligence community – an embarrassing blow (ibid.). Furthermore, the Schlickenrieder case was discussed in Prime Minister Schröder's weekly meeting with the German secret services, the so-called *Dienstagsrunde* on 6 February 2001. This is a confidential meeting where pressing issues are discussed, held every Tuesday – hence the *Dienstag* – for which no minutes are published[27] (Diederichs, 2001). Later that week, the parliamentary committee monitoring the German secret services discussed the case, also behind closed doors, Diederichs confirmed (interview by email, 22 January 2001).

The references in this chapter link to an overview of the available Manfred Schlickenrieder documents (MS docs), in Appendix 1. Translations are by the author, unless stated otherwise.

INTELLIGENCE FOR SALE

The company Schlickenrieder worked for is itself a perfect example of the grey area between public and private in the field of intelligence operations. Hakluyt & Company Ltd was established in 1995 by former members of the British foreign secret service, MI6. To quote Christopher James, one of its founders, 'the idea was to do for industry what we had done for the government' (Overell, 2000). Hakluyt filled a niche in the intelligence sector by specializing in upmarket business, where it has been very successful. The company started in a one-room office in 1995; in 2001, it claimed that its clients included one-quarter of the FTSE 100 companies (ibid.). Today, Hakluyt is housed in a stylish Victorian house in Upper Brook Street in London and its customers are treated as members of an exclusive club. Its founders have always cultivated secrecy, its executives almost never appear in public, and the firm did not have a web site until 2007 (*Intelligence Online*, 2006a). In 2009, the company hosted a one-screen internet presence providing nothing but the contact details for the firm at www.hakluyt.co.uk. Nicholas Rufford, investigative journalist for the *Sunday Times,* was among the first to profile Hakluyt, for *Management Today* in 1999. He followed the company closely through the years – together with his colleague Maurice Chittenden. Hakluyt hardly ever gives interviews to the press; the only – known – exception was made for Christopher James of the *Financial Times* (Overell, 2000), in effect some PR for the company. Necessarily this profile is based on what the company wishes to share, combined with what others in the business have to say about them. Specialized outlets such as *Intelligence Newsletter* and *Intelligence Online* provided additional details on the career profiles of some of Hakluyt's staff. To appreciate the Schlickenrieder files some understanding of the methods of this agency and how it deals with critics is necessary.

The London company was named after an economic intelligence specialist *avant la lettre*. Richard Hakluyt was a sixteenth-century geographer, born in London, who wrote up the tales told by returning explorers such as Drake and Frobisher as 'Hakluyt's Voyages'. He was one of the principal inspirations for the East India Company (Willcock, 1998). In 1582, Richard Hakluyt argued for the colonization of North America as a base for discovering the Orient. So the *FT* asked director Christopher James if Hakluyt was attempting to recapture a fading imperial grandeur. His answer was: 'When we set up, it was to help British companies stay ahead of the competition. We now have international clients, but there is still something in staying ahead of the game, of expansion in our message' (Overell, 2000). James' description of the ancient geographer's characteristics also classifies the present company. 'He is the silent man, seated in the dark corner, who is content to listen and remember' (ibid.).

The first directors, Christopher James and Mike Reynolds, were both former members of MI6, the British foreign intelligence service. Reynolds founded its counter-terrorism branch and was the head of station in Berlin. Richard Dearlove, head of MI6 from 1999 to 2005, is a close friend of his, according to *Intelligence Online* (1999). James led a section of MI6 that liaised with British firms. Over his 20-year career, he got to know the chief executives and directors of many of Britain's top companies. In return for a few tips that helped them operate in various foreign markets, James persuaded them to pass on intelligence from their overseas operations (Rufford, 1999). After the Cold War, James argued that MI6 should expand this role, but others in the organization feared that this could be mistaken for 'economic espionage' (ibid.). James subsequently left MI6 in 1995, applying his intelligence expertise for the private sector. He explained that support had come from a roll-call of establishment grandees – which also gives a clue to the contacts Hakluyt can muster, the *Financial Times* wrote in 2000.

> Former foreign secretary Malcolm Rifkind was supportive of the project; so too was Ian Lang, former secretary of state at the Department of Trade and Industry. The late Earl Jellicoe, president of the SAS Association, provided early encouragement. [...] The current DTI 'likes the idea'. (Overell, 2000)

Hakluyt was set up with the blessing of Sir David Spedding, the then chief of MI6 (who died in June 2001). The first management board demonstrated the kind of reputation the company was aiming for, closely linked to the world of intelligence veterans. The prestigious supervisory board, the Hakluyt Foundation, would help the firm to establish solid contacts across the boardrooms of leading multinationals. (The Foundation has since been renamed The Hakluyt International Advisory Board.)

Michael Maclay joined Hakluyt in 1997 as one of its directors. His career included work as a journalist and a diplomat; he was special adviser to Douglas Hurd, former foreign secretary, and Carl Bildt, UN high representative in Bosnia (Chittenden and Rufford, 2001). Another member was Winston Churchill's personal envoy to Marshall Tito during the Second World War, former soldier, spy and diplomat, the late Sir Fitzroy Maclean – also Ian Fleming's model for James Bond.

The first boards also showed that the oil companies were involved at the early stage of setting up this private intelligence company. Sir William Purves, CEO of Shell Transport (until 2002) has been chair of the Hakluyt Foundation since 1999 and director of the company since 2002. Sir Peter Holmes, former chair of Shell, was president of the Hakluyt foundation from 1997 until he died in 2002. Former deputy chair of BP Sir Peter Cazalet helped to establish Hakluyt in 1995 and was chair of the company and the foundation, before he retired in 2000. BP itself has long-standing ties to MI6: its director of government and public affairs, John Gerson, was at one time a leading candidate to succeed Sir David Spedding as chief of MI6 (ibid.; see also *Intelligence Online*, 2005).

Christopher James explained to the *Financial Times* how Hakluyt functions, stressing the careful way the company evaluates information and turns it into intelligence. 'The company has over 100 "associates" on its books – some based in London, others at stations worldwide. They might be investigative journalists, diplomats' wives, senior business people, former diplomats or consultants' (Overell, 2000). For each assignment, Hakluyt calls up to five associates back to London to be briefed and then 'deploys' them. The work essentially involves talking to the right people, according to James. Each associate is given different questions and works independently. When the associates come back with contradictory information, the directors make a careful judgement of the material in London before submitting a final report (ibid.).

Hakluyt tries to distinguish itself from other business intelligence consultants, spin masters and clipping services. 'We do not take anything off the shelf, nothing off the Net – we assume that any company worth its salt has done all of that,' Hakluyt's Michael Maclay explained to students in the Netherlands. 'We go with the judgement of people who know the countries, the elites, the industries, the local media, the local environmentalists, all the factors that will feed into big decisions being made' (Maclay, 1999). Manfred Schlickenrieder was one of those people who 'knew the local environmentalists'. His documents disclose additional details on Hakluyt's intelligence-gathering arrangements, and the development of subsequent covert strategy for their clients.

'Content to Listen and Remember'

Shell International was one of Hakluyt's first clients in 1995. The Brent Spar crisis and the execution of Ken Saro-Wiwa in Nigeria had become PR nightmares not easily forgotten. The company wanted to make sure it would not be caught unawares again (see also Chapter 5). Early in 1996, Hakluyt asked Manfred Schlickenrieder to make an inventory of the activist agenda for Shell International. To fulfil this assignment, Schlickenrieder used his cover 'gruppe 2' to start a research project described as 'shell in Nigeria/Environment damage/ Human right violation etc' (MS docs: 43, 56). In the letters he wrote to ask groups for interviews, he claimed his research would result in a video documentary (ibid.).

Posing as a film-maker working on a documentary about campaigning after 1995 had several advantages. Arguably, the most important was that nobody would think it strange that Schlicken-rieder was asking questions. He traded on his image as a veteran left-wing political activist on his various information-gathering missions. In addition, he made maximum use of the fact that the loose network of activists in Europe is (as it is elsewhere) a pattern of connections based on trust. Mentioning a joint acquaintance or referring to a demonstration participated in can be sufficient to gain entry (Juris, 2008: 17–18). This offered an easy way to widen the range of contacts for Schlickenrieder as well as the opportunity to map various networks, by outlining the various connections (or non-connections) as they occurred.

For instance, Schlickenrieder exchanged letters with EarthWatch, the foreign desk of Friends of the Earth in the Netherlands (MS docs: 56). He paid them a visit, obtained information, and used this contact to introduce himself to his next target, cosmetics company the Body Shop. In a letter to the head of the German branch of the company, Schlickenrieder mentioned organizations already engaged in his project. He then praised the company for their long-term involvement with the campaign against Shell in Nigeria, and for their concern for human rights and the environment. For his film about Shell, he requested an interview with a representative of the Body Shop about its activities so far, its future plans, its experiences with Shell, and about clients' feedback regarding this engagement (MS docs: 43). Schlickenrieder got his answers, and not just for the documentary.

Anita Roddick, founder of the Body Shop, was furious when she eventually read about this operation and the exposure of Schlickenrieder in the *Sunday Times*. 'Of course my company is merely a front to campaign on behalf of the environment and human rights,' she retorted in a letter to the editor.

> Shock, horror! We have been saying that to anyone who'd listen for the past 25 years. The outrage is rather that self-styled, 'socially responsible' corporations BP and Shell should have been working hand in glove with Hakluyt, a semi-official nest of ex-MI6 spooks, one of whom is quoted as saying: 'We don't ever talk about anything we do'. Not quite in the spirit of stakeholder dialogue, chaps. (Roddick, 2001)

By way of apology for setting these 'grubby little bin-riflers' on to her, she demanded that the fees paid to Hakluyt plus interest be donated to the public campaign against a real 'enemy of the people', Exxon-Mobil, for its irresponsible stance as No. 1 global warming villain (ibid.).

Schlickenrieder travelled around Europe, filmed protest actions and documented meetings, either on camera, or by making notes. He interviewed relatives and friends of Ken Saro-Wiwa, and other people central to the campaign against Shell operating in Nigeria. The project that served as a cover for the investigation eventually resulted in a documentary video, *Business as Usual: The Arrogance of Power* (gruppe 2, 1997) – a rather superficial overview of the European campaign against Shell. The next section shows how the information was used.

Counterstrategy

Intelligence gathered by people like Schlickenrieder was used by Hakluyt to help client companies develop strategies to counter the effect of planned campaigns, in this case the environmental movement. The ability to anticipate criticism is very useful for lobbying and public relations. Chapter 7, for instance, details how British Aerospace used intelligence to counteract specific plans of the

Campaign Against Arms Trade to undermine their campaign. After the confrontations of 1995 around Brent Spar and Ken Saro-Wiwa, other oil companies feared being targeted by Greenpeace. BP turned to Hakluyt for help after it learned that a campaign was planned to stop the development of new deep sea drilling sites in the Atlantic Ocean north-west of the UK, the so-called Atlantic Frontier. Hakluyt subsequently asked Schlickenrieder to deliver details about what was going to happen, and to assess how Greenpeace might respond to legal damage claims. Schlickenrieder delivered and billed the London company DM20,000 for 'the Greenpeace research' (MS docs: 44).

The intelligence was used for – at least – two separate proactive strategies prepared for BP. For the first strategy inside information from the environmental movement was effectively used to polish its press and PR communications. Hakluyt combined Schlickenrieder's information about Greenpeace with material from other sources. Reynolds claimed, for instance, to have obtained a copy of *Putting the Lid on Fossil Fuels* (Greenpeace, 1997) even before the ink was dry (MS docs: 45). This document was meant to kick off the Atlantic Frontier campaign, and apparently it provided timely and relevant material for the oil company. 'BP countered the campaign in an unusually fast and smart way,' Greenpeace Germany spokesperson Stefan Krug said (Diederichs and Stark, 2000; Strehle, 2000/2001). 'We continuously had the feeling that every step we took was already known by the target of our campaign in Britain,' Jan Rispens from the Energy Unit at Greenpeace Germany told Aufbau (MS docs: 56). Since the company knew what was coming in advance, BP was never taken by surprise.

Second, BP used Hakluyt's information to plan a lawsuit against Greenpeace. In an email message to Schlickenrieder, Hakluyt's director Mike Reynolds inquired about the possible impact of suing the environmentalists for mounting a campaign such as Brent Spar, asking whether Greenpeace was taking legal steps to protect its assets against seizure in the event of being sued by an oil company (MS docs: 45). The answer to that question is not among the leaked documents. However, when BP's Stena Dee oil installation in the Atlantic Ocean was occupied two months later, the company sued Greenpeace for DM4.2 million in damages, insisting that its work was being delayed. BP got an injunction to block Greenpeace UK's bank accounts, which caused serious financial problems for the group. (This may have been the first times an injunction was used to threaten activists with possible arrest. It has since become an increasingly popular way to stop a campaign, Mark Stephens, one of Greenpeace's lawyers in London, explained in an interview by email, 17 February 2009.)

Damage Control and Plausible Deniability

The exposure of Manfred Schlickenrieder put the spotlight on Hakluyt, a company that prefers a low profile. All parties involved, including Greenpeace, tried to downplay the damage by denying the infiltration.

Asked for a comment about the exposure of its spy, Hakluyt first denied knowing him. However, the email correspondence that surfaced clearly suggested a working relationship. Schlickenrieder and Reynolds addressed each other as 'Liebe Manfred' and 'Liebe Mike' – the meaning of the German '*liebe*' is more intimate than its English equivalent 'dear'. Confronted with this evidence, Hakluyt reluctantly admitted that it had employed the freelancer but claimed that it had only been for *one* assignment, and for a limited period. This was not true either, as detailed below. When asked which companies were involved, Hakluyt claimed not to be able to reveal details about its clients – but added that they were *not* Shell or BP (Diederichs, 2000; Strehle, 2000). Nevertheless, when the *Sunday Times* broke the story in Britain almost six months later, both BP and Shell acknowledged having hired Hakluyt. Both claimed, however, that they had been unaware of the tactics used (Chittenden and Rufford, 2001; confirmed by spokesperson from both Shell and BP in June 2001). BP acknowledged that it had hired Hakluyt, but claimed to have asked for a report based on published material only. This contradicted the specific questions Hakluyt asked Schlickenrieder and the detailed reports he subsequently delivered. Delegating dirty work allowed Hakluyt's clients, Shell and BP, to maintain that they had not been aware of the methods used. This damage control operation recalled Shell's efforts to distance itself from the *Neptune Strategy*, as detailed in Chapter 3.

Communication with Fouad Hamdan, spokesperson for Greenpeace Germany, documents the change of heart in the organization's public relations strategy following the exposure in Britain. First Hamdan said Manfred Schlickenrieder was trusted within the organization, that everybody knew him and many people had talked to him. Because he was seen as someone sympathetic to Greenpeace, he was kept up to date about upcoming campaigns. He had planned to make a film about the Atlantic Frontier campaign. Hamdan confided that he had told the *Sunday Times* that 'the bastard was good' (interview by phone, 16 June 2001). However, within a few days, Hamdan sent me the official Greenpeace statement on Schlickenrieder and the organization's instructions on how to deal with the press. This statement denies any involvement and encourages members of Greenpeace to react '*gelassen*', which translates as calm, composed and unconcerned. Schlickenrieder had visited Greenpeace in 1997, 'presumably for an interview', but 'nobody here can remember him' and 'No, we don't know if he has delivered information of any importance about our campaigns to Hakluyt' (Hamdan, 2001a). The quote that Schlickenrieder's activities had effectively sunk the Greenpeace campaign against BP's exploration in the Atlantic (Chittenden and Rufford, 2001), was retracted too and attributed to a mix-up between the German press association *dpa* and the *Sunday Times* (Hamdan, 2001a). When confronted about his efforts to downplay the damage Schlickenrieder had done, Hamdan claimed it was all a misunderstanding. 'After double checking with the oil campaigner at the time we discovered that no one remembered the guy' (interview by email, 18 June 2001).

Hakluyt added a level to the damage control operation, insisting that Schlickenrieder worked for the company for only a few months between 1996 and 1997, and just on the Greenpeace research commissioned by BP. However, this does not correspond with the findings of Swiss business journalist Res Strehle, who evaluated the available Schlickenrieder documents. Strehle (2000, 2000/2001) discovered that the German spy worked for Hakluyt for at least four years, up until he was exposed in 2000, and possibly even longer. The year before he was exposed he received three cheques from Hakluyt totalling more than DM9000. Hakluyt was his best client and hired him regularly for consultancy work, mostly due diligence. In 1999, he did research for the former German state telephone company Deutsche Telekom to prepare acquisitions – confirmed by an invoice Schlickenrieder sent to Hakluyt (MS docs: 57). In the same year, Schlickenrieder investigated Gunter Zöbel, the then owner of the petrol supplement producer Märkische Phasen, for a competitor interested in acquiring the company, according to Strehle. Also in 1999, Schlickenrieder was commissioned to work on the business relations between commodity trader Mark Rich and Glencore, the company Rich had founded more than 30 years previously. At the time, Rio Tinto, a Hakluyt client, was interested in a take-over of Glencore. In 1998, Schlickenrieder investigated Martin Ebener, the controversial Swiss financier and asset stripper who wanted to take over the tyre producer Pirelli. In 2000, he explored the current market and take-over options for the German beer brand Becks. Also in 2001, he undertook an investigation into the Bank für Gewerkschaft (owned by Crédit Lyonnais) for a client interested in a take-over (MS docs: 58).

In 1996, Schlickenrieder started mapping resistance against Freeport and Rio Tinto, the world leaders in finding, mining and processing mineral resources. He assessed the possible resistance to a Rio Tinto project planned in Liberia. He evaluated local opinions and contacted the Unrepresented Nations and Peoples Organization (UNPO) and the International Federation of Chemical, Energy, Mine and General Workers' Unions (ICEM) (Keine Friede, 2000). In a letter to Friends of the Earth, Schlickenrieder asked for information about their work against the mining companies in Irian Jaya and in Madagascar (MS docs: 56). In March 1999, Schlickenrieder sent Hakluyt an invoice for 'the Rio Tinto research in January' to be followed by an additional report (MS docs: 57). The Swiss Aufbau group found evidence that he continued billing Hakluyt for Rio Tinto research until he was exposed (Keine Friede, 2000). This is supported by the experiences of the West Papua Network in Wuppertal, Germany. Schlickenrieder subscribed to their newsletter and contacted them more than once to be updated. The last time he called to get a video about Freeport had been in June 2000 – just months before his cover was blown (Zöllner, 2004).

Both Freeport and Rio Tinto have been involved in controversy over their mining activities for many years. Both have engaged several strategies to co-opt or counter their adversaries, with or without the advice of Hakluyt (Global Witness, 2005; Perlez and Bonner, 2005, 2006, Seelye, 2006).

'HE IS A SILENT MAN'

Schlickenrieder had built up spying experience during his years of working for Germany's domestic and foreign intelligence services, the Landesamt für Verfassungsschutz and the Bundesnachrichten-dienst respectively. He frequented meetings of radical left groups, including the Red Army Faction (RAF), from the early 1980s until his cover was blown in 2000. He also developed contacts with Italian revolutionary groups. For 20-odd years Manfred Schlickenrieder was able to move around in radical left-wing and revolutionary circles, without raising suspicion.

Schlickenrieder's political career began and ended in Munich. He was briefly a member of the Maoist KPD/ML. By the end of 1975,

Schlickenrieder had managed to pass the admission procedure to enter the Rote Hilfe (Red Help) as well as the Kommunistischen Studentenbund (Communist Student Union), two of the many leftist groups that sprang up in Germany in the 1970s. When the Verfassungsschutz, the domestic intelligence service, knocked on his door, he told them to go to hell. Or so he claimed, according to Diederichs and Stark. For his Maoist comrades this encounter was enough to expel him from their organizations. But the story of his experiences delivered a convenient cover for his next project. Schlickenrieder laid the groundwork for approaching sympathizers of the Red Army Faction. In 1982, he published a pamphlet proclaiming solidarity with RAF members Christian Klar, Adelheid Schulz and Brigitte Monhaupt after their arrest.

The main explanation for Schlickenrieder's enduring career can be found in the way he worked. It seemed that he was a reticent character. He was what the Germans call an *Einzelgänger*, a loner, preferring to work on his own. He was known as an intelligent person, engaging and interesting to talk to. He would not ask too many questions at once, but would use what he heard on one occasion as a resource for cultivating future contacts. Taking advantage of activists' trust, he had a well-developed ability to piece together fragments of information to compile a fairly accurate picture, Steinbacher and Stauffacher explained in January 2001 (also see Keine Friede, 2000).

Other explanations can be found in the organization of his work. The 'Documenting Archive *gruppe 2*', was a flexible and plausible cover that offered a wide range of opportunities. Documentary making was one part of the business. Under the cover of providing an alternative to 'state propaganda', Schlickenrieder was allowed to be present – with camera and microphone – while police and others were excluded. He filmed the occupation of squats, sympathizers of the Italian Red Brigades, secret meetings, and many other events. He was intimate with the *Umfeld* (the environs), family and friends of the RAF. He made several documentaries for Revolutionäre Aufbau, including one video about the dockers strike in Britain. Another about the RAF, called 'Wass aber wären wir für Menschen' ('What kind of people were we?') featured solidarity groups and relatives of convicted comrades, following several of them from the moment they were released from prison. His film about Italy's Red Brigades, which he had been working on since 1985, was never finished, but served as an introduction to revive contacts in Italy's radical circles whenever necessary. Apart from that, as explained above, stills from video footage served as a photo database, accompanied by personal details about the many people he had met (MS files: 34–42). Over the years, he must have filmed hundreds, perhaps thousands of people who took the integrity of the producer for granted. Documenting the activists' struggle, Schlickenrieder's video tapes evolved into an extended illustrated archive of the radical left in Europe (Keine Friede, 2000).

Collecting and disseminating printed material was another important part of business at gruppe 2. This was a simple, but very effective way of gathering information. Most left-wing groups would send him their publications, either prompted or unprompted. From the mid-1980s until the mid-1990s, Schlickenrieder also published a magazine, or rather a series of pamphlets, called *texte* (see MS docs: 4, 5). The content mainly consisted of the writings of groups involved in armed resistance, including American political prisoners like Mumia Abu Jamal, Black Panther activist Dorouba, and discussion pieces by members of the Italian Red Brigades. To be the editor and publisher of *texte* was effective from an intelligence-gathering point of view. The content offered an insight into what kind of texts were of importance to the subscribers. It also revealed who were the ideological and strategic thinkers in a group, and how they could be reached to ask for a contribution for the magazine. The distribution of pamphlets gave an overview of who was interested in reading such material in Germany, Switzerland, and elsewhere in Europe. Apart from that, reproducing work from others excused Schlickenrieder from contributing substantial content himself.

For groups that ceased to exist Schlickenrieder readily offered to archive their legacy. He was about to receive the archive of Vreni Lauterbach, a long-term activist of the Gruppe der Angehörigen der politischen Gefängenen in der BRD ('Group of Family members of Political Prisoners in Germany'). After Lauterbach's death it was decided gruppe 2 would inherit the archive; Schlickenrieder's exposure only just prevented this, Steinbacher and Stauffacher explained in January 2001 (also see Keine Friede, 2000).

Schlickenrieder offered the kinds of practical support that resource poor groups needed. He offered to establish a postal address at the office of gruppe 2 for local activist groups. This convenient arrangement would deliver interesting mail right to Schlickenrieder's desk. The anti-fascist magazine *Pro K* was one of the groups that took up the offer. The magazine was sued for libel after it called a named plain clothes police officer a 'kleines mieses Bullenschwein' ('small mean police pig'). A search under warrant for copies of the contested issue at the gruppe 2 office did not deliver any evidence, but the incident was functional in reinforcing the idea of police repression against gruppe 2, and as such doubtless helped to secure Schlickenrieder's cover (MS docs: 59).

Ironically, Schlickenrieder was the person who spread the news in Germany about the exposure of an infiltrator and spy in the Netherlands, Lex Hester (MS docs: 2, 3). To uncover another spy provided more cover. On this occasion, there was actually a clear and present danger, because Lex Hester fulfilled a similar role within networks of radical groups in the Netherlands: collecting radical publications, working in an anarchist bookshop and functioning as a contact address for people who were interested in radical writing as well as action. In a pamphlet describing his contacts with the exposed spy, Schlickenrieder explained that he had exchanged information with Hester in the past and had visited him in the Netherlands – but claimed he stopped trusting him shortly before the exposure (ibid.).

The cover of gruppe 2 had more advantages. It forestalled questions about the political background of Schlickenrieder and his own radical achievements. Gruppe 2 was the answer: the documentary maker accommodates the process of struggle; he does not initiate or determine it. Questions about the name of his organization were explained by referring to a clandestine arrangement. A part of his group – presumably 'gruppe 1' – had been forced to go underground in 1977, due to severe and continuing police repression. In the 1970s, the RAF (dubbed the Baader–Meinhof group by the media), a left-wing collective born of the student revolutions of the 1960s, undertook a series of bombings, assassinations and hijackings in Germany. The repression this provoked is known as the *Deutschen Herbst* (German autumn). Schlickenrieder was the only one who could operate in public – or so he claimed until the very end, conveniently playing with the illusion that for him the *Deutschen Herbst* had never ended. The legacy of those turbulent years is still the subject of discussion today. The release of the last prisoners, new films and books about the period made Neal Ascherson, the *Observer*'s correspondent in Germany at the time, reflect 'on the legacy of those turbulent years and the strange hold they had – and still have – on the national psyche' (Ascherson, 2008). The secrecy and the presumed radicalism associated with gruppe 1 guaranteed no further questions asked (Revolutionäre Aufbau, 2000a).

The projects detailed here appeared to help sustain and confirm his cover as a political activist and trustworthy comrade, while at the same time providing opportunities to gather intelligence and expand his network. In the end, however, the same qualifications that made Schlickenrieder perfectly suitable for his role as 'fellow traveller' and information-gathering spy made it difficult for him to become a full member of a radical group. His distance, his failure to provide an acceptable political analysis assessing the current state of the anti-imperialist struggle, or a clear political praxis against the capitalist system, gave him away eventually. His lack of ability to get really involved ultimately caused the suspicion that led to his exposure (Revolutionäre Aufbau, 2000a; Keine Friede, 2000).

Members of the 'solidarity campaign Libertad!' – with hindsight – said Schlickenrieder had problems connecting with them when he joined their working group 'International Contacts'. From the available documents now, it transpired that Schlickenrieder was interested in their preparations for resistance against the G8 summit in Naples, in 1994. When he left the group within a year, no tears were shed. Schlickenrieder's contribution to the group was never substantial, Libertad claimed – he never took any initiative and he kept his alleged highly valuable contacts in Italy to himself (Keine Friede, 2000).

The Swiss Aufbau group had similar experiences. In the two years before his exposure, they tried to integrate Schlickenrieder into their structures; he was to become the Munich desk of Aufbau. Schlickenrieder agreed, but did not manage to keep appointments or to deliver promised work and his contributions to the discussions did not satisfy the Swiss. He was unable, or unwilling, to integrate, and this raised suspicion. After the first documents implicating Schlickenrieder's foul play found their way to the Swiss office, an internal investigation led to his exposure as a spy (Revolutionäre Aufbau, 2000a).

HIGHLY VALUED AGENT

Schlickenrieder was a special kind of agent, and not only because he managed to stay in business for such a long time. He had access to secret official documents and personal intelligence files on radicals to help him navigate in their circles. Among the documents is an official intelligence file detailing the contacts of specific individuals in Italian radical groups. The original document has numbered pages (1–16) but some pages or parts of pages are missing. It is written in German, has no heading and is not signed. It lists the names of 18 Italian activists, detailing their history and activities.

Schlickenrieder not only had access to intelligence files, but was also able to request further information about the people he spied on. His handlers in the German agencies would contact their Italian colleagues on his behalf. The file has two sections with remarks that are obviously answers to earlier questions. 'Referring to your request to be informed about additional extremists with possible foreign contacts, we can mention to you the following individuals: [list of names]' (MS docs: 31). The second set of questions refers to a specific house, where certain named contacts allegedly lived from time to time; and to an arms cache in Rome from which 'weapons and munitions may be obtainable'. The use of the subjunctive in the German original[28] suggests that the questions address gathered information, rumours or tips that need confirmation. The answer read: 'unfortunately no information is available yet. We have forwarded the request to SISDE [Italian intelligence service], but have until this moment received no reply' (ibid.).

Schlickenrieder's ways of working for state and business were similar. He made proposals to his employers, or provided them with reports they had not even asked for. For instance, in a September 1997 email to Hakluyt, the German spy explained how he had 'used the opportunity of visiting Hamburg to talk to two separate people within Greenpeace'. In closing, he wrote: 'That was your free "mood report" supplement from Hamburg' (MS docs: 47). In 1995, Schlickenrieder wrote an extensive strategy report with detailed proposals for state agencies, suggesting new fields of research among radical movements. He proposed taking up the project of making a video about the Red Brigades, because it would provide him with the possibility of getting in touch with almost any level of the movement (MS docs: 10). This is yet another example of a project that merged sustaining his cover and opportunities for intelligence gathering.

Additionally, Schlickenrieder's work was highly valued. The rewards allowed him to live in a spacious rooftop flat overlooking a park and to hire a four-room office equipped with up-to-date computers and video-editing equipment. Schlickenrieder drove two cars when he was exposed in 2000, a VW Sharon (a large MPV or people carrier) and a BMW Z3, the model of sports car driven by James Bond in *GoldenEye*. He declared an average of 1.600 DM of expenses every month and his budget was calculated at 10.000 DM monthly.[29] The average wage in 2000 in Germany was 54.256 DM per year (Monetos, 2009).

Not only was he well paid, the intelligence services also proved willing to invest in his ventures. In his 1995 strategy plan, Schlickenrieder emphasized the importance of producing and publishing a German translation of the *Rapporti Sociali*. This was an extensive Italian discussion paper assessing the current conditions for revolutionary struggle. The publishing project would 'offer the opportunity to establish direct contacts with the original publishers. The participation in the international meeting would be ensured [...] and above that taking up the distribution of it in Germany would lead to the contacts involved in this project in Switzerland and Germany' (MS docs: 10). Schlickenrieder provided the translations and the Swiss Aufbau group corrected them and wrote the preface for the German version.

The Schlickenrieder documents include copies of the test translations, which were prepared by an official translation service, judging by the marks and codes used. The Aufbau people calculated that the translation alone must have cost Schlickenrieder and/or his employer about 10.000 DM. This sum can be seen as a price to be paid to secure further access. Judging by the proposals Schlickenrieder wrote at that time, the Aufbau group concluded that the translation was '*sozusagen das Eintrittsbillet in die internationale kommunistische Bewegung*' – 'it was so to say an admission fee, a ticket to the international revolutionary movement' (Revolutionäre Aufbau, 2000a).

Searching for an explanation of why the *Revolutionäre Aufbau* had not been more careful, the group explained that the offer to translate and publish the German edition came at just the right moment. The French and Italian versions were ready to be published, and 'especially for Germany it was very important to have a Marxist analysis of the crisis in capitalism based on objective conditions' (Revolutionäre Aufbau, 2000b).

The assistance with the translation and publishing of these documents implicates secret services in assisting and facilitating the revolutionary movement. Instead of just monitoring developments, intelligence agencies played a more active role. Such active interference raises the question as to what extent the secret service influenced or controlled this movement in Germany.

Schlickenrieder was a proactive agent, at times also playing the role of agent provocateur. A 1994 report described how he tried to make a weapons deal with Dev Sol (MS docs: 9). This small Marxist-Leninist party in Turkey was originally formed in 1978 by Dursun Karataş as Revolutionary Left (Turkish: Devrimci Sol or Dev Sol), a splinter group from a larger organization. It is now known as DHKP/C, the Revolutionary People's Liberation Party Front, or

Devrimci Halk Kurtuluş Partisi-Cephesi in Turkish. Schlickenrieder offered Dev Sol a small amount of handguns – Sig Sauer or Heckler Koch – at 1200 DM apiece. There was one condition, he wrote in his report: '*Allerdings wurden diese Lieferanten darauf bestehen, zu erfahren, wohin die Waffen gingen (politisch/persönlich).*' – 'the suppliers insisted on getting to know what the weapons would be used for (political/personal)'. The revolutionary Turkish splinter group was at the time involved in an internal power struggle, resulting in serious casualties and fatalities – specifically in Germany, one of the lawyers of members of Dev Sol (and DHKP/C since) Marq Wijngaarden explained (interview by email, 25 April 2007). In the same period, the magazine *texte* – part of Schlickenrieder's cover – included a debut contribution from Dev Sol (Keine Friede, 2000). It is not clear if this deal was concluded; further documentation is lacking. Either way, the offer exemplifies a serious attempt at provocation involving intelligence agencies and weapons. It also raises questions about the extent of Schlickenrieder's work in this specific field. Was he prepared to act as provocateur in his dealings with other revolutionary or activist groups as well?

Dangerous Liaisons

The exposure of Manfred Schlickenrieder was an embarrassing blow for the intelligence community. The case was discussed in two separate parliamentary forums. If Schlickenrieder was indeed working for both the Bundesnachrichtendienst (BND) and the Bayern section of the Landesambt für Verfassungsschutz (LfV), he worked for two agencies whose tasks are separated by law. The BND is the foreign intelligence agency, while the LfV is supposed to focus on domestic matters. Two agencies simultaneously working with the same agent providing him with similar assignments is highly unusual, according to Otto Diederichs from the Institute for Civil Rights and Public Security. Indeed, they would be operating in a hitherto unknown grey area. Such an overlap could occur only under special circumstances, for instance when dealing with the fight against terrorism. In such cases it would be difficult – or impossible – to separate the origin of information, either by borders or by agencies. The supposition of alleged links with 'terrorism' would justify the joint 'running' of an agent. Apparently, the Revolutionäre Aufbau Schweiz was such a case (Diederichs, 2001). Intelligence sources allege that the group has good contacts with the remnants of terrorist networks in Italy, Spain, France, Belgium and Germany, but experts such as Diederichs know of no evidence to support such claims (ibid.). The Aufbau Gruppe was – and is – engaged in solidarity work for political prisoners in various European countries, according to their website. Moreover:

> We fight against capitalism in general, against dismissals, against keeping down wages, against discrimination of women. We also fight against pressure to perform in schools, against state repression, against the disturbance of the environment, against the fascists, against the imperialist war and against the reactionary witch-hunt specifically. (Revolutionäre Aufbau, 2006)

CONCLUSION

Manfred Schlickenrieder is an early example of the modern freelance spy. He started working for German and foreign intelligence services, later for privatized employers like Hakluyt, smoothly shifting gear between the two, as well as between political intelligence gathering and the more classic financial consultancy work. Schlickenrieder provided reports and strategy plans on his own initiative as well. More than a manifestation of individualism, or rather an odd example of precarious working conditions, the way Schlickenrieder operated can be seen as a practical and apparently workable response to continuing problems with hierarchy and modernization within state secret services.

Although their goals may differ depending on their clients' needs, business intelligence agencies – and their hired agents – often use much the same *modus operandi* in surveillance and spying as do governments. No matter whether he was working for secret services or for big business, when approaching his targets Schlickenrieder traded on the trust built up through the years. He was able to move around without raising suspicion for a very long time, in spite of security awareness within the various groups.

Furthermore, spying on the greens – as Schlickenrieder was commissioned to do for Shell and BP – is a good example of the need not just for intelligence, but for appropriate answers too. Hakluyt does not just gather intelligence to know what is coming, but also develops proactive strategies that require information of their own; the agency provides services to implement these counterstrategies as well.

The story about the Jobbing Spy indeed illustrates the intersection of state and corporate intelligence; in fact, it is an example of privatized intelligence and outsourcing. Hakluyt's first board of directors comprised a gallery of retiring public servants aiming at a new career. Shell and BP played a role in the founding of Hakluyt. They supplied high-profile CEOs (often with close links to the intelligence agencies themselves) to take seats on the corporate intelligence board or its advising Foundation. The oil companies were also clients and provided a number of assignments for the company, as was illustrated by the work of their freelance spy. As the Tofflers (1990) predicted, as the informal links between corporate security and state intelligence increase, they generate incestuous relationships. The restructuring of world business leads to complex cross-national business alliances, while globalization adds dimensions to the complicated political issues that corporations have to deal with. In other words, the challenges of the current timeframe increase the need for inside information and intelligence. Schlickenrieder and Hakluyt operated at the forefront of the information wars (ibid.), while their activities exemplify the workings of the network society (Castells, 1996; 2003; Sassen, 1996).

As such, Hakluyt is an excellent example of the specific area of grey intelligence under investigation here: former intelligence officials hired by private companies to do intelligence work exclusively defending the interests of that specific company. The people professionally involved in activist intelligence and covert corporate strategy tend to share similar backgrounds in police, the military or intelligence agencies. Both Pagan and his colleague Pattakos had had long careers in military intelligence advising various presidents, while Mongoven studied military strategy in his own time. The McDonald's security staff shared a police background and closely cooperated with Special Branch. The data collectors in the other two case studies also have close connections with law enforcement and the intelligence world.

The case studies in this book confirm that most private investigators and privatized intelligence agents see such a background as a selling point and do not hesitate to use connections with former colleagues or friends. The result is an informal circuit of information exchange through a form of 'old boys' network'. The high-ranking officials who go private have been privy to classified and top secret information for years. They take that knowledge with them and potentially retain continuing access to it through their networks within government intelligence agencies, at home and abroad. They have a knowledge of intelligence programmes, covert operations and the internal affairs of various countries that few can claim. Their experience, knowledge and networks appear to determine their value in the job market. Theoretically, the profit motive also includes a change of loyalty. The duty of serving the greater good seems to transform into serving the interest of a few (Shorrock, 2008). In practice, however, the same collection of people resurfaces in multiple roles, both inside and outside government, as Wedel (2004b) pointed out.

More research is required to map the political economy of these privatized intelligence networks, characterized by secrecy, insider or privileged knowledge and power. A defining element of intelligence, secrecy complicates research because it tends to deny access to oral and documentary sources. Organizations attempt to protect their information. Intelligence agencies are prone to mislead and to limit what can be discovered, but any organization with information to protect is advised to have a strategy to control the damage of exposure. When covert action is involved, the costs of public disclosure are even higher. As a result, critical research is confronted with situations in which powerful groups and organizations deliberately withhold or distort information that would serve the wider public interest (Lee, 1993: 150; also see Young, 1971). Staff involved in intelligence usually include specialists in maintaining secrecy and deception (Marx, 1984). Indeed, disclosure of source material for this book was hampered by efforts to mislead and obscure, as the case studies show. Ideally, the imbalances in the provision of information, favouring powerful organizations, can be overcome by using lawsuits and freedom of information legislation. However, the McSpy story proved that the law prefers to protect secrecy – something we'll see again in the next chapter. Moreover, private intelligence agencies operate in the absence of a legal framework and specialize in secrecy. Occasionally less conventional methods are required to secure data about the covert operations of large bureaucratic agencies and corporations, and their specialised undercover agencies.

Hakluyt provided a beautiful example of 'plausible deniability'. After the exposure, the company tried to put maximum distance between itself and its freelance spy. Outsourcing the corporate spying allowed the consultants and their clients to keep a distance from the actual intelligence gathering, the deception and other dirty tricks. Confronted with the facts, however, Hakluyt was forced to change its story several times. Despite the precautions, exposure facilitated discovery – in this story as well as in the others.

7
The Threat Response Spy Files: Case Study

The Campaign Against Arms Trade (CAAT) is a well-respected Quaker and Christian-based pacifist group, which believes in non-violent protest. One of their campaigns was aimed against the £500m sale of British Aerospace (BAe) fighter jets to Indonesia. The Hawk aircrafts would be used to crush resistance in East Timor, which was seeking independence at the time. When CAAT stepped up its campaign in the mid-1990s, BAe hired a private intelligence agency to spy on the group. The *Sunday Times* revealed in September 2003 that six to eight agents infiltrated the group between 1995 and 1999, while further research showed the spying went on until the date of exposure. The intelligence company was called Threat Response International (TRI) and was owned by Evelyn le Chêne, a woman with considerable intelligence connections. She sent daily reports on activists' whereabouts to Britain's largest arms dealer. The *Sunday Times* got hold of a large selection of these spy reports through a whistleblower; I was allowed on site access to the files because of my involvement in a related investigation in the case, as will be explained below.

The first two sections of this chapter are based on a detailed analysis of Evelyn le Chêne's reports. The files show how CAAT was subverted by infiltrators passing on information and manipulating the activists. The covert corporate strategies ranged from advance warning on lobbying to anticipating direct action, to the use of an agent provocateur to undermine the building of broader coalitions. The third part of the chapter outlines some of the consequences of the exposure of the spy files for the targeted group. It focuses on CAAT's internal investigation into a suspected infiltrator. TRI also spied on the road protests, specifically on the battles around the Newbury bypass. The fourth section highlights those activities. The final section profiles Evelyn le Chêne, and her history with the intelligence community. Her links with the world of covert action and propaganda set corporate strategy against activism and resistance in a wider perspective. Her work can be understood in an ideological context, as a Cold War type of activity, the ring-fencing of mainstream politics away from the politics of the left.

BACKGROUND

This case is based on two separate investigations into the same intelligence operation, five years apart, on both sides of the Channel. The set of spy reports provided to the *Sunday Times* in 2003 confirmed the outcomes of an investigation I had been involved in earlier. Back in 1998, buro Jansen & Janssen exposed a Frenchman calling himself Adrian Franks who had infiltrated European networks of peace campaigners and climate groups. As detailed below, Frank's consultancy was discovered to be a subsidiary of Le Chêne's agency. And Evelyn and Adrian were related not only by business: they turned out to be mother and son.

The research into Adrian Franks started with two anonymous letters containing warnings about him. The letters arrived several months apart, and seemed to originate from entirely different directions. The first was written by the assistant of the head of security of a multinational oil company. 'He said that he worked as a free-lance security consultant and acted as an adviser to a number of multinational corporations i.e. British Aerospace, Rio Tinto and a defence company in France.' The letter included details of his business card and the name of his company. It transpired that his first name and his address were identical to the details of someone known as an activist called Adrian Franks. French public databases confirmed that the company was registered at his home address. The fact that someone active in campaign groups on the Continent owned a company that allegedly sold information to corporations was indeed disturbing. The question was: did it provide conclusive evidence to expose him as a spy?

The letter ignited existing feelings of unease within groups that worked with Adrian Franks, because of the many inconsistencies between his stories and his life. He claimed to be in favour of radical action, but never took part. His income did not match his expenses. His decision to travel by plane and by car did not go well with environmentalism. His outspoken preference for meat dishes did not chime with his claim to be involved in radical animal liberation activism, which usually involves a vegetarian or vegan lifestyle. The feelings of unease were backed up by a second anonymous letter a few months later. This came from a French activist now spending a year in the United Kingdom. She pointed at another inconsistency in the image Adrian Franks painted of himself. In England, he claimed to be the representative of activist groups in France that in her experience were all but non-existent. In activist circles in France, he said he cooperated with well-known British groups such as Corporate Watch, which in fact had never heard of him.

Together, the contents of the letters explained most if not all of the simmering suspicion against Adrian Franks. But a situation that seems to be too good to be true requires even more caution. Anonymous letters can be written by anybody with a grievance, and need to be handled with care. Although the registration details in the letter had proved to be correct, the allegations about selling information to corporations needed to be confirmed by other sources. With a suspected spy operating in several countries, a part of the investigation needs to happen abroad. Before the rise of low-cost flights and the widespread use of internet (it was 1998!), this implied strained resources caused by the need to travel and high telephone bills for essential communication – circumstances that seriously hampered the investigation.

A surprise visit to his house did not reveal any additional facts – just more stories and inconsistencies. Confronting Adrian Franks with our findings seemed to be the only option left, but even that did not lead to compelling evidence. Although we were convinced that Adrian Franks was a spy, the secrecy surrounding the operation, and his bluff, taught us how difficult it is expose someone convincingly. The fact that Adrian's outfit was a subsidiary of a company in the United Kingdom, and his use of the name Le Chêne (by accident, or so it seemed), were in fact the last leads. Unfortunately, that track proved a dead end. Because the British Companies House database was not online at the time, the investigation depended on the cooperation of clerks, and none of the English groups involved was willing or able to help us with the investigation. When we published our findings, some of the people who knew him were unconvinced, and blamed the messenger – as has happened in other cases.

Evelyn le Chêne's spy files provided the final pieces of the puzzle, revealing that Franks was indeed selling activist intelligence to companies. The files also showed the extent of the operation. Franks was only one spy out of many. Le Chêne had recruited at least half a dozen agents to infiltrate CAAT's headquarters in Finsbury Park, north London, and a number of regional offices, according to the *Sunday Times* (Connett and Gillard, 2003a). Two other infiltrators have been identified publicly since. One was Martin Hogbin, who started as a volunteer and ended up working at CAAT's office in London as a paid campaign coordinator. He was a spy from 1997 until the exposure in 2003. A third infiltrator using the name Alan Fossey became secretary of the Hull Against Hawks group shortly after moving to the town. Fossey's profile is typical of an informer's in that he made himself indispensable within the group. The outline of Fossey's career includes his move in 1997 to Liverpool, where he had the task of undermining the local religious peace initiatives against BAe's Warton plant.

THE SPY FILES

The main sources for this chapter consist of intelligence reports compiled by Le Chêne – about 350 pages of printed material that the *Sunday Times* obtained from a whistleblower. Between 1995 and the end of 1997, and probably longer, she filed hundreds of pages of reports to BAe. Le Chêne initially sent her briefings on an encrypted fax to the BAe security offices on the ground floor of Lancaster House at the Farnborough airfield. Later BAe set up software on her office computer so that the company could access the reports directly from her database. The *Sunday Times* cited a source – whose name was withheld – claiming the firm paid her £120,000 a year. The recipient of the reports was Mike McGinty, an ex–RAF officer who headed security at BAe Systems. The files have frequent references to 'MM'. Dick Evans, then chief executive (and Chair of BAe Systems since 1994 until he stepped down in 2004), would also receive regular verbal briefings on the contents of Le Chêne's reports from Mike McGinty (Connett and Gillard, 2003a). Apparently, the intelligence material was important enough to find its way to the top of the company.

The CAAT Committee made the following summary of the subjects covered. The reports contain:

- information about CAAT as an organization, such as bank details, computer files, publications, Steering Committee agendas and minutes, the email password;
- information about CAAT and other anti-arms trade activists and supporters, MPs and other public figures who might be sympathetic to CAAT;
- comments made by one person about another, details about partners and flatmates;

- transcript of a person's diary;
- information about CAAT and other anti-arms trade actions and campaign planning, mostly, but not exclusively, protests;
- a printout of names and addresses from a database, apparently Le Chêne's or BAe's profile of activists. (CAAT Steering Committee, 2005a: 6)

Le Chêne's company TRI collated intelligence on the identities and confidential details of thousands of activists and marketed it to British industrial companies. In March 1996, Le Chêne claimed to have 148,900 names (ElC, 5 Mar 1996: 474.1).

Not on this list, but just as essential, is the personal input of Le Chêne, her comments and advice to the company. The analysis of the collected information combined with Le Chêne's added insights offers a better understanding of the consequences of an infiltration operation at this scale.

The references in this chapter consist of the abbreviation ElC, for Evelyn le Chêne – the author of the reports – and the dates mentioned on the reports. Appendix 2 includes a chronological list with the complete headings of the reports.

Daily Reports

In late 1995, John Major's Conservative government was deciding whether to grant licences for the sale of Hawk fighter jets to Indonesia. By then the intelligence reports on CAAT's activities were flowing into BAe's offices at Farnborough, Hampshire, on an almost daily basis. The infiltrators did not only report on what they heard, did or organized themselves, but collected any possible snippet of information they could lay their hands on. Banking details, the contents of computers, the whereabouts of colleagues, it all found its way to BAe eventually through Le Chêne's reports.

The accounts of meetings are pretty detailed. They describe people, their habits and their willingness to participate in CAAT. They report people not having much time to engage themselves in campaign activities and cite familiar reasons such as illness, study, family and work commitments:

- A. is recovering from influenza and is not participating at all for the moment. She is still interested in doing CAAT 'things.' […] However, this year she has been crying off sick or as being

too tired or that she has something else to do when she is asked to participate in meetings and liaisons.
- B. is increasingly tied up with writing a research dissertation for a degree and since her hernia operation has not been very active. She has been seldom [*sic*] at home when contact has been attempted. (ElC, 9 June 1997: 1734)

New members of the group get a lively description: who they are, where they come from, where they have been active before, known addresses, etc.:

- X. is considered, at 25, to be a 'veteran' of the protest movement, having previously 'worked' Faslane Peace Camp. [...] Her speciality appears to be the stopping of convoys of nuclear missiles but she seems to be capable of turning her hand to anything. She is a white female approximately 5'6" tall and quite slim. Her long wavy light brown hair was tied back. She wears loose ethnic clothing.
- Y. is a white male about 21 years old. He is over 6' tall and slim and looks fit. Has a long face with a Roman nose and thick lips. He looks slightly Mediterranean and wears an unkempt straggly beard with sideburns beneath a shock of long, thick brown hair. [...] He declares he is 'new to the protesting game' but is eager to try. He does not appear to fear arrest. (ElC, 30 Oct 1996)

The early reports show a mix of detailed information and comments by Le Chêne. Later on, she would add a separate paragraph or document headed 'comment'. The comments usually provide an analysis of the information, and a request to discuss strategy to counter activists' plans. Every now and then, however, her comments offer a glimpse into the opinions and background of Le Chêne herself.

Occasionally she pokes fun at the activists monitored, mocking their looks, outfits or behaviour. 'X is not very erudite. He cannot spell for a start. He has a spell-checker on his computer, but each time he wrote Finnish it came up that way when he had meant, of course, finish' (ElC, 23 Sep 1997, 1.4, Comment). When an activist pleaded guilty on minor charges, Le Chêne commented: 'The reason she pleaded guilty was that she is going on a three months tour of America for Ploughshares. It apparently seem [*sic*] ok to sacrifice your principles if there is something else that you would rather be doing!' (ElC, 18 Nov 1997). Le Chêne repeatedly showed her disapproval of activists living on unemployment benefit and of groups funded by the taxpayer. About a charity activity of CAAT, she said: 'This permits CAAT to off-set the programme under education which comes under charity thus avoiding paying tax on donations. It also means of course that the taxpayer is subsidising CAAT activism' (ElC, 27 Jan 1997). About people from East Timor, in the UK to protest against the sale of Hawk jets to Indonesia, she suggested: 'There could be a case for deportation under these circumstances as they must be costing the British taxpayer a great deal of money' (ElC, 12 Aug 1997: Comment).

Followed Home

'Desks were rifled, diaries were read and address books photocopied so information could be passed to BAe. People were followed, their houses were observed, their friends spied upon, their habits evaluated' (Connett and Gillard, 2003a). One such target was Anna B., described in one report as a 'good-looking' 25-year-old, who was a key activist and networker for CAAT and student groups. The *Sunday Times* heard a tape recording of a phone conversation between Le Chêne and a senior officer in BAe group security discussing having Anna B. followed. Reports on Anna B. give details of her addresses, housemates, hairstyles, the contents of her diary and her alleged habit of smoking marijuana in the corridor.

The reports contained further indications that people were followed. When new people joined CAAT, Le Chêne provided BAe with as many personal details as possible. When not available, those details needed to be obtained. Known addresses of CAAT members were checked and counterchecked with official registries ('The telephone number does not appear to be listed or is a very recent new addition.' – ElC, 30 Oct 1996).

When public sources failed, surveillance was used. It is highly unlikely that the same people who posed as activists performed this part of the surveillance work themselves. The risk of recognition would be unacceptably high. Hence, another observation team would have been involved in the surveillance.

Digital Data

The files show that Le Chêne's agents gained access to CAAT's IT system and databases. With Martin Hogbin staffing CAAT's main office in London, and another spy, Allan Fossey, as the secretary of the group in Hull, obtaining information from the various computers at the offices must have been relatively easy. However, the reports indicate that computers and software were specifically prepared to allow outside access. Another striking aspect of the files is the repeated offer by one of the infiltrators to install a new computer system at CAAT's offices and members' homes.

The report dated 27 January 1997 has the full directory of several computers at the London office attached – several pages each, a complete list of members of CAAT, their home addresses as well as those of the Steering Committee. One of the appendices is 'handwritten (due to circumstances)' and includes the assurance that the incomprehensible points 'will be rectified shortly' (ElC, 27 Jan 1997). The files also include the email password current at that time (ElC: 28 Jan 1997: 1451) and state 'several discs of importance have been obtained from the CAAT office in London' (ElC, first report after 10 Feb 1997: 1472).

Several reports indicate that Evelyn le Chêne had computers placed within the organization that were prepared in such a way that they were easy to access by her collaborators in order to copy their contents. There is this early note, dated February 1996, in which Le Chêne showed relief that nobody technical took a good look at a specific computer:

> The computer did not receive any attention at all in Manchester. Given that X.Y. has shown an interest in obtaining a computer, she is to receive the one in question. She is not a computer buff. The person installing it within her home will also be producing, for her, a new liaison newssheet on the machine. The transfer is expected to take place sometime during the course of next week. (ElC, 19 Feb 1996)

Le Chêne's agency seemed eager to be involved in placing new computers in CAAT offices, or at people's homes. The discussion within the activist group about the installation of a new computer system at CAAT's offices one year later appears to be of considerable importance. The detailed reporting on this issue suggested that Le Chêne's intelligence agency had a stake in whose tender was to be accepted. Le Chêne reports to BAe that A.K. has 'consistently pushed' that her boyfriend be the one to install the new system under the form of a maintenance contract at x amount pounds per quarter. This has not been well received by the rest of the group, hence the decision to use C. to do the job. (ElC, 27 Jan 1997: 1435)

A fortnight later Le Chêne reported that C.'s tender was accepted – 'because it is so cheap!' And she urged: 'Please let us talk about this' (ElC, 10 Feb. 1997: 1469).

COVERT CORPORATE STRATEGY

Groups like CAAT prefer to label themselves as 'open organizations'. Everybody is welcome, and there are never enough volunteers. Any screening of new members is considered a direct threat to participation. This principle of openness is often strongly connected to the belief that groups like CAAT have nothing to hide. The second part of this case study explores how details about the preparation of campaigns, as well as informal information about the organization, were used to undermine CAAT's campaigning work.

Advance Warnings on Lobbying

Le Chêne's agents took a particular interest in connections between anti-arms trade pressure groups and the House of Commons. Her agents collected a series of letters, including correspondence discussing British policy on the sale of arms to Indonesia, with a number of leading Labour politicians such as David Clark, then Shadow Defence Secretary, Jeremy Hanley, then Foreign Office Minister, and Jack Straw, then Home Secretary (Connett and Gillard, 2003a). Le Chêne closely monitored meetings and correspondence with MPs of all three parties, and forwarded advance warnings of any parliamentary events to BAe. Internal CAAT discussions on lobbying were repeated in the spy files.[30]

CAAT and two other pressure groups hired solicitors Bindman and Partners to seek a judicial review of the granting of export licences for arms companies. BAe was alerted to the contents of a letter sent by the firm to the then Trade Minister, Ian Lang. BAe's security department filtered the information, and passed it on to their in-house government relations teams. As a result BAe could be one step ahead of the campaigners when lobbying in parliament (ibid.).

Even links with celebrities were noted. The files mention the actors Helen Mirren and Prunella Scales and their opposition to the torture trade. A letter from the Clean Investment Campaign promoting ethical investments addressed to Anita Roddick, owner of the Body Shop, received special attention too:

> This is a very important document. The request is for the Body Shop to have declarations in their shop windows against the arms trade. If this is granted by the shops, then the Clean Investment Campaign's first success will be notched up. (quoted in Connett and Gillard, op. cit.)

Countering CAAT

Evelyn le Chêne tried to counter CAAT on every front, no matter how small the opportunity.

When she heard that CAAT always received BAe press releases immediately after they were sent out through the BBC, her advice was: 'Don't send them or leave them to the last when it no longer matters' (ElC, 11 June 1997: 1754).

When CAAT campaigners requested a copy of the Defence Manufacturers Association (DMA) members list, Le Chêne was consulted by its Director General. She advised him not to cooperate. In her report to BAe she explained why: 'having such a comprehensive and up-to-date listing of all the defence support industries would cut down their own research time by 100% and likewise their expenditure for it by 200%' (ElC, 14 May 1997: 1662.1). However, Le Chêne found out her recommendation was 'not heeded' (ibid.).

According to the *Sunday Times*, the names and addresses of activists were routinely run through the BAe computers to check if any were shareholders. In addition, the BAe switchboard was configured to flag up any calls from telephone numbers associated with the activists (Connett and Gillard, 2003a).

Anticipating Direct Action

Information on events and actions planned by CAAT was also highly prized by BAe. Often the reports detailed plans for upcoming demonstrations at BAe's sites or gatherings such as the company's AGM. Sometimes the files reported how activists intended to walk through the site, leaving behind some sign or trace of their action – varying from symbols of protest to the destruction of a Hawk. In one case, the files detailed exactly how a small group planned such an 'incursion'. A map with the planned route was attached:

HULL. The HAH Group has organised an action for Brough after their meeting on Friday 13th. It is likely to be about five or six strong. It will be non-violent and there will be a banner and some leaflets, all relating to items in the recent TV programmes World In Action. The timing is likely to be 23.00 hrs. Entry into the premises will be via the footpath that cuts across the runway. They do not intend any criminal damage nor to remain there. Comment: Please discuss. (EIC, 11 June 1997: 1755)

By infiltrating CAAT so thoroughly, BAe were well placed to deal with the various protest tactics. Le Chêne provided BAe with elaborate advice on how to deal with certain situations. Often, the reports ask for a face-to-face meeting with BAe officials ('Please discuss') but sometimes the files included her recommendations. Every occasion required a different tactic.

In March 1996 CAAT set up a Rapid Response Network to organize a 'die-in' outside Parliament. This event was to happen on the first Thursday after BAe announced the delivery of Hawk fighters to Indonesia. Le Chêne advised caution in timing the press release. The longer BAe waited, the more effective the CAAT protest would be. More time would allow the campaigners to mobilize more people, while the warmer weather would also increase the turnout. Le Chêne suggested that BAe announce the delivery to coincide with the Parliamentary Easter recess. That way, she thought, the 'die-in' would be 'a largely pointless exercise' (EIC, 8 March 1996: 493).

Sometimes activists wanted to get arrested, planning to use the resulting court case to draw more attention to their cause. In that case, Le Chêne suggested that BAe pressure the police to 'avoid arresting protesters, or at least not charging them' (ibid.: 494).

A similar pattern is evident in the BAe response to CAAT's 'snowball' strategy, which planned that each direct action that resulted in arrests would lead to further and larger actions. The resulting court cases were to be used to argue that activists were committing a crime (criminal damage) in order to prevent a greater crime (genocide) and that they were therefore not guilty. This defence was successful for Chris Cole in his 1993 'BAe Ploughshares' protest, and Le Chêne was afraid that it would work for the four women activists awaiting trial for 'disarming' a Hawk fighter with hammers on 29 January 1996 (ibid.: 495; see also Pilger, 1998: 313–22). Le Chêne advised that the corporate response to these actions be decided in relation to its effect on the longer-term protest. When two protesters went to a BAe site seeking to be arrested, the police merely confiscated their wire-cutters. They were reported to be annoyed, not least because they failed to generate publicity. Le Chêne wrote:

> It is therefore difficult not to conclude that arresting activists does play into their hands and leads ultimately to larger protests in the future. On the other hand one does accept that to offer no counter would be unsustainable from a company point of view. Alternatives need to be discussed. (Le Chêne, 8 March 1996)

BAe also used Le Chêne's insider knowledge to manage larger protests. Demonstrations outside more than 60 UK BAe sites were thwarted by tip-offs from infiltrators: a key tactic was to ambush trespassers, who were then served with injunctions preventing them from returning.

To reduce publicity for the activist cause seems to be one goal, but '[b]y the same token, if any activists are arrested for assaulting a police officer, it would significantly discredit their cause' (ibid.: 494). Here Le Chêne seems to suggest that a violent confrontation between police and activists could have benefits for her client, BAe.

Provocation

As an infiltrator, Franks had a disturbing influence on the coalition building within the European Network Against Arms Trade (ENAAT). His behaviour at meetings had aroused suspicion in 1998. The spy files provide evidence that this behaviour was part of a preconceived strategy to counter the efforts of the activist groups involved.

In November 1996, ENAAT started to organize a protest against the large international arms fair Eurosatory in Paris in June 1998. Because of his alleged contacts in the French movement, Franks assigned himself the task of involving the more moderate French peace organizations in the campaign. However, the leaflet he produced was thought too radical, even after repeated editorial interventions from Amsterdam. It was full of empty words and bombastic language, in poor English:

> We, Members of ENAAT (European Network Against Arms Trade) unanimously decided at our International meeting in Zurich on the 16–17th November 1996 to open a campaign of preparation, information and sensitisation of the public opinion

to the imperative necessity of stopping and to denounce the big market of death and mutilation that is represented by the arms industry in a world drifting constantly towards totalitarianism, dictatorship, oppression and genocide. (Eco-Action, 1996b)

This kind of language frustrated efforts to involve Amnesty International and Agir Ici (a moderate French NGO, now part of Oxfam France). The two had just started a campaign against electric shock torture, and could well have become partners.

Furthermore, his domineering behaviour during meetings made Franks unpopular. He had rather unsubtle and oversimplified opinions on the dynamics of the arms trade, banking world and the oil industry, as the quote above shows, and vented them often (Lubbers and van der Schans, 1998; Eco-Action, 1996a, 1996b, 1996c). This added to the feeling of unease that people had about him. He also strongly criticized the campaign against the arms trade to Indonesia, the only joint campaign ENAAT had got off the ground as a network at that time.

At Eurosatory meetings, he repeatedly tried to incite people toward direct action, and more violence than they intended to use. Given the pacifist origins of the groups involved, they tended to eschew violence. This was another reason for people to become suspicious in 1998. A member of the International Peace Bureau asked the Dutch antimilitarist partner in the network, AMOK, what kind of person he was (email to Buro Jansen & Janssen, 1998). In addition, an activist from Bangkok, with a different culture and background, politely asked after Franks' legitimacy (ibid.).

The spy files reveal that Franks was indeed a man with a mission. A detailed account of a meeting of anti-defence groups reported there was 'no sign of any interest' in a more radical approach. In this assessment, marked 'Addressee – eyes only', it said:

As at time of writing this report there would appear to be NO sign of any action taking place at the Paris Air show against any company including your own. [...] The issue of doing something was raised three times. To have pressed harder would have been impolitic from a security point of view. (ElC, 19 May 1997: 1665)

Franks knew he risked his cover by pushing the issue, but he kept trying. One can only guess the strategy behind this. It could have been a tactic to provoke police action at a picket line and thus disturb the peaceful character of the protest. If the strategy was to undermine the building of broader coalitions, it was successful. Franks' proposals had a negative effect on the 'spadework' of CAAT and AMOK within ENAAT. People got irritated and vital coalitions were thwarted due to an alleged lack of agreement on basic issues such as the character of the protests they were to organize. Franks' position as a troublemaker within the network was thus effective. The fact that he risked being sidelined because of his behaviour was apparently of less importance. Information would keep coming in, because CAAT was also a member of the Network, with Martin Hogbin present at most, if not all, international meetings.

In this role, disrupting the meetings of the network, undermining coalition building, and provoking more radical action, Franks was more than an infiltrator; this was work of an agent provocateur.

EFFECTS OF EXPOSURE

This section focuses on CAAT's internal investigation into Martin Hogbin, his job as the staff action coordinator and the difficulties some of his fellow activists had in accepting that he had been a spy. The *Sunday Times* journalists informed CAAT about the existence of the spy files on the Friday afternoon before publication (Connett and Gillard had planned the publication of the article for one or two weeks later; but on the Saturday, the editor of the paper decided otherwise). The consequences of the exposure of the spy files for CAAT were numerous and far-reaching. The group was confronted with the details of betrayal and the leaking of essential information, and had the painful task of identifying the spies in their midst.

Martin Hogbin

Hogbin was an active volunteer with CAAT from spring 1997, and joined CAAT's staff in November 2001. He was suspended in early October 2003, after the revelations in the *Sunday Times*. Hogbin resigned and left immediately after the initial internal investigation implicated him as a suspect, two days after his suspension (CAAT, 2003).

He started his surveillance work soon after he became involved with CAAT. The first surveillance report attributed to him described a trip to Farnborough. The report – long and detailed – was dated 19 June 1997, one day after the trip took place. Submitting reports so soon in his CAAT career implies that Hogbin was brought in as an infiltrator, as opposed to someone who was 'turned' and persuaded to secretly pass on information.

In 2005, the Information Commissioner confirmed that Hogbin was forwarding information by email to a company with links to Le Chêne. He did this during his time as a volunteer, in 1999–2000, and in the last year he was with CAAT (due to a change of systems at CAAT, no further information was available). Hogbin's email logs prove that he continued to forward information to Le Chêne until the exposure in the *Sunday Times* in September 2003.

How did CAAT find out that Hogbin was the main suspect? After the disclosures in the *Sunday Times*, CAAT's Steering Committee started an investigation. In an attempt to discover who had provided Evelyn le Chêne with information, CAAT staff checked the office email log and discovered records of suspicious activity in Hogbin's email account. Since early 1999, he had been forwarding large numbers of emails either to his home address, or to one specific email address (CAAT Steering Committee, 2005b). In December 2004, the Information Commissioner would link this email account to Evelyn le Chêne (Thomas, 2004, 2005), but CAAT had to investigate without this evidence. Hogbin agreed that he had sent the emails, insisting that they were to go to an ex-CAAT volunteer, but went to an unrelated address by mistake. He blamed the email programme's address book, but CAAT Steering Committee (2005a: 3) concluded that his explanation lacked credibility since hundreds of emails cannot go to the wrong address 'by mistake'.

CAAT had the difficult task of linking concrete details in spy files to specific members of the campaigning team. The investigation team closely examined some excerpts from the spy files they got from the *Sunday Times*. Although Hogbin declined to cooperate with the investigation, the intention of CAAT's researchers was to find information that could exonerate him. They were unable to find any (ibid.: 12). The report detailing CAAT's internal investigation presented several cases where Hogbin

appears to be one of a small group where we can with reasonable confidence eliminate most or all other possible sources within that group, or when he was one of a small number of people with access to private information reflected in Le Chêne's file. (CAAT Steering Committee, 2005a: 6)

The CAAT report refers to the detailed report on the trip to Farnborough mentioned above. Apart from Hogbin, only three other people were present; the information and the frequent references to the content of private conversations in the file could not but originate from one of them. The others were cleared of suspicion in a complicated process of assessing the spy files and interviewing the people involved, after which the committee decided it was fair to attribute this report to Hogbin (ibid.: 7–9).

The description of the trip included a lot of detailed planning of action: how to get in, where the BAe complex would be hit, the non-violent role of the Steering Committee, and the leaflets to be published. Detailed information like this offered the security staff of BAe the opportunity to take countermeasures in order to minimize the effect of the protests. The caveat of source sensitivity added by Le Chêne is of significance in hindsight. She warned: 'Only a very few people are aware of all above. Extra caution is requested in handling the information in order to protect excellent source' (19 June 1997, quoted in CAAT Steering Committee, 2005a: 7–8). Knowing now that CAAT's research connects this report to Hogbin, and that the Information Commissioner confirmed the connection between Hogbin and Le Chêne's company, the 'excellent source' Le Chêne seeks to protect here is Hogbin.

Several entries in the files traced back to Hogbin are related to his work at the CAAT office taking care of banking affairs. On 16 September 1997, Evelyn le Chêne reported to BAe: 'At the CAAT London office a cheque for £5,542 was banked. This was from the share handout ex Halifax account' (CAAT Steering Committee, 2005a: 10–11). The details refer to a cheque from the stockbrokers Waters Lunniss, who handled the sale of Halifax shares. Owning shares offered CAAT the possibility of attending an AGM and asking critical questions – on clean investment policy, for instance. Eventually such shares were sold again. Only the person who entered the cheque in the cashbook and the person who banked it would have known the exact amount of the cheque. CAAT investigators concluded it 'most likely' that it was Hogbin who provided this information to Evelyn le Chêne (ibid.).

The spy files also contain a detailed report of the protest against the fair of hi-tech defence equipment organized by the Armed Forces Communication Electronics Association (AFCEA), taking place in Brussels at the end of October 1997. The report includes details on the sources to finance the trip: 'Person G withdrew £250 from a "special account" about which he said, "no-one knew" to pay for the minibus to take volunteers to Brussels for the AFCEA action' (CAAT, Steering Committee, 2005a: 11). Hogbin was one of four

UK volunteers to attend the AFCEA protest, and he was the driver of the minibus. The Steering Committee investigation found out that Hogbin was the only one told about the source of the money (ibid.: 11).

CAAT's internal investigation concluded that Martin Hogbin played a pivotal role in providing BAe with information. The Information Commissioner later confirmed that Hogbin had sent information to an email account connected to Evelyn le Chêne, as detailed below.

'Excellent Source'

Hogbin had several ways of providing Le Chêne with information. Forwarding emails and writing surveillance reports were only two of them. The fact that he was one of the few paid staff campaigners meant that Hogbin had access to almost anything that passed through the office. As was mentioned, BAe got detailed information on cheques and (anonymous) donations, and on the possible sources of money used for actions. The content of the emails forwarded was wide-ranging. Examples are CAAT plans, CAAT National Forum Reports, nominations to CAAT Steering Committee, and notes about three legal cases, a press release, and email list circulars. It also included minutes from the Disarm DSEi network, a network of people mobilizing against the huge Defence Systems and Equipment international fair held annually in the UK. Around half of the emails concerned information about CAAT and half were about other organizations and networks (CAAT Steering Committee, 2005a: 3).

Additionally, as national campaigns and events co-coordinator, Hogbin was involved in much if not all campaigning against the arms trade. He was the main organizer of protests at BAe annual meetings. He would arrange the purchase of token shares in BAe or other companies in order to attend those meetings and publicly challenge directors on arms sales to repressive regimes. He was involved in organizing protests against BAe plants and arms fairs, his work varying from mobilizing activists to the practical preparations, such as organizing the transport of fellow activists to demonstrations or taking part in 'recce's' to explore the terrain of action – as detailed above. Hogbin also was a key networker in the movement, both in the UK and at the European level. He played an important role in mobilizing against the DSEi Arms Fair, the largest protest of its kind in the UK. Hogbin usually represented CAAT at meetings of the European Network Against Arms Trade

(ENAAT) and coordinated the UK mobilizing against Eurosatory, the large defence fair held in Paris. (Many ENAAT meetings in 1997 and 1998 were attended by Hogbin and Franks, who were both working for Le Chêne.)

With Hogbin's double role as a spy confirmed, it is possible to analyse the spy files again, and make an inventory of the information gathered by Hogbin – as opposed to by other infiltrators.

Difficult to Believe

At the CAAT office Hogbin was a well-respected colleague and a much-liked member of the small staff. People thought they knew him well, including his family and children. Hogbin, in his fifties, seemed like an open and honest person, devoted to the cause. He made no secret of his past career at the South African arms manufacturer Denel; his apparent change of views only added to his credibility (Thomas, 2007; Terry, 2005; Lewis, 2005).

Hogbin's exposure caused much upheaval within the CAAT network. For most people it is hard to believe that someone they have been working with for such a long time, on such a personal basis, could be collaborating with 'the enemy' – essentially betraying his fellow activists and friends. This usually hinders further research, as it did in this case. Some continued to trust Hogbin, even against the evidence. This was one of the reasons for the decision against a broader investigation. In an atmosphere where part of the team believed that the entire investigation into Hogbin's background was a political manoeuvre to set him up, it was impossible to get support to pursue the search for other infiltrators (see also Thomas, 2007).

Understandably, CAAT chose to avoid publicity on the matter. As mentioned, the group heard about the spy files on the Friday afternoon prior to the Sunday of publication. Avoiding publicity is a response typical of groups dealing with infiltration and spying. In this case, the delay in communicating the findings that confirmed Hogbin's work as a spy nourished the belief in his innocence. The CAAT Steering Committee decided not to publish the results of their internal investigation until the Information Commissioner had finished its investigation. The exposure in the *Sunday Times* was in September 2003; CAAT's internal investigation was finished in January 2004, but not published until July 2005, together with the results from the Information Commissioner (CAAT Steering Committee, 2004, 2005b).

The fact that Hogbin continued to be trusted did not just complicate the investigations against him. He also continued to come to anti-arms trade events after he left CAAT. The fact that the Information Commissioner linked him to Evelyn le Chêne did not stop people from other campaigns, both anti-arms trade and environmental, from working with him. In July 2005, almost two years after the *Sunday Times* articles, he was still working for the Disarm DSEi campaign, according to Mike Lewis, CAAT's media coordinator and other activists (Lewis, 2005; Terry, 2005).

It was Mark Thomas, the activist and comedian, who managed to convince more people. His column in the *Guardian* describing his growing doubts about Hogbin was widely circulated on the internet. Mark Thomas had believed Martin Hogbin when he claimed the accusations of him spying 'were bollocks'.

> For more than a year, in fact, I defended him and once again, when it was time to tour with my stand-up show, Martin came along. Touring the country, sharing hotel rooms and kipping on the floor in a sleeping bag, Martin helped raise thousands of pounds that funded anti-arms-trade groups and trade unionists visits to Colombia. (Thomas, 2007)

It would feel like an act of treachery on his part, Thomas wrote, to look at the file of evidence CAAT said they had on him. Nevertheless, the questions remained, and Thomas read the file in 2005. It dawned on him that Hogbin was indeed a spy. However, it took him another two years to go to Hogbin's house to confront him. In the meantime, the evidence piled up. The Information Commissioner found that 'a former member' of CAAT had been forwarding information to an email address at a company with links to Le Chêne. The careful phrasing was justified in the legal context: technically, anyone could have forwarded the emails from Hogbin's account. With Hogbin having admitted the forwarding, however, the findings formed a confirmation. And in 2006, BAe acknowledged hiring Evelyn le Chêne to spy on CAAT in legal documents filed in a court case, as detailed below (*Campaign Against Arms Trade* vs. *Paul Mercer and LigneDeux Associates*, 2007).

Thomas's column sharing his doubts was published in December 2007 – more than four years after the initial exposure in the *Sunday Times*. His column and the time it took him to write it are indicators of the denial and the doubts and the destruction of a friendship.

Infiltration and covert action can do a lot of harm, not only on the political front, but also on the personal level.

SPYING ON ROAD PROTESTS

CAAT was not the only group Threat Response spied on. The road protests against the Newbury bypass, for instance, receive more than average attention in the surveillance reports. Important events are reported on in great detail, to warn BAe against the danger of involvement of groups against the arms trade with the environmental movement.

In the late 1990s the Newbury bypass became the focus of anti-roads groups when thousands occupied the woodland earmarked for destruction. The 8-mile bypass finally opened in 1998 after years of protests delayed completion. The total cost of the project was £74m, of which nearly a third, £24m, was spent on security.

The *Sunday Times* heard tape-recorded conversations involving Le Chêne reveal that she regularly passed information from her network of agents to Group 4. She said she had agents posted permanently at Newbury and passed on highly confidential personal information about protesters to the company. These included accommodation addresses, vehicle registration details, National Insurance numbers, unemployment benefit details and income support information (Connett and Gillard, 2003b). The spy files reflect this work for Group 4. The detailed reports show that she forwarded advance warnings about the road protesters' plans to the private security forces involved, and to the police as well. Much to her frustration, Le Chêne's information was not used in the most adequate way – or rather: the way she thought was best:

The policing level was low for the amount of people present and the security guard reaction was insufficient. In fairness to the latter, it has to be said that there were not enough of them to reasonably expect control of the situation with even half the protesters present. In addition, the company concerned lacks a background of control to such groups and it showed. For protesters, this is an ideal double situation. On the police side, it was evident that they tried to make up for the lack of numbers by the use of horses – environmentalists being animal lovers. But this showed as well and when the police, on the second occasion, charged the oncoming handslinked protesters, the horses naturally bumped them and this led to an increase in tension and the rest is history. (ElC: 13 Jan 1997, Special Comment)

The eviction of the protesters' camp ended in an extremely violent confrontation with the police, now remembered as the Third Battle of Newbury (the first two took place in the seventeenth century). Had the authorities listened to Le Chêne's advice, it would not have got that far – or so it seemed:

> The numbers expected and what they would be doing and how they would do it, was known well in time and notified. It was apparently a decision on the part of the Highways Authority on how to deal with the situation that led to the low manning of police and security guards, although we are of opinion that where security guards were concerned, it was more a case of penny-scrimping by cash-strapped Costain. (ibid.)

Le Chêne claimed she had at least two people infiltrated in the Newbury bypass camp: 'According to two sources at Newbury on Saturday – neither of whom knows the other – the incident that led to the arsons was the police rush with horses' (ibid.).

Why a report to BAe would include detailed coverage of police dealing with anti-road protests is not entirely clear. Evelyn le Chêne tried to promote herself and her knowledge of both movements – while warning BAe that the presence and the influence of CND and other anti-defence groups in the road protests 'is *most* prominent so far' [italics in original]. She is proud to have infiltrated both movements; a rhetorical question in the comment of this report testifies to that: 'Exactly who has a good knowledge of the background to both BAe's problems and the anti-road protest movements [can be anyone's guess]' (ElC: 19 Feb 1996, Comment).

Over the years, Le Chêne tried to convince BAe of alleged dangerous liaisons; she claimed that peace groups were increasingly involved in the anti-road protest movement. As early as July 1995, Le Chêne thinks she has discovered a new trend of activists 'tiring of anti-road campaigns, need[ing] something that is more challenging and more confrontational with government and security' (ElC, 8 July 1995). Her analyses proved to be completely beside the point. The battles of Newbury had yet to come, and the tension around road protest was still building up.

A few months later, Le Chêne points at the networking between radicals again:

It is not the first time of course that CND or other anti-defence groups have been involved in the anti-road protest movement, but their presence and/or influence at Newbury is the most prominent so far. [...] One thing is certain. No networking is conducted without quid pro quo. (EIC, 19 Feb 1996, Comment)

Le Chêne traced the involvement of the anti-defence groups with the environmental movement to the EF! conference held in June 1996. In her view, the leader of the first Rainforest Action Network mass demonstration at the House of Commons in 1990 was now trying to persuade the most militant of the EF! activists to link with the anti-defence groups (EIC: 13 Jan 1997, Special Comment).

Group 4 admitted buying information on protesters. An unnamed spokesman told the *Sunday Times*: 'We have certainly been obtaining information about protests at our customers' sites. It is the sort of information that would be obtained in the pub about activities that may affect our customers; people or property,' he said. 'We were getting information about where protesters would be and what times in advance. We would have paid for that information' (Connett and Gillard, 2003a).

Le Chêne had close contacts with Group 4. Threat Response had Barrie Gane on the board from the very beginning; he also worked for Group 4 Securitas.[31] At the time, Group 4 was Britain's largest security firm whose clients ranged from the prison service to the royal family and the government. It advertised its ability to guard its customers against espionage, sabotage and subversion.

Gane is a former deputy head of MI6, once tipped to succeed Sir Collin McColl. However, he decided to leave the service on early retirement after a rationalization in 1993, and open up his knowledge and network for privatized intelligence companies. Group 4 called Gane one of the most important former intelligence men switching to the private branch of the business (Lynas, 1999). *The Times* concluded his appointment signalled an upgrading of its international operation. 'Mr Gane can bring the company knowledge of international terrorism, commercial espionage and risk assessment' (Elliott, Ford and Lanale, 1993).

According to the Highways Agency, the government had funded security operations around road-building sites, but the contractors involved held the responsibility for it. 'Clearly we worked closely with the police and the contractors to ensure that this was carried out in a lawful way', (spokesman cited in Connett and Gillard, 2003a). Group 4 carried out work on behalf of the Highways Agency as well as construction companies such as Costain and Tarmac, but other security firms were involved as well. The Transport department, working on orders from Treasury solicitors, spent more than £700,000 in the early 1990s employing the Southampton-based detective agency Bray's to help them identify protesters. Private detectives were seen filming people and noting down public conversations. 'Despite this, campaigners believed this type of surveillance alone could not account for some of the information contained in the dossiers issued by the department to support legal injunctions against them' (Connett and Gillard, 2003a).

The authorities had other ways to find information too. In 2002, BBC2 reporter Peter Taylor revealed how the Thames Valley police hired a spy to stop the Newbury protest. On TV, Sir Charles Pollard, then Chief Constable of Thames Valley Police, explained why Newbury was a line in the sand. The protesters could not be allowed to win once the government had approved the building of the bypass the previous year. 'The ones who were planning and tried to carry out seriously illegal acts are very subversive in a sense of subversive to democracy,' Pollard said (in Taylor, 2002). Special Branch resorted to their usual methods of gaining information and recruited informers paying anything from £25 to larger sums of money – up to £1,000 a week. Despite this, stalemate still loomed and costs were rising:

> Thames Valley took the unprecedented step of recruiting an agent outside normal procedures. They had heard of a particular individual who worked for a private security company with unique skills and a perfect pedigree to infiltrate the protesters. The police normally keep such private security companies at arm's length as they are in the business of making money from intelligence they gain. (Taylor, 2002)

Calculating that the value of his intelligence would far outweigh the cost of hiring him, the Thames Valley Chief Constable gave permission to proceed. A contract was drawn up with the individual and the security company for which he worked. According to Taylor (ibid.), the agent's main task was to get as close as possible to the leaders, and in particular to let his handlers know of the best time to take the main tunnel that was holding up the contractors' operations.

Whether Threat Response was the company involved in this particular infiltration operation proved next to impossible to verify. Peter Taylor went through his old notebooks, and came back with three other companies involved in the road protests: 'Reliance Security plus Brays and Pinkertons both of whom apparently ran their own agents' (email to the author, 9 April 2006).

A Freedom of Information request about the possible involvement of Le Chêne with Thames Valley Police came back negative.[32] Nor was it possible to 'trace or locate any specific records or documents to answer the question whether or not Thames Valley Police hired an agent to infiltrate the protest groups during the building of the Newbury bypass' (Picking, 2006).

The chief constable who confirmed contracting the private agent on BBC television in 2002, Sir Charles Pollard, claims he cannot remember any more details. He is however not surprised no paper trail can be found: 'Of course at the time it was a very closely-guarded secret [...] so secret in fact that the company was only referred to within the few people who knew about it under a codeword!' he explained when asked for more details (interview by email, 22 June 2006).

Whatever happened to the Newbury agent? 'His cover was so good and his information so accurate, that Special Branch then directed him to infiltrate the animal rights movement,' Taylor (2006) wrote on the BBC website. This correlates with the interests Adrian voiced at the time. But then again, Adrian was interested in everything that involved radical activism.

EVELYN LE CHÊNE

Evelyn le Chêne is linked to today's intelligence world by the members of the board of her company Threat Response International (the company was dissolved in early 2006), and Risk and Crisis Analysis before that. The board of Threat Response International included Barrie Gane and Robert Hodges. The first was introduced above, the latter is a former major-general in the British Army and a director of Rubicon (founded in 1996, and bought by Aegis Defence Services in 2005). Rubicon provides people to serve in the war in Iraq and hires mostly from the SAS, especially those with experience in Northern Ireland. As the former Commander of British Land Forces in Northern Ireland, Hodge has experience with guerrilla-style, urban warfare (Pallister, 2003; Aegis, 2005).

However, Le Chêne's own links to the intelligence services go a long way back. She has moved in government circles since, as a young woman, she married Pierre le Chêne, many years her senior. As a British agent in Nazi-occupied France, he was captured and interrogated by Klaus Barbie (also known as the 'butcher of Lyon' for his torture practices; Le Chêne went to his trial to testify in 1987); subsequently he survived the Mauthausen concentration camp (Dawe, 1987). Evelyn met Pierre at the end of the 1950s, when she interviewed him for her research into the history of this camp. Her extensive and often-quoted book *Mauthausen: The History of a Death Camp* was published in 1971. Two years later *Watch For Me by Moonlight: A British Agent with the French Resistance* (Le Chêne, 1973) appeared, an anecdotal novel based on the biography of Robert Burdett (formerly Boiteux), who was Pierre Le Chêne's superior in the Special Operations Executive (SOE). The two men were dropped together behind enemy lines in occupied France (ibid., 1973: 7). She wrote one more war-related book (Le Chêne, 1994a; another one never got beyond being announced, according to the publisher: Le Chêne and Her, 2001). Meanwhile she had two sons, Christopher and Adrian-Paul, the latter born in 1959.

Fierce Anti-Communism

Evelyn le Chêne's career shows that propaganda, lobbying and covert operations are closely related, and often difficult to disentangle. In the 1980s, she was the director of the West European Defence Association (Le Chêne, 1986c), an organization committed to exposing the dangers of communism and the left. WEDA was officially set up in July 1985 as a forum for pro-defence organizations. In her own words, its role was to act as a clearing house and point of contact between new pro-NATO bodies, to keep each other informed and to spread the word. Apart from books and articles, WEDA was holding seminars 'on topics such as NATO defence policy, Warsaw Pact capabilities, the chemical threat, and Soviet propaganda and disinformation' (Le Chêne, 1986b). Exactly how close the organization was to NATO is shown by the fact that in 1985, WEDA held a conference at NATO Headquarters in Brussels where representatives of similar anti-communist organizations from all over Europe exchanged thoughts with NATO specialists assessing the situation in the various countries. The second day of the conference took the participants to SHAPE in Mons, the operational headquarters of the Allied Powers in Europe (Le Chêne, 1985a). For 1986, two further NATO conferences were planned, on civil defence and chemical warfare. Another event on the agenda was a seminar on 'subversion and terrorism' to be held at the Conservative Party's headquarters (Le Chêne, 1986a).

In her WEDA capacity, Le Chêne did PR work for Jonas Savimbi and his Union for the Total Independence of Angola (Unita) in their fight against Angola's socialist government (see for instance her letter to the editor of *The Times*; Le Chêne, 1985b). She visited network meetings of likeminded organizations, such as the Dutch ICTO, Interchurch Committee Unilateral Disarmament, the German Bonner Friedensforum, Peace through NATO and the European Institute for Peace and Security, and helped organize press conferences on behalf of Soviet dissidents or victims of alleged communist influence in Cuba, South Africa or Nicaragua.

WEDA was a small organization. Serving as Joint Presidents were Monique Garnier-Lançot and the Rt. Hon. Lord Chalfont, PC, OBE, MC. Garnier-Lançot was the vice-chair of the Paris-based European Institute for Security at the time, while Lord Chalfont had been Minister of State at the Foreign Office from 1964 to 1970; his name will come up at the end of this chapter. Garnier-Lançot donated her archives to the Hoover Institution in California, including her correspondence with Evelyn le Chêne. The letters reveal some interesting details about her work and background.

First, the letters disclose that Le Chêne was in a position to arrange access to the Special Forces Club for her friend Monique Garnier-Lançot; she put in a word and succeeded (Le Chêne, 1985c). Membership of the Club is limited to current and former members of the military and intelligence elite from Britain, the United States and selected allies.

Le Chêne also copied Brian Crozier into her correspondence with the joint presidents of WEDA. Garnier-Lançot had started working with Crozier a few years earlier, in 1982, while he appeared in Le Chêne's correspondence (or the selection accessed for this research) in 1987, actively engaging in WEDA's work. In his autobiography, called *Free Agent: The Unseen War 1941–1991*, Crozier (1993) portrays himself as independent from the CIA and MI5. Meanwhile, he had direct access to Margaret Thatcher when she was PM to advise her on countering Soviet subversion in the UK, more specifically on dealing with the miners' strike, for instance. Crozier formed a covert operational group, called 'the 6I', 'a private sector operational intelligence agency' to 'provide intelligence in areas which governments were barred from investigating' and 'to conduct secret counter-subversion operations in any country in which such actions were deemed feasible' (Goulden, 1994; 6I is short for the 'Sixth International', the next in line after the Fourth – by the followers of Trotsky in 1938 – split up according to Crozier;

Evans, 1993). When the *Guardian* wrote that the 6I were funded by the CIA, Crozier stated that: 'The bulk of its funds came from rich individuals and a few private companies. The CIA's share of its budget – in the 10 years it existed – never exceeded 5 per cent' (Crozier, 1998). Among 6I's successes was, according to the four full-page extracts published in *The Times* when *Free Agent* appeared in 1993, 'the planting of moles in the Militant Tendency and the Campaign for Nuclear Disarmament (CND)' (Evans, 1993).

One more revealing detail in Le Chêne's correspondence is the letterhead. It shows that in 1985 and 1986, WEDA had an office address in London, while the telephone number is Le Chêne's home number in Gravesend, Kent. At the time, the second floor at 35 Westminster Bridge Road was home to two organizations led by Julian Lewis, one of which was the Coalition for Peace through Security. According to the biographical notes at his website, Lewis 'waged a campaign to expose the activities of Trotskyist Militants in the Labour Party in the late 1970s – a decade before they were eventually expelled'. Between 1981 and 1985, he was a leader of the anti-CND campaigns waged by the Coalition. 'In 1985, he became director of the political consultancy Policy Research Associates, which successfully campaigned for changes in the law on Educational Indoctrination, Media Bias, Propaganda on the Rates, and Trade Union Democracy.' From November 2002 until May 2010, he was the Shadow Defence Minister for the Royal Navy, the nuclear deterrent and strategic issues. At present, Lewis is the Conservative MP for New Forest East, in Hampshire. In September 2010, he was appointed to the Intelligence and Security Committee (Lewis, 2011).

Le Chêne had many functions. She was a consultant to the Defence Manufacturers Association, on questions of military economic stability in Third World countries (Le Chêne, 1987a). This contact is corroborated by entries in the spy files, mentioned above. Another clue to her closeness to defence contractors is her negotiation with Macdonald Douglas for financial support for WEDA. Lord Chalfont (1987) mentioned this in his resignation letter – it would present him a conflict of interest in his business activities. (In her answer, Le Chêne (1987b) denied the meeting with the American defence contractor had anything to do with WEDA.)

She also claims to have served as technical adviser to the UK National Council for Civil Protection (Le Chêne, 1989: 5). In the 1980s, the Council operated as an all-party Parliamentary group, concerned with the protection of the citizens of the UK against disasters, major incidents or acts of war. At the end of the Second World War, civil defence concerns were typically directed towards the nuclear threat of the Cold War; the organization has since all but ceased to exist (British Civil Defence website, last updated in 2003; the only reference to Le Chêne is one of her books mentioned as source of information in a brochure on the history of the organization).

Chemical and Biological Warfare, and Wouter Basson

The red thread in Le Chêne's work is her interest in chemical and biological warfare (CBW). According to biographical information in one of her books (Le Chêne, 1994, inner back cover), she has 'an Honorary Degree in National Security Studies from Kiel University where her thesis was on *Chemical and Biological Weapons – Threat of the Future*'. A 31-page brochure with the same title was published in 1989 by the Toronto-based Mackenzie Institute for the Study of Terrorism, Revolution and Propaganda (Le Chêne, 1989). However, no thesis is required for an honorary degree, and Kiel University has never heard of her, or the title she claimed to have.[33]

At conferences, she invariably warned against the danger of CBW in the hands of communists, terrorists, activists and the like. The European Round Table in Strasbourg invited her to a conference on 'the security of the citizen due to a possible abuse of the environment' (Le Chêne, 1994c). The Wilton Park Conference asked her to speak on 'the growing danger of biological weapons' (Le Chêne, 2000). In 2005, she was one of the five 'Fellows' who had donated half of their subscription of £2,000 to the Koeppler Appeal, a trust founded with a £150,000 gift from BP, the oil company (Wilton Park, 2005). On the occasion of Wilton Park's sixtieth anniversary, the BBC described the place as 'a secret retreat' and 'a diplomatic hideaway' (Horsley, 2006). Annual reports and accounts of the Wilton Park International Association, however, are presented to the House of Commons, because officially the organization is an 'executive agency of the Foreign and Commonwealth Office' (ibid.: i).

More remarkable still is Le Chêne's regular presence at the yearly conferences of the Chemical and Biological Medical Treatments Symposia (CBMTS), the first in 1998. The CBMTS website documents her presence in 2001, 2002 and 2003 (Applied Science and Analyses, 2009; the website provides no details on speakers at conferences since). Her papers – again – focus on analysing the terrorist threat (see for instance Le Chêne, 1998). The organizer and chair of the conference was Brian Davey. Until recently, Davey worked for the Organisation for the Prohibition of Chemical Weapons (OPCW) as its Head of Health and Safety. Since 1 January 2007 he has been Medical Director with the United Nations in New York (*Applied Science and Analyses Newsletter*, 2006). Davey's career, however, started in the South African Defence Force during the apartheid era. In 1986, he joined the 7 Medical Battalion under Dr Wouter Basson's command (Gould and Burger, 2000; Burger and Gould, 2002: 177). After two years, Basson appointed him director of Lifestyle Management, one of a network of front-companies founded to secure the funding and continuation of Project Coast. This secret programme supplied South African Special Forces and death squads with experimental chemical and biological poisons to use against enemies of the state. A special investigation of the Truth and Reconciliation Commission (1998) concluded that amongst other things the Project tried to develop – incredible as it sounds – bacteria that would kill only blacks, and vaccines to make black women infertile (ibid.; see also Gould and Burger, 2000; Gould and Folb, 2002; Singh, 2008). Davey was responsible for developing protective clothing and training programmes, and for drafting a defensive CBW philosophy for the SADF. This was an important task because international treaties forbid countries to develop CBW programmes for offensive use (Gould and Burger, 2000). Project Coast continued to exist in the 1990s, after the release of Nelson Mandela, and it still existed when Brian Davey started to work for the OPCW (Truth and Reconciliation Commission, 1998: 33). The project was officially shut down in 1995, although the public knew nothing about it until Basson's arrest in early 1997, which culminated in the TRC hearings on Project Coast in Cape Town in June and July 1998 (Singh, 2008, see also Purkitt and Burgess, 2005).

Le Chêne had another, even more direct link to South Africa's chemical and biological war programme, Project Coast and Brian Davey, through her propaganda work for Savimbi and Unita. Research by the Truth and Reconciliation Commission revealed that the justification for Basson's Project Coast, the potential threat of chemical attacks on South Africa, was solely based on research by the Flemish toxicologist Aubin Heyndrickx (Gould and Folb, 2002: 23, 39–40). The latter claimed that Angola used chemical agents against the CIA-backed rebels of the Unita movement of Jonas Savimbi. For a few years his claim was widely believed, published by *Jane's Weekly*, an authoritative publication dealing with military matters worldwide, and repeatedly quoted (see for instance Heyndrickx, 1989; Eppink, 1990a; Hallerbach, 1989; Branscheidt, 1989: 1, 3). This fitted well with the propaganda plan to undermine the MPLA government. With the Soviet Union falling apart and Cuba recalling its troops from the area, Unita feared the support of the Americans and the South Africans would fade away. Accordingly, Heyndrickx' travels to Angola and his scientific teams were funded by Savimbi (Eppink, 1990a).

However, evidence for Heyndrickx's claims became untenable, and were no longer taken seriously within the scientific world. The toxicologist countered the criticism by inviting a group of 'European experts' to prove he was right. Of the physicians who were part of the original delegation, the German, Spanish and Belgians did not endorse the final report. However, there *was* a 'British researcher' who *did* confirm the use of CBW in Angola. According to the Dutch paper *NRC Handelsblad*, this was Evelyn le Chêne of 'the laboratory of the Institute for Risk and Crisis Analysis' (Eppink, 1990b). For the occasion, her small company doubled as an institute with a laboratory to safeguard the work of Basson and Davey for Project Coast.

Undercover in Southern Africa, with Mercenaries

Evelyn le Chêne took part in covert operations in Southern Africa herself as well. The scheme was exposed in national papers in the Netherlands and the UK by Stephen Ellis (1991a, 1991b), a specialist on political violence at the African Studies Centre at Leiden University (who generously shared his sources for this research).

In the late 1980s Le Chêne was involved in Operation Lock, a secret scheme to put an end to rhino horn and ivory smuggling. The operation was initiated in 1987 by John Hanks, then in charge of the World Wide Fund for Nature in Africa, and the late Prince Bernhard of the Netherlands, former president of the WWF. The latter funded the operation in a private capacity with £800,000. Both were worried about the alarming decline in the number of rhinos. The Prince wanted men who could effectively put a halt to the smuggling. Hanks recruited KAS Enterprises, a London based security firm founded by Sir David Stirling, best known as the founder of the SAS, the Special Forces corps of the British army. KAS key personnel were former SAS soldiers, now operating on the private market as mercenaries. The aim of the operation was to infiltrate the black market of poachers by going undercover.

The would-be traders worked from safe houses in Pretoria and Johannesburg and had a stock of ivory and horn at their disposal, which was provided by South African and Namibian game parks. The operation was secret, not only out of necessity for it to succeed. Fearful for their respective reputations, neither the head of the WWF in Africa nor His Royal Highness of the Netherlands wanted to be publicly associated with setting up mercenaries to trade in ivory. Under the command of Colonel Ian Crooke, a decorated veteran of the Falklands war, the secret operation uncovered a web of smuggling routes in the four years of its existence. However, in the unstable Southern African area of the late 1980s, both South African military and guerrilla forces also used this network of routes. Inevitably, Operation Lock got entangled with South African military forces and their counterinsurgency warfare. The Operation Lock team recruited informers with experience in the field, such as ex-poachers, corrupt game wardens and officials of firms suspected of smuggling. Inadvertently, as several authors pointed out, it also recruited spies from the South African military intelligence active in the region (Brown, 1992: 2; Boggan and Williams, 1991: 6, Ellis, 1991a: 8, 1991b; Koch, 1996). The South Africans had two main concerns about the scheme: 'one was the possibility that KAS was working as a covert arm of the British secret service; the second was the chance that KAS might expose the smuggling South Africa conducted on behalf of Unita and Renamo' (Naylor, 2004: 281–2). To head off that danger, the two sides agreed that South African military intelligence would trade tips about smuggling rings (run by its competitors) for information KAS found regarding anti-apartheid activists (ibid.).

Although the initial aim was to gather intelligence, Project Lock developed into a more ambitious project to employ former SAS men for paramilitary anti-poaching work throughout Southern Africa. In 1996, an inquiry by the Kumleben Commission, appointed by then President Mandela, concluded that the country's defence forces were involved in wide-scale ivory and rhino horn smuggling. And many of the game traffickers in Southern Africa were also known to deal in drugs, weapons and ammunition, sometimes with the connivance or involvement of senior officers of the South African Defence Force. As far back as 1978, General Magnus Malan, ex-military Commander-in-Chief, gave the green light in 1978 to the forces' illegal dealing in animal products to bankroll Unita rebels' war against the Angolan government. The Kumleben report also confirmed the paramilitary training of game wardens in South African tribal 'homelands'. After being recruited as nature conservation officers, young people were in fact trained as soldiers at secret military sites (Koch, 1996; Brown, 1992: 2; Boggan and Williams, 1991: 6; Ellis, 1991a: 8; see also Kumleben Commission, 1995).

The public outcry at the brutal poaching of rhino gave the military a perfect excuse to maintain its presence in an area. It was a simple matter to claim that military training bases were, in fact, for the purpose of anti-poaching training. Internal KAS documents stated that operations ran in Zambia, Zimbabwe, Namibia, Swaziland and Botswana. The team also approached game authorities in Tanzania and Kenya (KAS/Crooke, 1989). In Namibia, KAS trained an anti-poaching team in mid-1989, when South African forces were being demobilized prior to independence elections. Stephen Ellis thought the trainees almost certainly included members of Koevoet (Crowbar), the South African counter-insurgency unit. KAS also trained game wardens for Mozambique inside South Africa, he wrote in the *Independent* (Ellis, 1991a).

Internal KAS documents (unpublished, courtesy of Ellis, in the archive of the author) reveal that Evelyn le Chêne was involved in Project Lock at a staff level; she took part from the beginning, in early 1988 until at least April 1989, when she was present at a board meeting. In July 1988, she accompanied Ian Crooke to the Dutch Royal Palace to bring Prince Bernard up to date. In a 'private and confidential' note to the Prince to thank him for further funding, Crook acknowledged the next phase of the project, mentioning a joint investigation with Le Chêne for 'a similar plan in the Western area [of Southern Africa]' (KAS/Crooke, 1988). At the same time, top priority was to be given to 'David Stirling's package for President Kaunda with concurrent activity by Mrs. Le Chêne on the political front' (ibid.).

Minutes of a KAS board meeting show that Le Chêne had a network of contacts in Africa, and that she travelled the continent to ease the way for Project Lock[34] (KAS, 1989, 4–6). She introduced Ian Crook to Craig Williamson, a South African intelligence man close to the then President Botha and Minister of Defence Malan.

Le Chêne billed KAS Enterprises for consultancy fees, travel to Africa and in-country expenses. For a period of two months in 1988, for instance, she charged £15,586.99 (Le Chêne, 1988). The invoice was issued by her company Risk and Crisis Analysis. The same company was hired by British Aerospace almost a decade later, to spy on peace activists and to infiltrate the Campaign Against Arms Trade. The company address was 65 Blandford Street in London, which happens to be the address WEDA had moved to early in 1987 (Le Chêne, 1987a, 1988).

A CONTINUUM IN UNDERMINING RESISTANCE

Evelyn le Chêne's career puts her in an anti-communist tradition and the legacy of anti-subversion activities of the SOE, the SAS and its secret operations, at home and abroad. She claims to be a specialist in the potential use of chemical and biological weapons by extremist groups, and headed a front-organization aimed at highlighting the red threat during the Cold War. She was also actively involved in fierce anti-Soviet propaganda and demonstrated a keen desire to neutralize dissent whilst defending the status quo. This means that there are not only parallels with historical events as described in Chapter 2. It seems fair to say that Le Chêne's background indicates a continuum in efforts to undermine resistance while defending the powers that be.

The assumption about a continuum at both the ideological and the practical levels is corroborated by a more recent episode involving BAe and CAAT. After the exposure of Evelyn le Chêne as a spymaster, the arms manufacturer hired yet another investigator to monitor the campaigners. He was called Paul Mercer, and his involvement was revealed in CAAT's campaign to reopen the investigation into the bribes the Saudi royal family paid to BAe. Mercer had access to confidential correspondence between CAAT and their lawyers discussing the legal strategy in this case. When he sent a CD with the correspondence to BAe security, the company recognised the legal risks of compromising confidentiality between lawyers and their clients, and informed CAAT. BAe subsequently also admitted having hired Evelyn le Chêne – something the company had not conceded up to that point (*Campaign Against Arms Trade vs. Paul Mercer and LigneDeux* associates, 2007; Thomas, 2007).

Le Chêne and Mercer share a common background, many details of which have not been revealed before (except for a well-researched piece at Nottingham Indymedia (2011), which I discovered at the very end of the investigation for this book).

Like Le Chêne, Mercer was active in anti-communist organizations during the 1980s. His book '*Peace' of the Dead: The Truth Behind the Nuclear Disarmers* (1986) was one of the many publications at the time, denouncing CND and the wider 'peace' movement' as communist fronts, attempting to disarm the UK, in the process furthering the foreign policy aims of the Soviet Union. The cover showed the peace symbol cut through the middle by a hammer and sickle.

Mercer made no explicit mention of infiltration as a research tool, but he claimed to have first-hand knowledge of key members of the organization. In the preface, Mercer stated that he had relied 'as much as possible on primary sources, including confidential and internal CND documents'. These files – which consist primarily of official letters, reports and minutes – are, Mercer added, 'not normally available to outsiders'. They have been 'obtained through careful research and from CND sources concerned about the developments within the Campaign for Nuclear Disarmament since its revival' (Mercer, 1986: 422). These may very well have been the same people who 'would rather not be named' in the acknowledgements (Nottingham Indymedia, 2011). Twenty-five years later, there is no need for such evasions. Early in 2011, in a 'rare appearance' at an event organized by the free market think-tank Policy Exchange, Mercer was introduced as 'UK's pre-eminent expert on extremist groups', someone who 'infiltrated CND many years ago, and is now advising leading companies on issues around protest' (Policy Exchange, 2011, 7 minutes into the video report).

There are, however, more links to the work of Evelyn le Chêne. Acknowledged for having 'done most in terms of proof-reading, copy-editing and acting as a source of inspiration' is Dr Julian Lewis. As pointed out above, Lewis' biography still features the Coalition for Peace Through Security and its campaign to undermine CND. 'One way he set about this was to assemble massive dossiers on leading members of CND, purporting to show that many had been associated with the Communist Party or various Communist fronts' (Hodgson, 1987, article in the *Observer* at Lewis' website). The organization disrupted events, sent a spy into the CND office and tried to link its then chair Bruce Kent with the IRA, while – as Kate Hudson, head of CND, wrote recently – the rumours of soviet funding persist to this day (Hudson, 2009).

Mercer's book was published by Policy Research Publications, one of the organizations Lewis ran from the second floor of 35 Westminster Bridge Road. As we have seen, Evelyn le Chêne also used this address for her WEDA correspondence.

When Mercer was exposed for spying on CAAT in 2007, Lewis (by then shadow defence minister) told the *Guardian* that he regarded him a friend. He said that he had 'worked closely with Paul in the 1980s', and that Mercer had done 'a lot of good work exposing the far left' (Evans and Leigh, 2004). Both of them were highly praised by Crozier in his biography as 'outstanding campaigners against CND' and Lewis as 'the 6I's leading activist in Britain' (Crozier, 1993: 243).

There is yet one more connection between Mercer and Le Chêne. The preface to Mercer's book was written by Lord Chalfont, who was one of the two joint presidents of Le Chêne's organization WEDA at that time. He was – among many other things – President of the UK Committee for the Free World and member of the Institute for European Defence and Strategic Studies. He combined these Cold War activities with the post of chairman of VSEL, builder of nuclear submarines and warships (Bowen, 1995). The company planned to merge with British Aerospace in 1995, and was eventually taken over by it in 1999.

What seemed to be a case-limited example – to the arms trade in the UK, and possibly even just to CAAT – was in fact linked horizontally across issue areas that included environmental activists and road protesters and also linked vertically from the UK to mainland Europe and even as far as sub-Saharan Africa. The ideological drive to undermine protest groups and campaigners links conservative groups on the right of the political spectrum with factions within police and intelligence circles. Together they seem to be 'focused on the perception that campaign groups present a threat to established western political traditions' (Dover, 2007: 1). In that sense, the contest seems to be focused around a very cold war type of activity, the ring-fencing of protest and activism away from mainstream politics. The strong anti-communist ideology of both Evelyn le Chêne and Paul Mercer and their common background puts their activities in the tradition of Operation Gladio. This secret 'stay behind' network – uncovered bit by bit since the end of the Soviet empire in 1989 – was to be activated in case of a communist invasion, but occasionally engaged in fighting what its members considered 'subversion' (Ganser, 2005). Maybe, Dover suggested, BAe-funded work provided a platform for Le Chêne and her successor to continue activities against the 'extreme' left that they had respectively engaged in during the Cold War and more specifically the 1980s (Dover, 2008: 4). This theory is corroborated by the more recently discovered facts about Le Chêne's close collaboration with NATO, as detailed above.

This section on Evelyn le Chêne opens a completely new avenue of research that is of major importance for the understanding of the position of the global corporation in pursuit of power, linking Cold War propaganda operations to covert corporate strategies today.

A quick summary underlines the links between the findings in this chapter and the Kennedy story featuring in the Preface. Paul Mercer was hired by BAe after Evelyn le Chêne was exposed, but his contract was finalized through private security firm Global Open. This firm was founded by Tod Leeming, who headed the Animal Rights National Index (ARNI) and infiltrated undercover officers into protest groups, until he left the police in 2001 (Evans et al., 2011). ARNI was the covert Metropolitan police unit that monitored London Greenpeace in close cooperation with private investigators hired by McDonald's, featured in Chapter 6.

Mark Kennedy, the undercover officer who infiltrated the climate movement, set up his own security agency just before he was exposed in 2010. Kennedy claims Leeming approached him for work; the agency was registered at the home address of another Global Open director. One of Leeming's clients was E.ON, looking for intelligence on climate groups. The very same climate groups were also infiltrated by Kennedy, for the same reason. Kennedy was – or should have been – supervised by one of the covert units of ACPO, called the National Public Order Intelligence Unit (NPOIU). This police unit exchanged information with E.ON, and with the department responsible for energy. And to close this circle, or rather, this attempt at mapping a network of influence, the ACPO units were set up at the special request of companies targeted by activist groups, companies that were dissatisfied with the work of ARNI and unconvinced by its results.

The next step is to link back the findings about the recent past presented here to the latest discoveries about Mark Kennedy and the six other infiltrators that have been exposed so far. The results of the official inquiries into the various aspects of these exposures have not yet been announced. Although there are no fewer than twelve different investigations into the covert infiltration of activist organizations (for an overview see Evans, 2011), none of these includes the risks and consequences of cooperation with corporate spies and former police, specifically Special Branch, changing to private security jobs.

One thing is clear. The network of cooperation between covert intelligence units and corporate spies continues to exist. The various vectors undermining resistance, the secret manoeuvres, are in urgent need of further investigation. The detailed mapping has only just begun.

8
Conclusion: Secrecy, Research and Resistance

A corporation does not spy on its critics just to know what is going on: it does so to be prepared and to defend itself. The crucial connection between surveillance and the gathering of intelligence on the one hand, and the subsequent corporate strategizing on the other, was the point of departure for this book. The concluding chapter outlines the essence of *activist intelligence and covert corporate strategy* as means of undermining public debate and engineering consent. The case studies offer a wide range of examples of spying on campaign groups, targeting activists, infiltrating their networks and reporting on their meetings and their strategy discussions. The gathering of intelligence on activists provides the building blocks, the knowledge, to develop covert strategy. The surveillance and infiltration take place in secret, and are not meant to be exposed, or known to the targeted people. On the contrary, the number of people privy to such confidential information is extremely limited. Creating more awareness of activist intelligence aims to break the silence of secrecy, and foster resistance against covert corporate strategies.

The last section explores how this all-pervading secrecy can be broken. The proposal for a specific multidisciplinary field of research is aimed at providing the means to collect more evidence and case studies, and to study the political economy of this specific branch of 'grey intelligence'. Furthermore, it is time to start the groundwork for a legal framework defining the responsibilities of those involved, and the legal rights of those targeted. Such a framework could provide institutionalised routes of discovery, aimed at supporting the people spied upon and at offering opportunities for research. Meanwhile, exposure of covert corporate strategy remains an important step towards transparency, as well as a form of resistance to secrecy.

SECRECY: A DANGER TO DEMOCRACY

Ironically, challenging TNCs about their lack of transparency and accountability is met with responses that rely on secrecy. The case studies illustrate unwillingness among corporations to change damaging business policies and illustrate the lengths companies under attack are prepared to go to evade public protest. While corporate critics become the target of intelligence gathering operations and covert actions aimed at undermining their work, secrecy enables the avoidance of responsibility and accountability for controversial actions. This section seeks to explain how activist intelligence and covert corporate strategy present a threat to democracy at various different levels.

Large corporations have a long tradition in fighting their critics with the help of propaganda and active interference, as Chapter 2 has shown. Today, public relations (PR) and lobbying are essential tools for the modern corporation, tools that afford the means to better anticipate and adapt to societal demands. Parts of the political activities of corporations, however, remain hidden. In particular, the covert actions laid out in this book are examples of dirty tricks by large corporations on a continuum with PR and lobbying.

Activist intelligence and covert corporate strategy overlap with a specific form of PR, issue management (IM). The literature in business studies on IM emphasizes the need for scanning, monitoring and tracking external forces that are a potential threat to the company, as well as the subsequent policy development and the implementation of action. However, most literature does not address the practice, or indeed ethics, of information gathering. The failure to address the issue in business studies is mirrored by the reluctance to discuss covert action in intelligence studies. The silence is an indicator of the secret character of intelligence gathering and the subsequent covert operations. It is also perhaps an indicator of the lack of awareness or concern among academics about the consequences and implications of privatized intelligence and non-state covert operations. To recognize IM as intelligence is an attempt to break this silence. More specifically, it puts activist intelligence and covert corporate strategy on the agenda as an important issue of research.

A key strategy for dealing with critical consumers and campaigners today is corporate social responsibility. CSR guidelines are currently embedded in voluntary pledges by TNCs to evaluate and better manage the wider impacts of their business on society. They are premised on dialogue and transparency as guiding principles in business policy. This brings up the question of how such principles relate to the use of covert techniques against corporate critics. Maybe it is best to understand activist intelligence and covert corporate strategy as the dark side of CSR. The relationship is not always clearly visible, and not always as obvious as in the examples below. Moreover, it is not always there, as not all corporations engage in such deception and manipulation.

Sometimes, however, complying with policies of responsible entrepreneurship can be a double-edged sword. The 'independent' commission auditing Nestlé served multiple purposes. While compliance helped restore the company's credibility, the commission also served to divert the media focus away from the activists, and to cause disarray amongst boycott groups. The dialogue Pagan set up with church groups was intended to end the 'shouting match' and enhance Nestlé's public image, while at the same time serving as an intelligence operation to gather information. After the Brent Spar débâcle and the execution of Ken Saro-Wiwa in Nigeria, Shell adopted a new set of business principles, including a code of conduct regarding human rights and environmental issues. One outcome of this new policy was the launch of a new website, shell.com, embodying the company's new philosophy of 'openness and honesty', with dialogue as the core concept. However, the online forum where everybody could have a say about Shell also served as a barometer for what people thought about the company. Meanwhile, in the same period, Shell hired Hakluyt to assess the plans of the environmental movement (Chapter 6) and online intelligence agencies to monitor the net (Chapter 5). Dialogue, one of the key instruments of CSR, doubles as a crucial tool to gather information, to keep critics engaged and ultimately to divide and rule, by talking to some and demonizing others (see Rowell, 2002b).

The rise of PR and other information industries marks a profound shift of political culture that offers a further threat to the disintegrating welfare state democracies and their legitimating social and political processes. Moreover, the case studies illustrate the use of corporate propaganda as means of protecting corporate power against democracy (Carey, 1978).

A corporate choice for covert action implies a refusal to discuss the damaging effects of production or trade in a public debate. Pagan's strategy focused on breaking boycotts, which in essence meant attempting to go back to business as usual without addressing the issue that provoked the boycott. The legal proceedings against London Greenpeace was only one part of the McDonald's strategy of intimidating critics: the company had a long history of libel litigation (see Armstrong, 2002). By countering the campaign for responsible disposal of toxic waste, the electronics industry hoped to avoid a public debate on the effects of their production policies, and to prevent regulation on waste disposal. Rather than negotiating employment conditions and contracts, Northwest Airlines monitored its workers and fired those whom they thought were the organizers of protest. Rather than discussing the risks of genetic engineering, Monsanto tried to circumvent criticism by blaming the messenger. Instead of joining the public debate about the pros and cons of drilling for oil in the Atlantic, BP prepared to tackle Greenpeace with legal damage claims for occupying an oil installation. BAe explored every possible way to evade the debate about the arms trade and to hinder the work of peaceful campaigners.

When the corporations investigated in this book *did* take part in public debates it was often under false pretences. The efforts to undermine the work of corporate critics qualify sometimes as efforts to keep issues off the public agenda, sometimes as attempts to diminish their effect once they are already in the public domain. As a result, decision-makers may make policies based on distorted information, or without awareness of alternatives. Moreover, with the work of corporate critics effectively thwarted, people might not even know that there is a problem. With the help of private intelligence agencies, some corporations develop strategies that attempt to damage the position of activist groups, the effectiveness of their work, their financial base or their credibility. Pagan's plan for Shell included a proactive strategy to influence the forming of ideas. The strategy suggested involving Shell in education to increase the impact of the corporate viewpoint at earlier stages and to persuade teachers to provide a 'balanced view' of the problems in South Africa. The issue of agenda setting relates to Beck's arguments about risk definition. Power is understood as who gets to decide, what counts as a 'risk' and who counts as the 'responsible party'. In the example of Sony and Infonics, for instance, the electronics industry perceived the campaigners as a risk for their business, while for the activists campaigning for responsible disposal, electronic waste is a risk for the environment. Power is in the hands of those who win this battle.

In short, the examples of corporate spying and strategizing presented here raise concerns about the 'engineering of consent'. The case studies detail many means that corporations have at their disposal to manipulate public debates and to exclude the voices of their critics. Deliberate democracy requires the participation of civil society, but if activists and campaigns are sabotaged in their work then the nature of policy and democratic decision-making are thrown into question.

The case studies point to a general intolerance of dissent, and a refusal of public scrutiny and accountability. It would be a mistake to think about this just in terms of a (new) media war, a battle fought in the public arena. It is not simply a matter of PR. The aim of covert corporate strategy is not to win an argument, but to contain, intimidate and ultimately eliminate opposition (Klein, 2002). The strategies to prevent civil society from getting real power and the secrecy surrounding it present a danger to democracy.

Dealing with resistance, or what is perceived – by some – as 'subversion' has traditionally been viewed as the state's responsibility. The case studies confirm that at least part of this mission has been transferred to organizations governed by profit. The academic focus on 'policy by proxy' is inadequate to describe recent shifts between public and private. Likewise, the term 'blurring boundaries' is insufficient to analyse the complex landscape of contemporary intelligence organizations. Social network analysis can provide further snapshots of the workings of governance and the complex entanglements of formal and informal state and private structures and processes, in the context of Wedel's flex power and flex groups. However, secrecy complicates such research in various ways.

Secrecy as the defining character of intelligence agencies, their activities, and the people working for them – either publicly or privately – is the last aspect discussed here.

The dynamics of governmental secrecy discussed in Tefft's edited volume (1980) demonstrate that intelligence units at both local and national levels operate to predict, control and manipulate their environment. The case studies show that this also applies to the dynamics of private and corporate secrecy. The internal security required to protect organizations from safety breaches or leaks creates problems such as preventing the flow of vital information (Wilensky, 1967). Such an office culture may lead to problems typical of intelligence agencies. Immersed in a world of deception and secrecy, intelligence agencies have been known to develop their own morals, norms and culture. In its exemplary report, the Church Committee (1976) noted the dangers of questionable activities justified by such intelligence morality. The Committee investigated complaints about spying and countering politically active citizens by the FBI and the Secret Service, part of a response to the emergence of the new social movements of the 1960s and the 1970s. The exposure of COINTELPRO (short for Counterintelligence Programme) or 'the war at home' can be attributed to the research of critical investigative journalists (Gelbspan, 1999; Glick, 1999, Churchill and Vander Wall, 2001; see also Donner, 1990). The Church Report extensively documented how American intelligence agencies tended to expand the scope of their activities, and how operations based on 'vague standards' could soon involve 'unsavoury and vicious tactics'. The Committee revealed that '[t]oo many people have been spied upon by too many government agencies and too much information has been collected' (Church Committee, 1976: 4–5). As a result of these critical reports, the US Congress and the President increased controls, requiring explicit authorizations at the highest levels for intelligence operations.

Private intelligence agencies also run the risk of over-identifying with their clients. Evelyn le Chêne's spy files display a certain narrow-mindedness about the position of campaigners and the value of protest in a democratic society. At several points, Le Chêne urges BAe to undermine public protests regardless of their peaceful character or the democratic context of the event. Her suggestions fit her background as an active anti-communist and anti-protest propagandist. Likewise, Pagan held strong opinions about his clients' opponents and tirelessly strove to counteract them.

In policing political activities, the concept of subversion is suitably amorphous, and often synonymous with left-wing dissent in liberal capitalist states (O'Reilly and Ellison, 2006). The case studies in this book confirm that this is so not only in the public realm, but in the private, corporate sphere. A system of governance that relies on secrecy may lead to a decline of social trust. The spread of deception throughout societal institutions promotes the kind of cynicism that undermines participation in the normal political process. Judged by the ultimate consequences for the state and its citizens, the costs of secrecy might seem greater than its benefits (Tefft, 1980). Activist intelligence and covert corporate strategy constitute part of a system of governance that relies on secrecy; the broad range of different aspects of secrecy profiled in this book threatens to erode trust in democracy.

RESISTANCE AND RESEARCH

While surveillance, power, knowledge and secrecy are interrelated elements that make up intelligence, resistance seems to be the odd one out. Lack of resistance can be attributed to the level of secrecy on various fronts, as argued above. Exposure is essentially a form of resistance in the context of activist intelligence. As the stories in this book show, the exposure of covert operations offers a form of resistance to surveillance as well as a valuable addition to intelligence studies.

Exploring the options for resistance in the context of activist intelligence while failing to address the power context in which the intelligence is produced seems inadequate. In the context of TNCs acting against their critics, usually the power – for instance the amount of time and money available – is unequally distributed. The level of secrecy is another aspect determining the power of TNCs in their use of covert corporate strategy – it is indeed a defining element. In order to be able to resist surveillance, you have to know that you are spied upon in the first place. However, most of the people featured in the case studies presented in this book had no idea that their groups were infiltrated, and thus did not even have the option to resist the gathering of information. And once they *did* know, exposure including legal action where possible was more likely to be the answer – rather than putting up fences.

Promoting greater awareness of activist intelligence is essential to enhance resistance to corporate surveillance. Proposing activist intelligence and corporate covert action as a specific field of research is a first step. The analyses of the case studies provide an initial plan, and inspired by the work of Richter (1991, 1998) – but also by Gill, Marx and Wedel – the following paragraph is a first outline of the research terrain.

Activist intelligence and covert corporate strategy refers to intelligence gathering and assessment of the sociopolitical climate in which the particular company is operating; activities to manipulate public debates in a direction favourable to the company; and activities to exclude what the industry perceives as diverging or antagonistic voices. Additionally, *activist intelligence* refers to the organization, and thus the people that collect and analyse the intelligence and are involved in the subsequent (covert) actions, a flex power force of privatized intelligence people now working for big business. This field of research focuses on intelligence gathering, the methods used and the people professionally involved. It also includes the processing of the information gathered and the subsequent strategic planning by corporations to make use of it: the *covert corporate strategy.*

The field of research not only covers the gathering of information, but relates to the development of covert strategy. The studies in this book confirm that the analysis of intelligence informs how the company deals with critics. This could be a proactive policy to stay ahead of possible problems, or to take action to prevent problems – or both. There is a need for research into what these policies entail. Of course, the wider context needs to be explained too. Why do companies choose to undermine their critics? How often does it happen? Which companies decide to employ covert strategies and what are the circumstances that determine such decisions? At what level in the company hierarchy is the decision to implement intelligence operations taken, and who else knows about it?

A multidisciplinary approach would have to include aspects of globalization and privatization, the power of TNCs, the movement for social justice, civil society and the internet, PR and issue management, and intelligence studies. Mapping the world of grey intelligence – or flex power if you wish – would benefit from research into the political economy of the private intelligence agencies and consultancies involved, while the informal contacts of former agents require social network analysis.

A deeper understanding of the grey area of activist intelligence and covert corporate strategy – and the extent to which it is integrated into wider policies of corporations under fire – would make a critical contribution to contemporary debates about power relations, governance, and opportunities for resistance in liberal democracy.

Another way to break through the secrecy surrounding this subject, while also providing opportunities for research and resistance, would be to implement a legal framework to regulate private intelligence. A system of accountability and transparency would have to include terms for access to information, and thus opportunities for discovery. Of no less importance would be provisions for the targets of surveillance, infiltration and corporate strategy to take legal action. What is required is a framework that acknowledges and warrants the rights of those people and groups who are or have been the objects of covert operations. Of course, this is easier said than done. The question is: how one can police the unseen? Given the covert nature of the work, how can any system of regulatory control ensure that laws and ethical standards are respected and observed (Gill and Hart, 1999: 259)? This dilemma exceeds the issue of activist intelligence; it applies to the wide spectrum of private investigators and intelligence contractors. A possible solution would be some form of licensing, including a law clearly defining the responsibilities for clients and a clear mechanism for dealing with complaints (ibid.). A law would have to include all parties involved in activist intelligence: the private covert agents, their corporate clients, and their targets – the critics. It would also have to aim at defining responsibilities and legal rights. However, this might not be enough. In order to expand transparency, the legal framework for private intelligence would have to include a registry with the obligation to publish client lists and keep record of contracts. And to expand accountability, it would have to guarantee access to financial and operational information on private intelligence contractors, a step towards establishing an information equilibrium between data holders and data subjects (Hamelink, 2000). An evaluation of existing laws regulating intelligence agencies and access to secret information, and their effectiveness in creating transparency could provide a first outline of a legal framework. The protection of constitutional rights such as the freedom of association and freedom of expression, in short universal rights to communicate, may require a more active role for an ombudsman or a privacy commissioner as an independent trusted third party.

Implementing such a framework would acknowledge the existence of activist intelligence and indeed increase the awareness of covert corporate strategy. Developing the framework would open up the debate about governance, about the role of civil society and the power of TNCs. This debate is essential because at least part of the difficulty in deciding what is appropriate is ideological. Essentially this is about transparency and privatization. Gill and Hart (1999: 245) wonder how much of what has traditionally been viewed as the state's responsibility can be transferred to corporate – for profit – entities. More than a decade later, it might be better to ask how much of this responsibility has already been transferred. The Mark Kennedy case outlined in the Preface allows a glimpse of today's flex power networks – while at the same time it shows that in the absence of a legal framework, the corporate intelligence connections are not part of the official reviews evaluating the many mistakes made.

In essence, the field of activist intelligence and covert corporate strategy requires a broad foundation of evidence. Without in-depth research and a larger collection of case studies, it is almost impossible to properly understand the issues of corporate spying. In other words: more stories of secret manoeuvres in the dark are needed!

What we are looking for are 'hidden and dirty data', as opposed to information that is publicly available. Marx (1984: 79) defines dirty data as 'information which is kept secret and whose revelation would be discrediting or costly in terms of various types of sanctioning'. One of the ways to collect dirty data is via accidents or mistakes that reveal underlying social patterns. Collecting accidents that happened in the past and taking the analysis beyond the media coverage is one research strategy. To discover the logic behind a collection of separate events can indeed inform academic projects as well as present new research questions. This book testifies to that.

More importantly, a technological accident, like an oil spill, does not always become a scandal by itself. It takes activist researchers monitoring oil companies, a mobilized affected community, investigative journalists, or a dedicated environmental movement – and ideally a combination of the four – to point out that the oil spill is a disaster for which someone should be held to account. Watergate did not fall out of heaven as a political scandal to provide 'strategic research sites' for revelations, as Marx put it; it was the other way round. If it had not been for Bernstein and Woodward piecing together facts and figures to contextualize the snippets supplied by their 'Deep Throat' source, there would not have been any further opportunity to reveal activities normally hidden from public view. Furthermore, it is not necessarily the accident or the scandal that brings about dirty data; it can also be the commitment of people (be they activist researchers or investigative journalists) that lays the foundations for secret information to emerge. The latter applies to most of the case studies in this book. The *Threat Response files* originated from a whistleblower in an unrelated event, but usually the leaking of documents does not take place in a political vacuum. The *Neptune Strategy* landed on the desk of the boycott campaign at the height of the anti-apartheid struggle. Sympathy for this campaign had apparently reached insiders at the offices of the corporations facing boycotts. Exposures of surveillance or infiltration operations do not happen unexpectedly; they are by definition embedded in the political conflicts that evoked those operations in the first place. Monsanto would not have resorted to digital machinations if the stakes were not high: public discussion about genetic engineering and 'Frankenstein food' threatened their business by making the possibility of tougher regulation more probable. The operation would not have been discovered if it had not been for the highly specialized investigative activists who had second thoughts about the sudden heat of the discussion and contributions from particular posters. The *McSpy files* surfaced in a court case as an annex in the libel claim filed by McDonald's – thanks to the perseverance of the defendants unearthing them. The exposure of Hakluyt's spy and his work could not have happened without the activists who acted on their suspicions and their political judgement of the situation. Likewise, the recent exposures of Mark Kennedy (plus six others in his wake) and Bob Lambert were the result of the diligence of people who no longer trusted him.

However, exposure of infiltration is not self-evident for all of the campaigning groups involved in such investigations. While most of them would agree to the importance of challenging disputable exercise of power, media coverage of is not always perceived to be in the best interests of the groups themselves, as detailed in the first chapter. Setting up an investigation team of dedicated activists and seeking cooperation with a third party might offer a solution in such a situation. Buro Jansen & Janssen offers years of experience in dealing with cases of infiltration of activist groups, and more specifically suspicions of spying. There is a body of knowledge and a set of tactical tools available, crucial for understanding cases like those presented in this book. Likewise, in the UK SpinWatch.org offers a secure platform for investigation and independent dissemination with a wide reach. The aim of investigating and publishing is the exposure of secret policies and covert action. Seeking publicity and openness is to address issues of secrecy and lack of accountability. More specifically, the aim of exposure is threefold. The first is raising security awareness amongst activist groups. Sharing the findings with others issues a warning about a specific individual and informs a wider audience about the risks of infiltration. The second aim of exposure is to hold the responsible parties to account. In the absence of legal frameworks, publicity is a way to build up pressure. A public outcry could encourage politicians to address responsible authorities, and maybe start some kind of investigation – the Mark Kennedy case is testimony to that. And third, related to the second aim, the exposure functions as the final option to get more information. Shaking the tree might evoke memories and reach people beyond the focus of the original investigation. Likewise, official investigations might produce more evidence, or fresh clues.

To develop activist intelligence and covert corporate strategy as a field of research, more detailed examples are required. However, original source material is – almost by definition – hard to access, maybe secret, and often difficult to comprehend. Intelligence operations necessarily take place in secret, under-cover. Data on such operations are confidential by nature, prepared for the client's 'eyes only'. Discovery of proof behind stories and controversies that surface in the media is essential to put the events in perspective and understand the wider context. But new research needs to be initiated too. While secrecy seriously hampers research in the field of activist intelligence, academics rely on the work of whistleblowers, investigative journalists and dedicated activists and other corporate critics. Why would it not be possible for a social researcher to play a more active role in this field? My work with buro Jansen & Janssen and SpinWatch.org made me into the activist researcher and the investigative academic that I am now. Ideally more research on different fronts results in publications that draw from the novelist, journalist or detective on the one hand, and the social researcher as an academic on the other. 'Such knowledge shares with the former the need to rely on non-rigorous and questionable data sources, the desire to raise issues, sensitise the public, and document problems, and a frequent reliance on individual cases. It shares with the latter respect for the logic of explanation and the need for empirical verification and generalisation' (Marx, 1984: 102).

Secret Manoeuvres in the Dark aims to be the first of many of such hybrid publications aimed at understanding activist intelligence and resisting corporate counterstrategies.

Appendix 1
Manfred Schlickenrieder Documents

This appendix consists of an overview of the Manfred Schlickenrieder documents, referred to as the 'MS docs' in Chapter 6. Most of the documents are available at the archived version of the Aufbau website dedicated to the exposure, called *GRUPPE 2 – ein Projekt des Bundesnachrichtendienst BND*. Since most documents lack a proper title or author, the Aufbau index and numbering are used as the key to the references. The files are listed below under their German titles; English translations are added by the author. So the reference 'MS doc 9' in the text refers to document number 9, translated 'Weapon deal'. It can be found through the Aufbau index online at <http://tinyurl.com/3bt8s7p> under '*Waffenköder*'.

Included at the end of this appendix are a few unpublished documents – courtesy of the Aufbau investigators who shared these for research purpose only. All quoted documents are in the archive of the author.

MANFRED SCHLICKENRIEDER DOCUMENTS, MS DOCS

1. *Ausweis Denkmalpflege*   False identity papers
2. *Die Enttarnung des Agenten Lex Hester*
    Exposure of Lex Hester as a spy
3. *Agent Schlickenrieder zum enttarnten Agenten Lex Hester*
    MS on the exposure of Lex Hester
4. *Zeitschrift – texte 1*   Magazine text 1
5. *Zeitschrift – texte 8*   Magazine text 8

Documents and Files Composed by Schlickenrieder

6. *Reisebericht*   Travel report
7. *Reise und Kontaktbericht 1*   Travel and contact report
8. *Reise und Kontaktbericht 2*   Travel and contact report
9. *Waffenköder*   Weapon deal
10. *Politische Lageanalyse und operative Vorschläg ital.*
    Political analyses and operational proposal/Italy
11. *Fiche mit Foto zu Personen des rev. Aufbau 1*
    Photo file of someone from Rev. Aufbau 1
12. *Fiche mit Foto zu Personen des rev. Aufbau 2*
    Photo file of someone from Rev. Aufbau
13. *Fiche mit Foto zu Personen des rev. Aufbau 3*
    Photo file of someone from Rev. Aufbau 3
14. *Fiche mit Foto zu Personen des rev. Aufbau 4*
    Photo file of someone from Rev. Aufbau 4
15. *Fiche mit Foto zu Personen des rev. Aufbau 5*
    Photo file of someone from Rev. Aufbau 5

16. *Korrektur zu personeller Zuordnung zum RAS*
                                      Correction of earlier report
17. *e-Mail-Verteiler*   Mailing list
18. *Reisespesen 1*   Expense claim 1
19. *Reisespesen 2*   Expense claim 2
20. *Notizen Angriff auf Neonazitreff*
                                        Notes on neo-Nazi meeting
21. *Österreich*   Travel and contact report from Austria
22. *Gesprächs- und Kntaktbericht – Kurze Zusammenfassung*
                                        Contact report, short summary

Zulieferung Anderer Dienste – Documents from Other Intelligence Agencies

Germany
22. *Postkontrolle 1*   Mail and visit overview of detained people 1
23. *Postkontrolle 2*   Mail and visit overview of detained people 2

France
24. *Interner Dienstbericht 1*   Internal Report 1
25. *Interner Dienstbericht 2*   Internal Report 2
26. *Interner Dienstbericht 3*   Internal Report 3
27. *Interner Dienstbericht 4*   Internal Report 4
28. *Mitteilung Front de la guerre rev. 1* – Message 1
29. *Mitteilung Front de la guerre rev. 2* – Message 2
30. *Mitteilung Front de la guerre rev. 3* – Message 3

Italy
31. *Berichte über italienische GenossInnen*
                                      Report on comrades in Italy
32. *Ticker zu Italien 1*   Telex message about Italy 1
33. *Ticker zu Italien 2*   Telex message about Italy 2
34. *Karteikarte 1*   Indexcard 1
35. *Karteikarte 2*   Indexcard 2
36. *Karteikarte 3*   Indexcard 3
37. *Fiche 1 mit Foto*   File 1 with Photo
38. *Fiche 2*   File 2
39. *Fiche 3*   File 3
40. *Fiche 4*   File 4
41. *Photo-Index Fichen*   Photo index file
42. *Namensverzeichnis*   List of names

Im Dienste Shells Gegen Greenpeace, Bodyshop, Grune ect.

Work for Hakluyt
43. *Brief an Body-Shop*   Letter to the Body Shop
44. *Honorarrechnung*   Invoice for Hakluyt
45. Ex-MI6 Agent Mike Reynolds and Manfred Schlickenrieder   email contact
46. Manfred Schlickenrieder and ex-MI6 Agent Mike Reynolds 1   email contact
47. Manfred Schlickenrieder and ex-MI6 Agent Mike Reynolds 2   email contact

Foto-Documentation

48. Manfred Schlickenrieder alias Camus
49. Ex-MAD Agent Karsten Banse
50. Mike Reynolds, Christopher James und Michael Maclay – Hakluyt
51. Büro der Gruppe 2   Office of Gruppe 2
52. Klingel, Büro der Gruppe 2   Door bell office Gruppe 2
53. Wohnung von Manfred Schlickenrieder – House of M.S.
54. Eingang zur Wohnung von Manfred Schlickenrieder

                                      Entrance to the house of M.S.
55. Schlickenrieder's Auto   Schlickenrieder's car

In the Archive of the Author

56. Letter to Irene Bloemink (1997) Vereniging Milieudefensie/Friends of the Earth Netherlands, 27 May.
57. Schlickenrieder, M/Gruppe 2 (1999) fax coversheet to Hakluyt & Co, Mike Reynolds, 11 March.
58. Dossier BfG (no date) from Schlickenrieders archive. Copies from page 1 and 2, containing the index of the report and a page of summary, in German.
59. *Gruppe 2 (1998) Ruhmlos – aber rastlos, Bekanntmachung und Presserklärung zu den Durchsuchungen durch den Staatschutz am 16. Juni 1998.* Two documents, press release from Gruppe 2, as well as the search warrant containing the offending citation.

Appendix 2
Evelyn le Chêne Documents

The Evelyn le Chêne spy files were exposed by a whistleblower, as explained in Chapter 7. Because of the buro Jansen & Janssen involvement in the case, the Insight team of the *Sunday Times* granted me on-site access to these files. I was allowed to copy what seemed the most important files; the quotes in Chapter 7 come from that selection. The quotes are reproduced exactly, including obvious typing errors. References that would invade the privacy of CAAT activists have been omitted; and names replaced with random initials.

Most of the reports are composed by Evelyn le Chêne, sometimes calling herself *Source P*. Each paragraph is numbered, and each 1–3 pages of report are dated. The intelligence reports went out a few times a week, covering the monitoring of the days in between. According to the numbering, the monitoring started early June 1995. However, the files mention reports about earlier dates – so maybe the numbering system was not as accurate before that time. The last document in the spy files is dated November 1997. The reports sometimes refer to appendices, but these were not included in the selection of files the *Sunday Times* obtained.

The documents used in this chapter, in chronological order.

8 July 1995	No title
November 1995	Source 'P' 265–71, comment
19 February 1996	Source 'P' 371–81
20 February 1996	Source 'P' 392–97.4
5 March 1996	Source 'P' 473–8
8 March 1996	Source 'P' 487–97
30 October 1996	Personal – In strict confidence
13 January 1997	Addressee – eyes only, 1387–91, Special Comment
27 January 1997	Addressee – eyes only, 1433–44
27 January 1997	Addressee – eyes only, 1445–51
10 February 1997	Addressee – eyes only, 1465–73
05 March 1996	Source 'P' 474.1
14 May 1997	Addressee – eyes only, 1661– 4
19 May 1997	Addressee – eyes only, 1665–81
09 June 1997	Addressee – eyes only, 1734 (B2) HULL SITREP. 1734
11 June 1997	Addressee – eyes only, 1735–56
13 June 1997	Addressee – eyes only, 1758–65
08 August 1997	Briefing note, 1. New Campaigns; 2. CAAT; 3. Other
11 August 1997	1. Court Case, Lytham St. Annes 11 August 1997, 1.1–1.9; 2. Possible weekend problem; 3. Hull Dinner, 3.1–3.4
12 August 1997	Court Case, Lytham St. Annes 11 August 1997
23 September 1997	Update, Comment
18 November 1997	BAe REPORT, 4. Arrests at Reenee Beenee

Notes

1. In due course, ACPO is to become subject to freedom of information law. Accountability will still be limited, because the law is known to exempt queries concerning police and intelligence.
2. Although the Toffler trilogy is not officially co-authored by his wife Heidi, Toffler (1990) emphasizes the importance of her contribution in the 'Personal preface' of Powershift. I appreciate this acknowledgement by referring to the both of them as the authors.
3. Republic's arsenal included 552 revolvers, 64 rifles, and 245 shotguns with 2,702 gas grenades, 143 gas guns, 4,033 gas projectiles, 2,707 gas grenades, and an undetermined number of nightsticks and gas revolvers (Auerbach, 1966: 101).
4. *Fifty Fighting Years* is an anonymous 24-page pamphlet published by the Economic League (Central Council) in 1969. It was written 50 years after the event, according to Mike Hughes, and its author was probably John Baker White, who was Director of the League from 1926 until the Second World War. The League's own records were not made available, and the historian Arthur McIvor was told that most of the early records had been destroyed (Hughes, 1994b: fn. 2).
5. Sethi (1994) attributes this observation to Pagan on page 70, and to Ernest Saunders, a Nestlé senior vice-president, on p. 218.
6. A duplicate of this paragraph also appears on pp. 69–70 (Sethi, 1994).
7. At the time, the Royal Dutch Shell group had 280 operating companies over 100 countries; Shell South Africa was a wholly owned subsidiary of Royal Dutch Shell (Pratt, 1997: 247).
8. According to his obituary, with the capture 'Rafael D. Pagan, 67, adviser to 5 presidents' he also worked for Presidents Nixon, Reagan and Bush on policies promoting Third World social and economical development (*Washington Times*, 1993).
9. In 1991, Pattakos was director of programmes integration at Beta Analytics, a national defence, security and intelligence support services firm primarily providing services to federal government agencies and organizations. In 2004, the 20-year-old company had 330 employees, all with security clearance; the biggest customer at the time was the U.S. Missile Defense Agency – the successor of the 'Star Wars' Programme (Herbst, 2004).
10. All court transcripts are available at www.mcspotlight.org, in the 'McLibel' section under 'Court Transcripts', www.mcspotlight.org/case/trial/transcripts/index.html. However, the results produced by the search engine need a small correction. Looking for 'Bishop, B. Day 259' one gets referred to www.mcspotlight.org/cgi-bin/zv/case/trial/transcripts/960610/86.htm By simply removing the cgi-bin/zv/ in the middle, the link does work again. The right URL is www.mcspotlight.org/case/trial/transcripts/960610/86.htm.
11. According to Nicholson (Day 249: 46), the Economic League may very well have sent McDonald's reports of employee involvement in union activities too;

staff were not allowed to carry out any overt union activity on McDonald's premises.

12. The new Poll Tax, announced on 1 April 1989, replaced a tax on households with one on individuals, which many people regarded as a tax on the poor. The Poll Tax aroused broad protests, its peak a carnivalesque gathering of 250,000 in London on 31 March 1990. It turned into a running battle with police that spread through the major commercial streets of central London. About 500 people were arrested, and police raided dozens of activists' homes over the next few weeks. Conservative Prime Minister Margaret Thatcher resigned in late November 1990, largely as a result of the damage to her credibility and strategy. By 1991, 18 million were refusing to pay the tax. New Prime Minister John Major understood that it was uncollectable and announced that the tax would be scrapped.

13. Simon May (1998) claimed that Shell hired both companies, although Roy Lipski of Infonic denied it (interview by email, 10 November 2000 and 5 February 2001; see also Lubbers, 1998b, 1998c). But, as this chapter will show, Lipski is fast to deny involvement in issues that could damage the image of his company.

14. Infonic appeared on the list from 19 December 1999 to 16 July 2000. It was not until early January 2001 that it appeared there again – for three solid months (Greenpeace, 1999/2000). Because Greenpeace does not keep statistics connecting visitors to specific pages, it is impossible to draw further conclusions. Unfortunately, none of the other groups campaigning against toxic waste kept similar statistics.

15. Archive.org makes duplicates of websites once a month to archive – and sometimes more often. The copy of the eWatch website made on 20 June 2000 still shows the promotion for the CyberSleuth service at the bottom of the right-hand column (eWatch, 2000a). On the next copy, made on 15 August, it is no longer there (eWatch, 2000b). The first time the CyberSleuth announcement appeared on archive.org was on 8 Feb 1999, (eWatch, 1999b); on the archive. org copy before that, 25 January it was not there yet (eWatch, 1999a).

16. In fact, the case was even more complicated. The two flight attendants who filed procedures against NWA, Kevin Griffin and Frank Reed, were not members of the union (the Teamsters), and were thus not represented at the first hearings. Additionally, they did not agree with the collective bargaining agreement. This made them a separate party in the legal proceedings, but this is not essential for the case discussed here.

17. The Netscape feature is similar to the Explorer 'properties' option. It registers the last update, but only for sites still online. See note 15.

18. A subscriber asked the AgBioView list to publish the *Nature* Editorial, because: 'Many people are going to need that reference, not least those who, like me, will be in the frontline fights for biotech in the coming weeks at the Conference of the Parties of the Biodiversity Convention and the ICCP3 of the Cartagena Protocol in The Hague' (De Greef, 2002).

19. This is not the only evidence as to Murphy's true identity. After making a passing defence of DDT on the AgBioView listserv, Murphy was drawn into correspondence off-list with another subscriber. The technical headers on these e-mails also show Murphy's mails as originating from bw6.bivwood. com (PowerBase, 2009e).

20. In the first months of the AgBioView list, messages were forwarded in such a way that it was possible to track the technical 'headers' that shows where a message comes from.

21. The full error message was: 'AgBioView E-mail Newsletter Archives Warning: MySQL Connection Failed: Cannot connect to MySQL server on 'apollo. bivings.com' (113) in functions.php online 5' Research Jonathan Matthews (PowerBase, 2009b).

22. Other companies mentioned were Mindshare Internet Campaigns and Issue Dynamics, both based in Washington, DC (Raney, 1999).

23. The German *Aufbau* translates as 'structure' as well as 'disposition'. The self-definition of the organization is: 'The Revolutionäre Aufbau fights for a revolutionary change of the political and economical existing order.' For a longer self-definition, see the über uns /about us section (Revolutionäre Aufbau, 2006).

24. While expenses billed to Hakluyt were invoiced in round numbers, these expenses were accounted for in detail and some items were claimed for just 75 per cent. Further research by the Swiss group led them to conclude Schlickenrieder was working for at least two German intelligence services, and was dividing his claims at a 75–25 per cent ratio (Nowak, 2001).

25. Federal Office for the Protection of the Constitution, official translation (*Bundesambt für Verfassungsschutz,* 2009).

26. Germany's Federal Criminal Police Office, official translation (*Bundeskriminalamt,* 2009).

27. The secret services present are the Bundesamtes für Verfassungsschutz, Militärische Abschirmdienst, and the Bundesnachtrichtendienst.

28. The text in German: 'Was die Wohnung in ORT anbelangt, die die bekannten *Name* und *Name* zeitweise bewohnen sollen, und das römische Waffenlager, das *Name* und *Name* kennen sollen und aus dem Waffen und Munition beschafft werden können, liegen uns leider noch keine Informationen vor. Wir haben die Anfrage an SISDE weitergeleitet, aber bis jetzt noch keie Antwort erhalten' (MS docs: 31).

29. Calculated by the Aufbau researchers, everything in German Marks: 1.800, – rent for his house; 1.700, – rent for the office; 1.000, – private health insurance; 600, – leasing VW Sharan; 500, – insurance and maintenance BMW Z3; 1.650,- expenses to be declared; totalled 7.250 DM, add food, cloths, holidays makes a budget of 10.000 DM.

30. 'Political. CAAT has produced a list of people as '"best contacts" in the FCO, MoD, DTI, in the House of Lords, among the Conservatives (1), Liberal Democrats, SNP, Plaid Cymru, Defence Select Committee and even the Academic Library. The list in the FCO includes Cook. Andy Hood, a political appointee who used to work for extreme left-winger Jeremy Corbyn; Dr David Mathieson, a special advisor to Cook etc (See Appendix 2)' (ElC, 8 Aug 1997: 2.2).

31. Gane worked for the Group 4 Securitas Head Office until the merger with Falck in 2000, at which point he transferred to Global Solutions Ltd, the custodial services division of Group 4 Falck. GSL was divested from the Group in 2004, after which Gane continued to work for them as a consultant, the head of communications for Group 4 Securicor explained (email to the author, 7 June 2006).

32. Unfortunately, the Department for Transport, incorporating the Highways Agency responsible for roadworks and their security in the 1990s, was not able

to provide information relating to the period before the Department had been formed in May 2002. Before that, the Department was merged with up to two other government departments and therefore records were difficult to access, the Department explained in a first assessment of a FOI request (Devine, 2006).

33. No proof of the thesis or the honorary degree could be found at the University of Kiel. At my request, the dean and the library of the Kiel University verified that no one by the name Evelyn le Chêne finished a doctoral dissertation in 1989 or before that. No work of hers on CBW could be found in the library or its databases (emails to the author: Gabriele Wenzel, Office of the Dean Social Sciences, 17 Nov 2011; Marion Koch, University Library, 9 Nov 2011). The managing director of the Institute for Security Policy at the University of Kiel explained that his is purely a research institute that does not offer any degree. Moreover, as far as he knew, the University of Kiel has never offered a degree in 'National Security Studies' (Stefan Hansen, email to the author, 19 Nov 2011).

34. Present at the KAS board meeting on 2 April 1989: 'D.S., I.C., K.E. E. Le C., J.H.' – referring to: David Stirling, Ian Crooke, Kenneth Edwards, Evelyn le Chêne, John Hanks (KAS, 1989).

Bibliography and References

N.B. All URLs were last visited in July 2011.

ACPO (2008) *Memorandum and articles of association*, version accepted by ballot in June 2008, <www.acpo.police.uk/documents/ArticlesofAssociation.pdf>.

ACPO (2009) Response to article in *Mail on Sunday*, 15 February, <http://tinyurl.com/5uxxb6j>.

Aegis (2005) *AEGIS announces the acquisition of Rubicon International*, 4 November, <http://tinyurl.com/3buh9k7>.

AgBioWorld (2000) *Declaration: Scientists in support of agricultural biotechnology, signers*, 31 January, <www.agbioworld.org/PHP/index.php>.

—— (2005) *Greg Conko biography*, <http://web.archive.org/web/*/www.agbioworld.org/about/greg-bio.html>.

—— (2009a) *About AgBioWorld*, <www.agbioworld.org/about/index.html>.

—— (2009b) *Archives AgBioView newsletter*, <www.agbioworld.org/newsletter_wm/index.php?caseid=archive>.

—— (2009c) *Dr. Channapatna S. Prakash*, <www.agbioworld.org/about/prakash-bio.html>.

—— (2009d) *Mexican maize resource library*, <www.agbioworld.org/biotech-info/articles/biotech-art/mexmaizeresource.html>.

Anderson, D.E. (1982) 'Washington', *United Press International (UPI)*, 11 November.

—— (1987) 'Shell mounts campaign against critics', *United Press International (UPI)*, 1 October.

'Angela B.' (1998) Anonymous letter addressed to Aseed Europe in Amsterdam, 11 May.

Applied Science and Analyses (2009) *The chemical and biological medical treatments symposia*, <www.asanltr.com/cbmts/default.htm>.

Applied Science and Analyses Newsletter (2006) 'Focal point News, ASA's professional associates are on the move in government, industry and academia, vol. 6, no. 117, <www.asanltr.com/newsletter/06-6/articles/Focal.htm>.

Armstrong, F. (1997) *McLibel: Two Worlds Collide*, documentary, 53 minutes, One-Off Productions, London.

—— (2002) 'Using libel laws to shut up critics', in E. Lubbers (ed.), *Battling Big Business: Countering Green Wash, Infiltration and Other Forms of Corporate Bullying*, Greenbooks, Devon, pp. 78–85.

Ascherson, N. (2008) 'A terror campaign of love and hate', *Observer*, 28 September, <www.guardian.co.uk/world/2008/sep/28/germany.terrorism>.

Auerbach, J.S. (1966) *Labor and Liberty: The La Follette Committee and the New Deal*, Bobbs-Merrill Company, Indianapolis, IN.

Baby Milk Action (2005) *Press release: Nestlé's public relation machine exposed*, 25 April, <www.babymilkaction.org/boycott/prmachine05.html>.

Ball, K. and F. Webster (2003) *The Intensification of Surveillance*, Pluto Press, London.

Barrett, J. (1987) 'Washington', *States News Service*, 1 October.

Bartimole, R. (1982) *Nestlé boycott. Nestlé pressures Notre Dame students. Tries splitting church critics,* September, vol. 3, iss. 9, <http://multinationalmonitor. org/hyper/issues/1982/09/bartimole.html>.

Baskin, O., C. Aronoff and D. Lattimore (1997) *Public Relations: The Profession and the Practice,* Brown & Benchmark Publishers, Madison WI.

Baynes, A. (2000) *NGO Strategy,* PowerPoint presentation at a meeting of the European Information and Communication Technology Industry Association, Brussels, 12 July, <http://web.archive.org/web/20070622065557/http://svtc.igc. org/cleancc/graphics/sonyspy.pdf>, currently available at <www.ban.org/whistle/ ee00708.pdf>.

BBC Radio 4 (2002) 'Seeds of Trouble', part one of a two part series on the politics and science of GM food production, 7 January, <www.bbc.co.uk/radio4/science/ seedsoftrouble.shtml>.

Bell, R. (Justice) (1997) *Verdict. The issue of publication of the leaflet,* 17 June, <www.mcspotlight.org/case/trial/verdict/verdict_jud1b.html>.

Beck, U. (2005) *Power in the Global Age: A New Global Political Economy,* Polity Press, Cambridge, UK and Malden, MA.

Beder, S. (1997) *Global Spin: The Corporate Assault on Environmentalism,* Green Books, Devon.

—— (2006) *Suiting Themselves: How Corporations Drive the Global Agenda,* Earthscan, London.

Bergh, E. van der (1995) 'The Dutch campaign against Shell', in R. Hengeveld and J. Rodenburg (eds), *Embargo: Apartheid's Oil Secrets Revealed,* Shipping Research Bureau, Amsterdam University Press, Amsterdam, pp. 306–24.

Bivings, F.G. (2002a) 'Bivings: we condemn online vandalism', *Guardian,* 12 June, <www.guardian.co.uk/theguardian/2002/jun/12/guardianletters5>.

—— (2002b) 'The maize feud', *New Scientist,* 2350, p. 29, <www.newscientist.com/ article/mg17523504.000-the-maize-feud.htm>.

Bivings Group (2002a) *Statement on the Ecologist story entitled 'Amaizing disgrace',* May, <www.ethicalinvesting.com/monsanto/news/10076.htm>.

—— (2006) *The Bivings Group. Wired.Global.Impact,* 3 August, <http://web. archive.org/web/20060803141224/http://bivings.com/>.

—— (2009) *Bivings client list,* <www.bivings.com/clients>.

Bleifuss, J. (1993) 'PR Spies', *In These Times,* 20 September, pp. 12–13.

Boggan, S. and F. Williams (1991) 'WWF bankrolled rhino mercenaries', *Independent,* 17 November, p. 6.

Bok, S. (1982) *Secrets: On the Ethics of Concealment and Revelation,* Pantheon Books, New York, NY.

Bowen, D. (1995) 'Profile: Lord Chalfort, Old soldier above the battle', *Independent,* 28 May, <http://tinyurl.com/7anxe55>.

Branscheidt, H. (1989) 'Gifgaseinsatz in Angola bewiesen, Kubanische Truppen haben chemische Kampfstoffe gegen die Zivilbevölkerung eingesetzt. Der Krieg in Angola dient als Testfeld für neue sowjetische Waffen, *die Tageszeitung,* 25 August, pp. 1, 3.

British Civil Defence (2003) *Welcome to the pages of British Civil Defence. Serving the community for more than 60 years. Motto: survive and protect,* <www. britishcivildefence.org>; more specifically the page on the National Council for Civil Protection, <www.britishcivildefence.org/NCP/ncp.html>.

Brodeur, J.P. (1983) 'High policing and low policing: remarks about the policing of political activities', *Social Problems,* vol. 30, no. 5, pp. 507–20.

Brown, P. (1992) 'Web of African intrigue foils ivory plot', *Guardian*, 2 March, p. 2.

—— (2002) 'Mexico's vital gene reservoir polluted by modified maize', *Guardian*, 19 April, <www.guardian.co.uk/gmdebate/Story/0,2763,686955,00.htm>.

Buckman, R. (1999) 'Gumshoe game on the internet. Companies hire private eyes to unmask online detractors', *Wall Street Journal*, 27 July, p. B1.

Bundesambt für Verfassungsschutz (2009) *Office for the Protection of the Constitution*, <www.verfassungsschutz.de/en/index_en.html>.

Bundeskriminalamt (2009) *International page, English version*, under: 'English', <www.bka.de/>.

Bunting, M. and R. Lipski (2000) 'Drowned out: rethinking corporate reputation management for the internet', *Journal of Communication Management*, vol. 5, no. 2, pp. 170–8.

Burger, M. and C. Gould (2002) *Secrets and Lies: Wouter Basson and South Africa's Chemical and Biological Warfare Programme*, Zebra, Cape Town.

Buro Jansen & Janssen (1990) *Regenjassendemokratie*, Ravijn, Amsterdam.

—— (1991) *De Vluchteling Achtervolgd*, Ravijn, Amsterdam.

—— (1993) *Opening van Zaken, een ander BVD-jaarverslag*, Ravijn, Amsterdam.

—— (1995) *Welingelichte Kringen, inlichtingendienstenjaarboek*, Ravijn, Amsterdam.

—— (1999) *Luisterrijk*, Papieren Tijger, Breda, <www.burojansen.nl/afluisteren/index.html>.

—— (2003) *Misleidende methode*, Papieren Tijger, Breda.

Business Wire (1985) 'Pagan-int formed by public affairs strategists who resolved Nestlé boycott', 10 May.

Bussey, J. (2006) 'Murder in Colombia prompts group to sue Nestlé units in Miami. The widow of a brutally murdered Nestlé worker joins others in a lawsuit against the firm over her husband's death', *Miami Herald*, 28 October, <www.laborrights.org/end-violence-against-trade-unions/colombia/969>.

Byrne, J. (2001) *Protecting your assets: an inside look at the perils and power of the internet*, PowerPoint presentation at the Ragan Strategic Public Relations Conference, v-Fluence Interactive Public Relations, December, <http://tinyurl.com/5tngvzf>.

—— (2002) *Web-savvy PR: the powers & perils of the internet*, PowerPoint presentation at the media relations boot camp for financial services firms, Boston, 24–25 October, <http://tinyurl.com/5wr9uao>.

—— (2003) *Money, marketing & the internet. Key unanticipated and unacknowledged factors influencing agricultural biotechnology public acceptance*, American Enterprise Institute, June, <http://tinyurl.com/6hmpl68>.

CAAT (2003) *Statement on the 'spying' report in the Sunday Times*, London, 28 September, <http://web.archive.org/web/20050308111251/www.caat.org.uk/spying.php>.

CAAT Steering Committee (2004) *Statement regarding Martin Hogbin*, 26 May, <http://web.archive.org/web/20050310235311/www.caat.org.uk/mh-may04.php>.

—— (2005a) *Report of an investigation into suspicious activity of Martin Hogbin*, London, July, <www.caat.org.uk/about/spying/spy-investigation-report.pdf>.

—— (2005b) *Summary of email log information, appendix to the Report of an investigation*, July, <www.caat.org.uk/about/spying/spy-email-breakdown.pdf>.

—— (2005c) *Statement on the spying, following the conclusion of investigations by both the Information Commissioner and the CAAT Steering Committee*, July, <www.caat.org.uk/about/spying.php>.

California Monthly (2002) 'Novartis revisited. Pro: Bob Buchanan – Con: Dr. Ignacio Chapela', February, vol. 112, no. 4, <www.cnr.berkeley.edu/~christos/espm118/articles/novartis_revisited_chapela.html>.

Calvert, J. and D. Connett (1997) 'Cloaks, daggers and Ms X appeal. McDonald's spy had affair with protester', *Observer*, cover story and inside exposé, 26 January, republished at <www.mcspotlight.org/media/press/observer_26jan97.html>.

Campaign Against Arms Trade vs. Paul Mercer and Lignedeux associates (2007) 14 March, <www.caat.org.uk/issues/sfo/CAATvMercer-documents.pdf>.

Campbell, M. and Ch. Gourlay (2009) 'French spies targeted UK Greenpeace', *Sunday Times*, 26 April, <http://business.timesonline.co.uk/tol/business/industry_sectors/utilities/article6169017.ece>.

Campbell, Ph. (2002) Letter to the editor, *Guardian*, 15 May, <www.guardian.co.uk/theguardian/2002/may/15/guardianletters>.

Carey, A. (1995) *Taking the Risk out of Democracy*, University of Illinois Press, Urbana and Chicago, IL.

Carter, S.M. (2002) 'Mongoven, Biscoe & Duchin: destroying tobacco control activism from the inside', *Tobacco Control*, vol. 11, issue 2, pp. 112–18, <www.tobaccofreekids.org/pressoffice/mbdpr.pdf>.

Castells, M. (1996) *The Rise of the Network Society. The Information Age: Economy, Society and Culture*, vol. I, Blackwell, Cambridge, MA.

—— (2003) *The Internet Galaxy: Reflections on the Internet, Business, and Society*, Oxford University Press, Oxford.

Catlin, B. (2000) 'How private is the home computer', *Minnesota Public Radio*, 8 February, <http://news.minnesota.publicradio.org/features/200002/08_catlinb_privacy/>.

Cawthra, G. and R. Luckham (2003) *Governing Insecurity: Democratic Control of Military and Security Establishments in Transitional Democracies*, Zed Books, London.

CEI (2001) *Annual report 2000*, Competitive Enterprise Institute, <www.cei.org/PDFs/2K_annual_report.pdf>.

—— *Gregory Conko biographical information*, Competitive Enterprise Institute, <http://cei.org/people/gregory-conko>.

Lord Chalfont (1987) Letter to Evelyn le Chêne, 28 April, Monique Garnier-Lançot collection, Box 7, Folder 18, Hoover Institution Archive, Stanford, CA.

Chamberlain, Ph. (2008) 'Enemy at the gates', *Guardian*, 28 June, <www.guardian.co.uk/money/2008/jun/28/workandcareers>.

—— (2009) Construction industry blacklisting: the fallout continues, *Guardian*, 21 November, <www.guardian.co.uk/money/2009/nov/21/construction-industry-blacklisting>

Chapman, D.W. (1939) 'Industrial conflict in Detroit', in G.W. Hartmann and T. Newcombe (eds), *Industrial Conflict*, Cordon, New York, NY, pp. 43–102.

Chêne, le, E. (1971) *Mauthausen: The History of a Death Camp*, Methuen, London.

—— (1973) *Watch For Me By Moonlight: A British Agent with the French Resistance*, Eyre Methuen, London.

—— (1985a) Letter to Monique Garnier-Lançot, 30 August, including programme for conference at NATO HQ, 18–19 September, Monique Garnier-Lançot collection, Box 7, Folder 18, Hoover Institution Archive, Stanford, CA.

—— (1985b) 'The outside forces propping up Angola', letter to the editor, *The Times*, 20 September.

—— (1985c) Letter to Monique Garnier-Lançot, 20 September, Monique Garnier-Lançot collection, Box 7, Folder 18, Hoover Institution Archive, Stanford, CA.

—— (1986a) Letter to Rt. Hon. Lord Chalfont at IBM, 31 January, Monique Garnier-Lançot collection, Box 7, Folder 18, Hoover Institution Archive, Stanford, CA.

—— (1986b) Text to go inside W.E.D.A. leaflet: West European Defence Association, cover sheet dated 12 April, Monique Garnier-Lançot collection, Box 7, Folder 18, Hoover Institution Archive, Stanford, CA.

—— (1986c) Covering letter from the director of the West European Defence Association to Menaul, 9 June, to go with Crozier, B. 'International terrorism: How NATO became impotent,' *American Legion Magazine*, the Menaul archives 7/1/465, King's College London, Liddell Hart Centre for Military Archives, <www.kcl.ac.uk/lhcma/cats/menaul/mn0701b.htm>.

—— (1987a) Memorandum to Lord Chalfont and Monique Garnier-Lançot (cc Brian Crozier), 6 March, Monique Garnier-Lançot collection, Box 7, Folder 18, Hoover Institution Archive, Stanford, CA.

—— (1987b) Letter to the Rt. Hon. The Lord Chalfont, 7 May, Monique Garnier-Lançot collection, Box 7, Folder 18, Hoover Institution Archive, Stanford, CA.

—— (1988) *Costing for Project Lock, 5 Jan–7 Mar 1988*, invoice for KAS Enterprises issued by Risk and Crisis Analysis, 9 March.

—— (1989) *Chemical and Biological Warfare: Threat of the Future*, Mackenzie Institute for the Study of Terrorism, Revolution and Propaganda, National Intelligence Book Center, Mackenzie Paper, no. 11, Toronto.

—— (1994a) *Silent Heroes: The Bravery and Devotion of Animals at War*, Souvenir Press, London.

—— (1994b) 'Security of populations from criminal use of the eco-terrorism', *Applied Science and Analyses Newsletter*, vol. 4, p. 4.

—— (1994c) 'The threat to society and the environment from use of chemical and biological agents by illegal organisations', paper presented at the European Round Table conference: the security of the citizen due to a possible abuse of the environment, Europe 2000, Freedom, Democracy, Stability, Strasbourg, 12–14 October.

—— (1998) *Eco-terrorism, industry, and civilian population*, paper presented at the Chemical and Biological Medical Treatment Symposium, 25–31 October, Dubrovnik, Croatia, Proceedings of the CB MTS Industry-I, Applied Science and Analysis, Portland, MA.

—— (2000) 'Growing danger of biological weapons', *Applied Science and Analyses Newsletter*, 27 October, vol. 5, no. 80, pp. 8–9.

Chêne, le, E. and H. Her (2001) *The Hidden Agenda: Anglo-Dutch affair – Penetration of the Dutch Secret Service by the Germans*, Pen & Sword Books/ Leo Cooper, London (announced, but never published).

Chetley, A. (1986) *The Politics of Baby Foods: Successful Challenges to an International Marketing Strategy*, Frances Pinter, London.

Chittenden, M. and N. Rufford (2001) 'MI6 "firm" spied on green groups', *Sunday Times*, 17 June, republished at <www.commondreams.org/headlines01/0617-01.htm>.

Chomsky, N. and E. Herman (1988) *Manufacturing Consent: The Political Economy of the Mass Media*, Pantheon Books, London.

Christen Democratische Verkenningen (1988) Vermaatschappelijking en het Zuid-Afrika-beleid, pp. 40–5.

Church Committee or Select Committee to Study Governmental Operations with respect to intelligcence activities, United State Senate (1976) *Intelligence Activities and the Rights of Americans,* Final Report, Book II, April, see for instance: <www.icdc.com/~paulwolf/cointelpro/churchfinalreportIIa.htm>.

Churchill, W. and J. Vander Wall (2001) *The COINTELPRO papers: documents from the FBI's secret wars against dissent in the United States,* South End Press, Cambridge, MA.

Clover, Ch. (2002) '"Worst ever" GM crop invasion', *Daily Telegraph,* 19 April, <http://tinyurl.com/5s9koxb>.

Committee on Interior and Insular Affairs (1992) *Alyeska Pipeline Service Company covert operation. Oversight hearings before the Committee on Interior and Insular Affairs, House of Representatives. One hundred second congress, first session. Hearings held in Washington, DC, November 4, 5, and 6, 1991,* United States Printing House, Washington, DC, viewed 12 June 2009, <www.alaskaforum.org/rowhist/Congress/102Congress.pdf>.

Companies House (2006) *R. & C. A. (Risk Crisis Analysis) Publications Ltd, file 02443409,* company information.

—— (2007) *Caprim. Abbreviated accounts for the year ended 30th April 2007 for Caprim Ltd. Registered Number: 2792569,* company information.

—— (2008) *Caprim. Annual Return. Company Number: 2792569,* 14 February, company information.

Connett, D. and M. Gillard (2003a) 'Arms firm waged dirty war on protesters. How the woman at no. 27 ran spy network for an arms firm', *Sunday Times,* Insight Team, 28 September, cover story, <www.timesonline.co.uk/tol/news/uk/article1164036.ece> and inside <www.timesonline.co.uk/tol/news/uk/article1163959.ece>.

—— (2003b) 'Security firm spied on road protesters', *Sunday Times,* Insight Team, 5 October, <www.timesonline.co.uk/tol/news/uk/article1166422.ece>.

Corporate Watch (2009) *Watching the corporations. Blacklisting workers in the construction industry,* 21 May, <www.corporatewatch.org.uk/?lid=3386>.

Cox, B. (2000) 'Be careful what you say online – Big Brother is probably listening', *eCommerce Guide,* 17 July, <www.ecommerce-guide.com/news/trends/article.php/415491>.

Crane, T.Y. (1977) *What is issue management? Clarification of terms,* Issue Management Council, <http://issuemanagement.org/learnmore/clarification-of-terms/>.

Cronin, B. and H. Crawford (1999) 'Raising the intelligence stakes: corporate information warfare and strategic surprise', *Competitive Intelligence Review,* vol. 10 no. 3, pp. 58–66.

Crozier, B. (1993) *Free Agent: The Unseen War 1941–1991,* HarperCollins, London.

—— (1998) 'Letters: Churchill, the CIA and Clinton', *Guardian,* 3 August.

Daragahi, B. (2000) 'Private eyes who watch the web', *Web Watch,* 11 July, <http://tinyurl.com/3e8ktuy>.

Dawe, T. (1987) 'British hero's widow to testify against Barbie', *The Times,* May 9.

Defense News (2009) *Defense news top 100,* (ranking based on 2007), Defense Revenue, <www.defensenews.com/static/features/top100/charts/top100_08.php?c=FEA&s=T1C>.

Delborne, J. (2005) 'Pathways of scientific dissent in agricultural biotechnology', PhD thesis, Environmental Science, Policy, and Management, University of California, Berkeley, CA, <http://tinyurl.com/3auaumx>.

Denig, E. and A. van der Meiden (eds) (1985) *A Geography of PR Trends: Selected Proceedings of the 10th PR world congress: 'Between People and Power'*, Martinus Nijhoff Publishers, Amsterdam and Dordrecht.

Detectives PI (2009) *About Us, Cameron H. Craig*, <www.detectivespi.com/index_files/AboutUS.htm>.

DeWitt, D. (2000) 'Corporate stalking', *Citizen Engineer*, EE Expert Lee Goldberg Technology, Society, and the Environment, 18 July.

Diederichs, O. (2001) 'Der Mann, der Camus war', *die Tageszeitung*, 3 February, republished at <www.libertad.de/inhalt/spezial/gruppe2/taz030201.shtml>.

Diederichs, O. and H. Stark, (2000) 'Greenpeace. Das Auge der Multies. Im Auftrag der Öl-Industrie soll ein Dokumentarfilmer die Umweltschützer ausspioniert haben', *die Tageszeitung,* 10 December, republished at <www.tagesspiegel.de/zeitung/greenpeace-das-auge-der-multis/185438.html>.

—— (2001) 'Der Top-informant – Im falschen Film', *Tagesspiegel,* 29 January, republished at <www.libertad.de/inhalt/spezial/gruppe2/tsp290101.shtml>.

Dieren, van, W. (1986) 'Pagan International vertelt wat management hoopt te horen', *NRC Handelsblad*, 24 December.

Digital Discovery team of Harvard Law School students (2000) *Case Study: North West Airlines*, The Berkman Centre of Internet & Society at Harvard Law School, <http://cyber.law.harvard.edu/digitaldiscovery/digdisc_library_1.html>.

Dimock, A. (2002a) *Viral marketing: how to infect the world,* [unedited version], Bivings Group, 1 April, <http://tinyurl.com/3ergmcb>.

—— (2002b) *Viral marketing: how to infect the world* [edited version], Bivings Group, 1 April, <www.bivingsreport.com/2002/viral-marketing-how-to-infect-the-world/>.

Dinan, W. and D. Miller (2007) *Thinker, Faker, Spinner, Spy: Corporate PR and the Assault on Democracy*, Pluto Press, London.

Doane, D. (2005a) 'The Myth of CSR. The problem with assuming that companies can do well while also doing good is that markets don't really work that way', *Stanford Social Innovation Review*, Fall, <www.ssireview.com/pdf/2005FA_Feature_Doane.pdf>.

—— (2005b) 'Beyond corporate social responsibility: minnows, mammoths and markets', *Futures*, vol. 27, no. 2–3, pp. 215–29, <www.corporation2020.org/documents/Resources/Doane_CSR.pdf>.

Dobbing, J. (1988) *Infant Feeding: Anatomy of a Controversy 1973–1984*, Springer Verlag, New York, NY.

Donner, F. (1990) *Protectors of Privilege: Red Squads and Police Repression in Urban America*, University of California Press, Berkeley, CA.

Dover, R.M. (2007) 'Grandma's army: arms trade intelligence and campaign groups', paper presented at the British International Studies Association Conference, Cambridge, December.

—— (2008) 'Digging for victory: BAE Systems and the Campaign Against the Arms Trade', [under review], *Intelligence and National Security.*

Draulans, D. (2009) '500.000 euro gevonden. Justitie', *Knack Magazine*, May 27, p. 16.

Drimmelen, van, R. (1987) Letter from the World Council of Churches to R. Pagan, Pagan International, Washington, DC, 16 October, held in the Aluka archives, <http://tinyurl.com/66pwktj>.

Drohan, M. (2003) *Making a Killing. How and Why Corporations Use Armed Force to do Business*, The Lyons Press, Guilford, CT.

Duchin, R.A. (1991) 'Take an activist apart and what do you have?' *CALF News Cattle Feeder*, June p. 9, p. 14.

Eco-Action (1996a) *Do killer profits exist?! Death, oil, banks and the $$$ game!* (author: Adrian Franks/Le Chêne).

—— (1996b) *Eurosatory '98 'Against the Arms Trade Campaign'* (author: Adrian Franks/Le Chêne).

—— (1996c) *Blood Oil, and Money – The Interests and Arms of the Petrol Industry* (author: Adrian Franks/Le Chêne).

Economist (2009) 'Big Brother bosses. More than ever, companies want to know what their employees are up to', 10 September, <www.economist.com/business-finance/displaystory.cfm?story_id=14413380>.

Edwards, R. (2009) Revealed: a web of police bids to infiltrate protest groups, *Sunday Herald,* 25 April, <www.heraldscotland.com/revealed-a-web-of-police-bids-to-infiltrate-protest-groups-1.826304>.

EICTA (2009a) *The recovery will be ... digital!,* Home page, <www.eicta.org/> see also <http://tinyurl.com/6fgzrh6>.

—— (2009b) *Members*, <www.eicta.org/index.php?id=8>.

Eine Deutsche Genossin (2001) *Erklärung einer deutschen Genossin*, News, Schweiz/Deutschland, Rev. Aufbau, 7 April, <www.libertad.de/inhalt/spezial/gruppe2/erkldtgen.shtml>.

Elliott, C., R. Ford and J. Lanale (1993) 'Senior appointment boosts Group 4's international work', *The Times*, 26 May.

Ellis, S. (1991a) 'Prince paid thousands into wildlife sting. The World Wide Fund for Nature is disowning a secret project to fight rhino poachers, which collapsed with funds and horn stocks missing', *Independent*, 8 January, p. 8.

—— (1991b) 'Prins Berharnd sponsored onbedoeld stropers. De lange arm van het Wereld Natuur Fonds', *Volkskrant,* 24 August.

Eppink, D-J. (1990a) 'Belgische geleerde zoekt in Angola een "chemische bom"', *NRC Handelsblad*, 3 March.

—— (1990b) 'Onderzoekers: leger Angola gebruikte chemische wapens', *NRC Handelsblad*, 19 April.

European Commission (2000) *Communication from the Commission on the precautionary principle*, 52000DC0001, EuroLex, <http://tinyurl.com/5rf8x28>.

Evans, M. (1993) 'Freelance who was KGB's enemy no. 1', *The Times*, 28 June.

Evans, R. (2009) 'Alan Wainwright: The lonely life of a construction industry whistleblower. Former manager exposed how workers were being secretly blacklisted. This week, Lord Mandelson acted', *Guardian*, 15 May, <http://tinyurl.com/qjpy8y>.

Evans, R. (2011) 'How many more inquiries will there be into the undercover infiltration? Twelve inquiries have so far been set up since the revelations about police spy Mark Kennedy emerged', *Guardian*, 2 november, <http://tinyurl.com/brrgfvy>.

Evans, R., S. Carrell and H. Carter (2009) 'Man behind illegal blacklist snooped on workers for 30 years. Investigator faces fine or jail for privacy breach. Leading construction firms bought data on workers', *Guardian*, 27 May, <www.guardian.co.uk/uk/2009/may/27/construction-worker-blacklist-database1>.

Evans, R., A. Hill, P. Lewis and P. Kingsley (2011) 'Mark Kennedy: secret policeman's sideline as corporate spy. Former undercover officer apparently also worked privately as a corporate spy using the same false identity', *Guardian*, 13 January, <www.guardian.co.uk/environment/2011/jan/12/mark-kennedy-policeman-corporate-spy>.

Evans, R. and D. Leigh (2004) 'Campaigner a BAE mole, anti-arms group says', *Guardian*, 29 May, <www.guardian.co.uk/uk/2004/may/29/politics.armstrade>.

—— (2007) 'BAE spy named by campaigners is friend of leading Tory', *Guardian*, 19 April, <www.guardian.co.uk/world/2007/apr/19/bae.armstrade>.

Evans, R. and P. Lewis (2011) 'Second undercover officer accused of misleading court. Bob Lambert, who ran a network of police spies in the protest movement, suspected of having been prosecuted under his alias', *Guardian*, 21 October, <http://tinyurl.com/7lq8vx3>.

Evans, R., P. Lewis and M. Taylor (2009) 'How police rebranded lawful protest as "domestic extremism" Forces gather details of single-issue protesters. Activists claim monitoring has echoes of the cold war', 25 October, <www.guardian.co.uk/uk/2009/oct/25/police-surveillance-protest-domestic-extremism>.

eWatch, (1999a) *Comprehensive, accurate, trusted internet monitoring. Making headlines,* 25 January, <http://web.archive.org/web/19990125095202/www.ewatch.com/>.

—— (1999b) *Comprehensive, accurate, trusted internet monitoring. Making headlines,* 8 February, <http://web.archive.org/web/19990208013034/www.ewatch.com/>.

—— (2000a) *Comprehensive, accurate, trusted internet monitoring. Making headlines*, 20 June, <http://web.archive.org/web/20000620091631/www.ewatch.com/>.

—— (2000b) *Comprehensive, accurate, trusted internet monitoring. Making headlines*, 15 Augustus, <http://web.archive.org/web/20000815073736/www.ewatch.com/>.

—— (2000c) *Cybersleuth*, <http://web.archive.org/web/20000818003808/www.ewatch.com/pop_sleuth.html>.

—— (2000d) 'Online monitoring goes beyond anonymous postings press release, investigative service to uncover identities of malicious attackers, press release announcing the agreement between eWatch and ICG', 18 June, *PRNewswire*, <www.e-commercealert.com/article79.shtml>.

—— (2000e) *Comprehensive, accurate, trusted internet monitoring. Making headlines,* 20 June, <http://web.archive.org/web/20000620091631/www.ewatch.com/>.

—— (2000f) *Comprehensive, accurate, trusted internet monitoring. Making headlines,* 15 September, <http://web.archive.org/web/20000815073736/www.ewatch.com/>.

—— (2009) *eWatch product information,* <http://info.prnewswire.com/ewatch/logincontent/product_info.shtml>.

Europe Intelligence Wire (1997) 'Monday profile. The detective with his eyes always on the inside view. Stan Hardy is a detective with a difference', *Yorkshire Post*, 19 May.

Foley, S. (2007) 'Fired Wal-Mart "spy" embroils retailer in surveillance scandal', *Independent*, 5 April, <www.independent.co.uk/news/business/news/fired-walmart-spy-embroils-retailer-in-surveillance-scandal-443441.html>.

Foot, P. (1991) Series of articles on blacklisting and the Economic League in the *Daily Mirror*, 25 September–3 October (in Scotland the *Daily Record* for the same period used the same sources for its exposé of the League's blacklist).

Ganser, D. (2005) NATO's Secret Armies: *Operation Gladio and Terrorism in Western Europe*, Frank Cass, London and New York.

Garland, D. (2001) *The Culture of Control*, Oxford University Press, Oxford.

Gelbspann, R. (1999) *Break-Ins, Death threaths and the FBI: The Covert War against the Central America Movement*, South End Press, Cambridge, MA.

Gifford, T. (2011) Unmasking the environmental infiltrators, SpinWatch.org, 19 January, <www.spinwatch.org/-articles-by-category-mainmenu-8/54-corporate-intelligence/5418-unmasking-the-environmental-infiltrators>.

Gill, M. and J. Hart (1999) 'Enforcing corporate security policy using private investigators', *European Journal on Criminal Policy and Research*, no. 7, pp. 245–61.

Gill, P. (2008) 'Theories of intelligence. Where are we, where should we go and how might we proceed?' in Gill, P., M. Phythian and S. Marrin (eds), *Intelligence Theory: Key Debates and Questions*, Taylor and Francis, London, pp. 208–26.

—— (2009) 'Knowing the self, knowing the other: the comparative analysis of security intelligence', in L. Johnson, *Handbook of intelligence studies*, Routledge, London. pp. 82–9.

Gill, P. and M. Phythian (2006) *Intelligence in an Insecure World*, Polity Press, Cambridge.

Glick, B. (1999) *War at Home: Covert Action against U.S. Activists and What We Can Do About It*, South End Press, Classics Series, Volume, 7, Cambridge, MA.

Global Witness (2005) *Paying for protection, the Freeport mine and the Indonesian security forces*, <www.globalwitness.org/media_library_detail.php/139/en/paying_for_protection>.

Gould, C. and M. Burger (2000) 'Hearing of Brian Davey', *The South African Chemical and Biological Warfare program, Truth and Reconciliation Commission, Trial report 28*, 4–8 September.

Gould, C. and P. Folb (2002) *Project Coast: Apartheid's Chemical and Biological Warfare Programme*, United Nations Institute for Disarmament, Geneva and Centre for Conflict Resolution, Cape Town, <www.unidir.org/pdf/ouvrages/pdf-1-92-9045-144-0-en.pdf>.

Goulden, J. (1994) 'Crozier, covert acts, CIA and Cold War', *Washington Times*, 15 May.

Gray, R. (2001) 'Thirty years of social accounting, reporting and auditing: what (if anything) have we learned?', *Business Ethics: A European Review*, no. 10, pp. 9–15.

Gray, R. and J. Bebbington (2007) 'Corporate sustainability, accountability and the pursuit of the impossible dream', in G.S. Atkinson, S. Dietz and E. Numeyer (eds), *Handbook of Sustainable Development,* Edward Elgar, Cheltenham.

Greef, de, W. (2002) 'Subject: Where is the *Nature* editorial?', list server, 24 April, AgBioView, <www.agbioworld.org/newsletter_wm/index.php?caseid=archive&newsid=1404>.

Green, S.D. (2000) 'Internet hoaxes', *Revolution, Business and Marketing in the Digital Economy*, <www.sherrigreen.com/Internet%20Hoaxes.htm>.

Greenpeace (1997) *Putting the lid on fossil fuels,* <http://archive.greenpeace.org/climate/atlantic/reports/lidful.html>.

—— (1999/2000) *Visitor statistics,* <http://web.archive.org/web/*/www.greenpeace.org/Admin/usage/>.

Gruner, S. (2001) 'He's not Sam Spade, but the web detective digs his work', *Wall Street Journal,* 17 January.

Gruppe 2 in cooperation with AutorInnenkollktiv (1997) *Business as usual oder die Arroganz der Macht. Shell und Nigeria – Ein Jahr nach der Ermorderung von Ken Saro Wiwa,* documentary, VHS/S-VHS, 60 min.

Haas, de, J. and M. Koolhoven (1993a) 'Autonoom Centrum op de korrel bij politie. onderzoek naar brand Grenshospitium', *Telegraaf,* 12 July.

—— (1993b) 'De tentakels van de RaRa, activistisch Nederland op de bres voor illegale vluchtelingen en asielzoekers', *Telegraaf,* 24 July.

Haas, de, J. (1994) 'Zuid Afrika missie ernstig in de problemen', *Telegraaf,* 22 April.

Haas, de, J and C. Sanders (1997b) 'De tentakels van de Tamils. Harde kern Nederlandse activisten steunt vluchtelingen uit Sri Lanka al sinds jaren '80', *Telegraaf,* 20 February.

—— (1997c) 'De bloedbroeders van de PKK. Ook Pax Christi onderhield jarenlang banden met Koerdische guerrilla', *Telegraaf,* 12 April.

Hager, N. and B. Burton (1999) *Secrets and Lies: Anatomy of an Anti-Environmental PR Campaign,* Graig Potton, Nelson.

Hallerbach, R. (1989) 'Angola als Versuchslabor für chemische Kampfstoffe?', Europäische Wehrkunde/WRR, vol. 7, pp. 433–5.

Hamdan, F. (2001a) *Mail to staff of GP Germany today to inform you about the case,* Greenpeace Germany, 18 June.

—— (2001b) *Zeitschiene zu Schlickenrieder bei GP,* Greenpeace Germany.

Hamelink, C.J. (1994) *The Politics of World Communication: A Human Rights Perspective,* Sage Publications, London.

—— (2000) *The Ethics of Cyberspace,* Sage Publications, London, originally published as *Digitaal fatsoen* (1999) Uitgeverij Boom, Holland.

Hamilton, P. (1997) *Putting the Pressure On: The Rise of Pressure Activism in Europe,* The Communication Group, Entente International Communication, London.

Hansen, S. (2007) 'From "common observation" to behavioural risk management: workplace surveillance and employee assistance 1914–2003', in S.P. Hier and J. Greenberg (eds), *The surveillance studies reader,* Open University Press, McGraw Hill, Maidenhead.

Harknett, J. (2006) *Decision on Freedom of Information Request reference no. 2006040007370,* signed by the Information Manager, Metropolitan Police Service, 5 October.

Harvard Law Review (1939) 'Industrial police and espionage', March, pp. 793–804.

Heath, R.L. (1997) *Strategic issue management, organisations and public policy challenges,* Sage, Thousands Oaks, CA.

Helvarg, D. (1994) *The War Against the Greens: The 'Wise Use' Movement, the New Right and Anti-environmental Violence,* Sierra Club Books, San Francisco.

Hencke, D. (2000) 'Left blacklist man joins euro fight', *Guardian,* 9 September, <www.guardian.co.uk/business/2000/sep/09/emu.theeuro>.

Hengeveld, R. and J. Rodenburg (eds) (1995) *Embargo: Apartheid's Oil Secrets Revealed,* Shipping Research Bureau, Amsterdam University Press, Amsterdam.

Herbst, J. (2004) 'Analex buys Beta Analytics', *Washington Business Journal*, 7 May, <http://washington.bizjournals.com/washington/stories/2004/05/03/daily35. html>.

Herman, M. (1996) *Intelligence Power in Peace and War*, Cambridge University Press in association with The Royal Institute of International Affairs, Cambridge.

Herron, O. (1990) *Interview with James Armstrong*, Chicago Sunday Evening Club, 11 November, <www.csec.org/csec/sermon/Armstrong_3406.htm>.

Hess, D. and T.W. Dunfee (2007) 'Corporate social reporting: implementing a standard of optimal truthful disclosure as a solution', *Business Ethics Quarterly*, vol. 17, no. 1, pp. 3–30.

Heyndrickx, A. (1989) 'Slachtoffers van chemische oorlog leven als planten', *NRC Handelsblad*, 9 November.

Hodgson, G. (1987) 'The BBC and the Politicians' (extract), *Observer*, 13 December, republished at <www.julianlewis.net/cuttings_detail.php?id=13>.

Hoff, van der, E. (2006) 'C&A tobt met de vergrijzing', *Algemeen Dagblad*, Rotterdam, 25 April.

Hollingsworth, M. and R. Norton-Taylor (1988) *Blacklist: The Inside Story of Political Vetting*, Hogarth Press, London.

Hollingsworth, M. and Ch. Tremayne (1989) *The Economic League: The Silent McCarthyism*, Liberty, London.

Holmes Report, The (1999) *PR agency report card*, <http://tinyurl.com/6fh5tgh>.

Hoogenboom, A.B. (1994) *Het politiecomplex. Over de samenwerking tussen politie, bijzondere opsporingsdiensten en particuliere recherche*, Gouda Quint, Arnhem.

—— (2005) '"Grey intelligence": de private toekomst van inlichtingendiensten', in ed. H. Matthijs, *Geheime diensten in Benelux, Israël en de Verenigde Staten: For your eyes only?* Die Keure, Brugge, 2005, pp. 161–78, <www.nisa-intelligence. nl/PDF-bestanden/GreyIntelligence.pdf>.

—— (2006) 'Grey intelligence', *Crime, Law and Social Change*, Springer Netherlands, vol. 45, no. 4–5, pp. 373–81.

Horsley, W. (2006) 'Secret retreat marks 60 years of diplomacy', *BBC news*, 12 January, <http://news.bbc.co.uk/2/hi/uk_news/4602986.stm>.

House of Commons Hansard (1990) 19 May, column 1081, <www.publications. parliament.uk/pa/cm198990/cmhansrd/1990-05-17/Debate-11.html>.

Hudson, K. (2009) Soviet funding? Rubbish, Campaign for Nuclear Disarmament, blog, 26 November, <www.cnduk.org/index.php/media/item/812-soviet-funding?-rubbish>.

Hughes, M. (1994a) *Spies at work*, 1 in 12 publications, Bradford, <www.PowerBase. info/index.php/Spies_at_Work>.

—— (1994b) 'Chapter 1: Origins and Early Days,', in *Spies at work, 1 in 12 publications*, Bradford, <www.PowerBase.info/index.php/Spies_at_Work%2C_Chapter_1:_Origins_and_Early_Days>.

—— (1994c) 'Chapter 2: The diehards' hidden hand', in *Spies at work*, 1 in 12 publications, Bradford, <http://tinyurl.com/74p6m8o>.

—— (1994d) 'Chapter 11: The fall', in *Spies at work*, 1 in 12 publications, Bradford, <www.PowerBase.info/index.php/Spies_at_Work%2C_Chapter_11:_The_Fall>.

Hyer, M. (1984) 'Former activist clergyman tries new corporate role', *Washington Post*, 22 December, p. F10.

INSEE (1998) *Company information for Risk Crisis Analysis,* Institut National de la Statistique et des études économiques (National Institute for Statistics and Economic Studies), no. Siren: 411 015 241.

Inside EPA Weekly Report (2000) 'Industry goes on global offensive against toxics activists: targeting funding, internet activities', vol. 21, no. 37, 15 September, <http://web.archive.org/web/20070709100851/http://svtc.igc.org/listserv/letter70.htm>.

Inside PR (1999) '1999 Agency report card Bivings Woodell', <http://web.archive.org/web/20000821171841/www.bivings.com/news/insidepr.html>.

Intelligence Newsletter (1999) 'Dearlove's appointment good news for some, Business intelligence notes: UK', 26 August.

—— (2000) 'Hakluyt a well-connected company', 15 June.

Intelligence Online (2005) 'Hakluyt talks to the bosses', 2 September.

—— (2006a) 'Hakluyt casts net wide for talent. Business intelligence and lobbying', 13 January.

—— (2006b) 'Hakluyt founder calls it a day', 10 February.

'Jeanne' (1998) anonymous letter warning against Adrian Franks/le Chêne, addressed to *Action Update*, Earth First! Newsletter, June.

Johnson, D. (1981) 'A glimpse at Nestlé's anti-boycott strategy', *Business and Society Review*, iss. 37, pp. 65–7.

Johnson, L.K. (ed.) (2009) *Handbook of Intelligence Studies*, Routledge, London.

Johnston, L. (2007) 'Glocal heroes: transnational private security companies in the twenty-first century', inaugural lecture at the Institute of Criminal Justice Studies, University of Portsmouth, 20 June.

Juris, J. (2008) *Networking futures, the movement against corporate globalisation*, Duke University Press, Durham, NC.

KAS (1989) *Confidential minutes of board meeting Operation Lock*, London, 2 April.

KAS/Crooke, I. (1988) *letter to HRH Prince Bernhard of the Netherlands* (marked: KAS/T/140 private and confidential), 25 July.

—— (1989) *Operation Lock, situation report*, covering period 18 January–31 May 1989 (marked: secret, no unauthorised dissemination, limited distribution), June.

Katholiek Nieuwsblad (1987) 'Zwarte geestelijken VS wijzen sancties tegen Z-Afrika af, Boycot zou niet-blanken het zwaarst treffen', 31 March.

Kean, Y.J. and A. Allain (eds) (2004) *Breaking the Rules, Stretching the Rules: Evidence of Violations of the International Code of Marketing of Breast Milk Substitutes and Subsequent Resolutions*, International Baby Food Action Network, Penang, Malaysia.

Kein Friede (2000) *Der Landeskonservator, Zur Enttarnung der „gruppe 2" und Manfred Schlickenrieder*, 3 December, <www.libertad.de/inhalt/spezial/gruppe2/kf031200.shtml>.

Kent, S. (1946) 'Prospects for the National Intelligence Service', *Yale Review*, vol. 36, no. 1, Autumn.

Kilmann, S. and H. Cooper (1999) 'Crops blight: Monsanto falls flat trying to sell Europe on bioengineered food. Its soybeans are safe, say trade officials, but public doesn't want to hear it. Mad-cow and Englishmen', *Wall Street Journal*, 11 May, p. A1, A10, republished at <www.organicconsumers.org/Monsanto/noselleuro.cfm>.

Kitchen Ph. J. (1997) *Public relations: Principles and Practice*, Cengage Learning EMEA, London.

Klein, N. (2000) *No Logo*, Random House, Toronto.

—— (2002) in E. Lubbers (ed.) *Battling Big Business: Countering Greenwash, Infiltration and Other Forms of Corporate Bullying*, Greenbooks, Devon.

Knight, D. (2000) 'Sony Corporation tracks environmental organisations', *Inter Press Service*, 15 September, <http://web.archive.org/web/20070709044541/http://svtc. igc.org/cleancc/sonyspy.htm>.

Koch, E. (1996) 'Military implicated in poaching', *IPS*, 22 January.

Koch, L.Z. (2000) 'Walking along a fine line; Opinion', NetInteractiveWeek, *Znet*, <http://web.archive.org/web/20021209103521/www.lzkoch.com/column_17. html>.

Koolhoven, M. (1996) 'BVD vreest terreur op Schiphol. En: Wijnand Duyvendak, een leven vol verzet', *Telegraaf*, 18 October.

—— (1997) 'Actiegroep steunt terroristen in Peru. Ambassade vraagt opheldering', *Telegraaf*, 24 January.

Kumleben Commission (1995) *Commission of Inquiry into the alleged smuggling of and illegal trade in ivory and rhinoceros horn in South Africa: Evidence presented to the Inquiry, (chairman: the Honourable Mr Justice M E Kumleben)*, Durban, September–October.

Kunczik, M. (1990) *Die Manipulierte Meinung: Nationale Image-Politik und Internationale Public Relations*, Böhlau Verlag, Cologne and Vienna.

Labour Notes (1988) 'Shell's "Neptune Strategy" aims at countering anti-apartheid boycott', no. 106, January, p. 1, <www.cpcs.umb.edu/labor_notes/files/10601. pdf> and p.11 <www.cpcs.umb.edu/labor_notes/files/10611.pdf>.

Lambert, R. (2011) Bob Lambert replies to Spinwatch open letter on police infiltration, *SpinWatch.org*, 24 October, <http://ow.ly/76gco>.

Laqueur, W. (1985) *A World of Secrets: The Uses and Limits of Intelligence*, Basic Books, New York, NY.

Lee, R.M. (1993) *Doing Research on Sensitive Topics*, Sage Publications, London.

Lewis, Jason (2009) Body in charge of UK policing policy is now an £18m-a-year brand charging the public £70 for a 60p criminal records check, *Mail on Sunday*, 15 February, <http://tinyurl.com/d39xjx>.

Lewis, Julian (2011) Dr Julian Lewis, MP, website, Bibliographical information, <www.julianlewis.net/biography.php>.

Lewis, M. (2005) 'Don't tar Disarm with this, media coordinator for CAAT in a statement,' list server Indymedia.uk, in the discussion following Terry, 2005, <www.indymedia.org.uk/en/2005/07/319686.html?c=on>.

Lewis, P. (2009) Police caught on tape trying to recruit Plane Stupid protester as spy. Climate change activist taped men who offered cash for information about group's members and activities, *Guardian*, 24 April, <http://tinyurl.com/6vmr5lg>.

Lewis, P. and R. Evans (2011a) Green groups targeted polluters as corporate agents hid in their ranks, Special report: After revelations of police spying, the focus turns to firms paid to infiltrate protesters, *Guardian*, 14 February, <http://tinyurl. com/7awctgm>.

—— (2011b) Police spy tricked lover with activist 'cover story'. Bob Lambert used false identity in 1980s to infiltrate protest movements while working for Metropolitan police special branch, *Guardian*, 23 October, <http://tinyurl. com/6wapcrg>.

—— (2011c) Undercover police: how 'romantic, attentive' impostor betrayed activist. I feel angry and violated, says woman apparently used as cover by officer who was trying to infiltrate Animal Liberation Front, *Guardian*, 23 October, <http:// tinyurl.com/6wapcrg>.

Lewis, P., R. Evans and M. Taylor (2009) Police in £9m scheme to log 'domestic extremists'. Thousands of activists monitored on network of overlapping databases, *Guardian*, 25 October, <www.guardian.co.uk/uk/2009/oct/25/police-domestic-extremists-database>.

Lewis, P. and R. Evans (2011) 'Police spy tricked lover with activist "cover story"', *Guardian*, 23 October, <http://ow.ly/76gn2>.

Lietz, G. (1997) *Agendasetting: PR-Kampf um Brent-Spar*, GRIN Verlag, Munchen.

Livesey, S.M. (2001) 'Eco-identity as discursive struggle: Royal Dutch/Shell, Brent Spar, and Nigeria', *Journal of Business Communication*, vol. 38, no. 1, pp. 58–91.

London Greenpeace (1986a) *What's wrong with McDonald's? Everything they don't want you to know* [long version] London, <www.mcspotlight.org/case/pretrial/factsheet.html>.

—— *What's wrong with McDonald's?* [short version] London, <www.mcspotlight.org/case/pretrial/factsheet_new.html>.

Losa, M. and J.P. Ceppi (2008) 'Securitas: un privé qui vous surveille', *Temps Présents*, 12 June, <www.tsr.ch/tsr/index.html?siteSect=370501&sid=9209396>.

Love, J. <love@cptech.org> (2000) 'eWatch and CyberSleuth', list server, 30 June, Random Bits, <http://lists.essential.org/pipermail/random-bits/2000-June/000180.html>.

Lovink, G. and E. Lubbers (1983) *'t Moet kunnen... Een skriptie over een bewegingsgebonden alternatief weekblad*, thesis, Faculty of Political Science, University of Amsterdam.

Lubbers, E. (1994a) 'Liefdewerk Oudpapier Spionage in de Derde-Wereldbeweging', *onzeWereld,* Amsterdam, July/August, <www.evel.nl/onzewer.htm>.

—— (1994b) 'Garbologie. Een alternatieve vorm van bedrijfsspionage', <www.evel.nl/bobh.htm>.

—— (1995a) 'Liefdewerk oudpapier wordt vervolgd,' in Buro Jansen & Janssen, *Welingelichte Kringen*, Ravijn, Amsterdam, <www.evel.nl/oudpap.htm>.

—— (1995b) 'Court Drama. McDonald's vindt het niet leuk meer', *Vrij Nederland*, Amsterdam, 2 December, <www.evel.nl/mclibel.htm>.

—— (1996) 'De Telegraaf, Milieudefensie, en de oud papier-affaire', *Ravage*, November, Amsterdam, <www.evel.nl/wijnand.htm>.

—— (1997a,) 'De Telegraaf en het links complot', *de Journalist*, 21 March, <www.evel.nl/jour.htm>.

—— (1997b) 'McSpy. Mag ik u infiltreren?', *de Groene Amsterdammer*, Amsterdam, 12 March, <www.evel.nl/mcspy.htm>.

—— (1998a) 'Het geweten van Shell. Politiek correct ondernemen in de jaren negentig', *Inzet*, Amsterdam, July, <www.evel.nl/inekenw.htm>.

—— (1998b) 'The Brent Spar syndrome, counterstrategies against online activism', *Telepolis,* 22 September, <www.heise.de/tp/r4/artikel/2/2469/1.html>.

—— (1998d) 'Shell is bang voor Internet', *Intermediair,* Amsterdam, 8 October, and (1998) *Ravage*, Amsterdam, 16 October, <www.evel.nl/simon.htm>.

—— (1998e) 'Shell vervalt in de oude fout. Tsjaad een tweede Nigeria?' *Intermediair*; 15 October, and (1998) *Ravage*, Amsterdam, 28 October, <www.evel.nl/tsjaad.htm>.

—— (1998g) 'Shell is making the same mistake. Chad a second Nigeria?' *Telepolis*, 4 November, <www.heise.de/tp/r4/artikel/2/2519/1.html>.

—— (1999) 'The Brent Spar syndrome', in eds G. Lovink and J. Bosma, *Read me, Filtered by Nettime: ASCII culture and the revenge of knowledge*, Autonomedia, Brooklyn, NY, pp. 281–5, <www.evel.nl/brenteng.htm>.

—— (2000a) 'eWatch, Shell & web intelligence', list server, 30 June, Random bits, <http://lists.essential.org/pipermail/random-bits/2000-June/000183.html>.

—— (2000b) 'NW Airlines & cybersleuths', list server, 10 November, Nettime, <www.nettime.org/Lists-Archives/nettime-l-0011/msg00074.html>.

—— (2001a) 'Wat waren wij eigenlijk voor mensen?' *Ravage,* 2 February, <www.evel.nl/camus1.htm>.

—— (2001b) 'Groene krijgers, spionage bij Greenpeace', *Ravage,* 2 February, <www.evel.nl/camus2.htm>.

—— (2001c) 'De mol, codenaam Camus', *Groene Amsterdammer,* 10 February, <www.evel.nl/camuskort.htm>.

—— (2001d) 'Vervagende grenzen. Oliegiganten erkennen spionage bij milieubeweging', *Ravage,* 6 July, <www.evel.nl/camusvervolg.htm>.

—— (ed.) (2002a) *Battling Big Business: Countering Greenwash, Infiltration and Other Forms of Corporate Bullying,* Greenbooks, Devon.

—— (2002b) 'Garbology: activist trash as corporate treasure', in E. Lubbers (ed.), *Battling Big Business,* pp. 98–106.

—— (2004a) 'Shell: modern schoon of ouderwetse PR?', *Volkskrant,* Amsterdam, 13 February, republished at <https://www.globalinfo.nl/content/view/332/40/>.

—— (2004b) 'Brits wapenbedrijf infiltreert, actiegroepen doelwit bedrijfsspionage', *Ravage,* 15 October, <www.evel.nl/spinwatch/TRdutch1.htm>.

—— (2004c) 'British Aerospace wapent zich tegen acties', *Ravage,* 5 November, <www.evel.nl/spinwatch/TRdutch2.htm>.

—— (2005) 'The Threat Response spy files: a case study about an arms manufacturer, a private intelligence company and many infiltrators', *Journal on Information Warfare,* vol. 4, no. 3, pp. 40–8.

—— (2006) Freedom of Information request to the Metropolitan Police Service, 25 April.

—— (2007) 'Fighting dirty wars, spying for the arms trade,' in eds W. Dinan, and D. Miller (2007) *Thinker, faker, spinner, spy. Corporate PR and the assault on democracy,* Pluto Press, London, pp. 138–54.

Lubbers, E. and W. van der Schans (1998) *Account of our research to infiltrator Adrian Franks in 1998,* Buro Jansen & Janssen, July, <www.evel.nl/spinwatch/TRFrontpage.htm.#part1>.

—— (2004) *Treath Response spy files dossier,* November, <www.evel.nl/spinwatch/TRFrontpage.htm>.

Lynas, M. (1999) 'Group 4: cry freedom', *CorporateWatch Magazine,* iss. 8, <http://archive.corporatewatch.org/magazine/issue8/cw8g4.html>.

Maclay, M. (1999) 'Recruiting political scientists', paper presented at the European Thematic Network Political Science Second Plenary Conference in Leiden, the Netherlands, 2–3 July, *TN-Discussion Papers n°1, Political Science Today,* second edition, <www.epsnet.org/publications/2%20Leiden.pdf>.

Mamou, Y. (2009) 'Jean-Marc Sabathé, directeur de la sécurité du groupe: "EDF n'a pas besoin de payer des hackers"', *Le Monde,* 20 April, <http://tinyurl.com/3uc6qrp>.

Margen S., V. Melnick, L. Neuhauser and E. Rios Espinosa (1991) *Infant Feeding in Mexico: A Study of Health Facility and Mothers' Practices in Three Regions,* Nestlé Infant Formula Audit Commission (NIFAC), Washington, DC.

Marquez, M. (1984) 'Nestlé boycott called off', *Washington News UPI,* 26 January.

Martens, J. and J. Schürkes (2004) *Human Security and Transnational Corporations: The Entanglement of Transnational Corporations in Wars, Human Rights Violations and Tax Evation,* DGB-Bildungswerk, Terre de Hommes,World Economy, Ecology & Development, WEED, Bonn.

Marx, G.T. (1974) 'Thoughts on a neglected category of social movement participant: the agent provocateur and the informant', *American Journal of Sociology*, vol. 80, no. 2, pp. 402–42, <http://web.mit.edu/gtmarx/www/neglected.html>.

—— (1979) 'External efforts to damage or facilitate social movements: some patterns, explanations, outcomes, and complications', in M.N. Zald and J.D. McCarthy, *The dynamics of social movements*, Winthrop Publishers, Cambridge, MA, pp. 94–125, <http://web.mit.edu/gtmarx/www/movement.html>.

—— (1984) 'Notes on the discovery, collection, and assessment of hidden and dirty data', in J.W. Schneider and J.I. Kitsuse (eds), *Studies in the Sociology of Social Problems*, Ablex, Norwood, NJ, <http://web.mit.edu/gtmarx/www/dirty.html>.

—— (1987) 'The interweaving of public and private police undercover work,' in C. Shearing and P. Stenning, *Private Policing*, Sage Publications, London, pp. 172–93, <http://web.mit.edu/gtmarx/www/private.html>.

—— (1988) *Undercover: Police Surveillance in America*, University of California Press, Berkeley and Los Angeles, CA.

—— (2004) 'Some concepts that may be useful in understanding the myriad forms and contexts of surveillance', *Intelligence and National Security*, vol. 19, no. 2, pp. 226–48.

Marx, G.T. and C. Fijnaut (1995) *Undercover: Police Surveillance in Comparative Perspective,* Kluwer Academic Publishers, Norwell, MA.

Marx, K. and F. Engels (1848) *Het communistisch manifest*, <www.marxists.org/nederlands/marx-engels/1848/manifest/manif1.htm>.

Matthews, J. (2002) 'The fake parade, under the banner of populist protest, multinational corporations manufacture the poor', *Environment*, 3 December, republished at <www.freezerbox.com/archive/article.php?id=254>.

—— (2003) 'Biotech's hall of mirrors: a very dirty game. From Berkeley to Johannesburg, India to Zambia, biotech's deceivers are playing a very dirty game', *GeneWatch,* vol. 16, no. 1, <http://ngin.tripod.com/080303b.htm>.

May, S. (1998) Presentation at the Putting the Pressure on conference in Brussels, 4 June.

Mayfield, K. (2001) 'Fire insurance for the internet', *Wired News*, 3 January, <www.wired.com/news/business/0,1367,40798,00.html>.

McDonald's Corporation (1990) McDonald's Corporation and McDonald's Restaurants Ltd. vs P. Gravett, H.M. Webster, A.J. Clarke, D. Morris and J. Parrell (1990) 1990 M-No. 5724, <www.mcspotlight.org/case/pretrial/writ.html>.

McIvor, A.J. (1988) '"A Crusade for Capitalism" – The Economic League, 1918–39,' *Journal of Contemporary History*, vol. 23, pp. 631–55.

McLibel Support Campaign (1998) *Press release. McLibel 2 sue Met Police Commissioner*, 17 September, <www.mcspotlight.org/media/press/msc_17sep98.html>.

—— (1999) *McLibel Trial story,* <www.mcspotlight.org//case/trial/story.html>.

—— (2000) *Press release. Met police pay £10.000 to McLibel 2 over disclosure of confidential info to McDonald's*, 5 July, <www.mcspotlight.org/listarc/0012.html>.

Medick, V. and M. Rosenbach (2011a) Deutsche Behörden forderten Briten-Spitzel an. Spionage in linker Scene, *der Spiegel*, 26 January, <www.spiegel.de/politik/deutschland/0,1518,741826,00.html>.

—— (2011b) Berlin Sent Five Undercover Police Officers to Scotland. German Agents at G-8 Summit, *der Spiegel*, 21 February, <www.spiegel.de/international/germany/0,1518,746766,00.html>.

Mercer, P. (1986) *'Peace' of the Dead: The Truth Behind the Nuclear Disarmers*, Policy Research Publications, London.

Miller, D. and W. Dinan (2003) 'Global public relations and global capitalism', in D. Demers (ed.), *Terrorism, Globalization and Mass Communication*, Marquette Books, Spokane, WA.

—— (2008) *A Century of Spin*, Pluto Press, London.

Miller, H.I. and G. Conko (2004) *The Frankenfood Myth: How Protest and Politics Threaten the Biotech Revolution*, Praeger Publishers, Santa Barbara, CA.

Miller, K.S. (1999) *The voice of business: Hill & Knowlton and postwar Public Relations*, University of North Carolina Press, Chapel Hill, NC.

Miller, W.H. (1987) 'Issue Management: "No longer a sideshow,"' *Industry Week*, vol. 235, no. 2 November, pp. 125–9.

Ministry of Justice (2009) Coroners and Justice Act 2009, 12 November, <http:/www.justice.gov.uk/publications/coroners-justice-bill.htm>.

Ministry of Justice (2011) 'Opening up public bodies to public scrutiny', press release, 7 January, <www.justice.gov.uk/news/press-releases/moj/press-release-070111a.htm>.

Mintz, M. (1981) 'Infant-formula maker battles boycotters by painting them red', *Washington Post*, 4 January, pp. A2, 23.

Mobbs, P. (2009) 'NETCU, WECTU and NPOIU: Britain's secretive Police Force. Politicising the policing of public expression in an era of economic change', electrohippies Paper Q2 The Free Range electrohippies Project, April, <http://tinyurl.com/d7d79on>.

Mohr, M. and K. Viehmann (eds) (2004) *Spitzel. Eine kleine Sozialgeschichte*, Assoziation A, Berlin.

Mokhiber, R. (1989) 'Nestlé undercover', *Multinational Monitor*, vol. 10, no. 5, <http://multinationalmonitor.org/hyper/issues/1989/05/mokhiber.html>.

Monbiot, G. (2002a) 'The fake persuaders. Companies are creating false citizens to try to change the way we think', *Guardian*, 14 May, <www.guardian.co.uk/politics/2002/may/14/greenpolitics.digitalmedia>.

—— (2002b) 'Corporate phantoms. The web of deceit over GM food has now drawn in the PM's speechwriters', *Guardian*, 29 May, <www.guardian.co.uk/education/2002/may/29/research.highereducation>.

—— (2002c) 'The covert biotech war. The battle to put a corporate GM padlock on our foodchain is being fought on the net', *Guardian*, 19 November, <www.guardian.co.uk/science/2002/nov/19/gm.food>.

Monetos (2009) *Independent information and research on the European private financial sector* (section statistiken, durchschnittseinkomen), <http://de.moneto.eu/altersvorsorge/grundsicherung/statistiken/>.

Montague, P. (1993) 'PR Firms for hire to undermine democracy', *Rachel's Hazardous Waste News*, News and resources for environmental justice, no. 361, 27 October, <www.rachel.org/files/rachel/Rachels_Environment_Health_News_767.pdf>.

Muncaster, Ph. (2009) CBI baulks at ICO's proposed new powers, V3.co.uk, 9 July, <www.v3.co.uk/v3-uk/news/1975670/cbi-baulks-icos-proposed-powers>.

'Murphy, M.' (2000) 'Activists change stance on GMOs after scientist genetically alter marijuana (AP)', list server, 9 July, FoxBGHsuit, <http://tinyurl.com/5v64s5z>.

—— (2001) 'Mexican corn – the new Starlink-Monarch-Mutant scare story', list server, 29 November, AgroBioView, <www.agbioworld.org/newsletter_wm/index.php?caseid=archive&newsid=1267>.

—— (2002) 'Re: Scientist claims vendetta over GM research', list server, 8 April, AgBioView, <www.agbioworld.org/newsletter_wm/index.php?caseid=archive& newsid=1398>.

Nature (2002) 'Editorial note', 4 April, p.1, available for subscribers at <www. nature.com>, republished at <www.agbioworld.org/newsletter_wm/index.php? caseid=archive&newsid=1404>.

Naylor, R.T. (2004) 'The underworld of ivory', *Crime, Law & Social Change*, Springer, vol. 42, no. 4–5, pp. 261–95.

NDH, Nederlands Duitse Handelskamer (2006) 'Persbericht. C&A verleidt de Duitsers', 17 July.

Nelson, J. (1989) *Sultans of Sleaze, Public Relations and the Media,* Between the Lines, Toronto.

Nelson-Horchler, J. (1984) 'Fighting a boycott. Image rebuilding. Swiss style,' *Industry Week*, 23 January, Vol. 220, pp. 54–6.

Networksolutions.com (2009a) *Domain registration details for bivwood.com*, 2009, <www.networksolutions.com/whois/results.jsp?domain=bivwood.com>.

—— (2009b) *Domain registration details for IP number 199.89.234.124*, <www. networksolutions.com/whois/results.jsp?ip=199.89.234.124>.

—— (2009c) *Domain registration details for bivings.com*, 2009, <www.network-solutions.com/whois-search/bivings.com>.

Newsletter on the Oil Embargo against South Africa (1987) Shipping Research Bureau, Amsterdam, October.

Newsnight (2002) 'Row over GM crops – Mexican scientist tells Newsnight he was threatened because he wanted to tell the truth', transcript of *Newsnight*, BBC, 7 June, republished at <http://ngin.tripod.com/080602d.htm>.

No Police Spies campaign (2011) 'Undercover Police Officers and the UK protest movement. A briefing by the No Police Spies campaign', February, <http:// nopolicespies.org.uk/wp-content/uploads/2011/02/Background-briefing-Feb-11. pdf>.

Northmore, D. (1996) *Lifting the Lid. A Guide to Investigative Research*, Cassell, New York, NY.

Norton-Taylor, R. (1993) 'Rightwing vetting agency disbanded', *Guardian*, 24 April, p. 9.

—— (1994) 'Blacklisters back in business', *Observer*, 3 April, p. 2.

Norwood, S.H. (2002) *Strikebreaking and Intimidation, Mercenaries and Masculinity in Twentieth-century America*, University of North Carolina Press, Chapel Hill and London.

Nottingham Indymedia UK (2011) 'Corporate spy was active in Nottingham', including additions by some calling him/herself 'Researcher' in the comments, 9 February, <www.indymedia.org.uk/en/2011/02/473761.html>.

Nowak, P. (2001) 'Rückschlag für Spionage gegen Linke? Interview mit Res Steinbacher von der Schweizer Organisation "Revolutionärer Aufbau"', *junge Welt*, <http://tinyurl.com/3fgslug>.

O'Donnell, S. (2002) 'Private spooks, Wackenhut vs. whistleblowers', in E. Lubbers (ed.), *Battling Big Business*, pp. 107–13.

O'Dwyers PR services report (1990) 'Ex-Nestlé firm goes bankrupt', November, p. 1.

O'Reilly, C. (2003) 'Brisbane activist targeted by British spooks while doing East Timor solidarity work in England', list server, 22 October, Indymedia Brisbane, <http://tinyurl.com/3gcg2ks>.

O'Reilly, C. and G. Ellison (2006) 'Eye spy private high: re-conceptualising high policing theory', *British Journal for Criminology*, vol. 46, no. 4, pp. 641–60.

Obbink, H. (1987) 'Er valt nog heel wat op te poetsen, Shell, Zuid-Afrika en de strijd om de publieke opinie', *HN-Magazine*, 24 October.

Osler, D. (1994) Economic League organisers return with revamped blacklisting outfit, *Tribune*, 1 April, <http://tinyurl.com/3rx55r4>.

Overell, S. (2000) 'Masters of the great game turn to business. Globalisation and cross border mergers are increasing demand for Hakluyt's brand of intelligence', *Financial Times*, 23 March, p. 21.

Owen, D., T. Swift, and K. Hunt (2001) 'Questioning the role of stakeholder engagement in social and ethical accounting, auditing, and reporting', *Accounting Forum*, vol. 25, no. 3, pp. 264–82.

Pagan Jr. R.D. (1982) 'Carrying the fight to the critics of multinational capitalism, think and act politically', paper presented at the Public Affairs Councils, New York, NY, 19 April.

—— (1983) 'The shaping of an issues strategy', paper presented at the Public Relations Student Society of America, New York, NY, 25 October.

—— (1985) 'The challenge to multinational marketing, a public relations response', in E. Denig and A. van der Meiden (eds), *A Geography of PR Trends*, pp. 373–9.

—— (1985) 'Why cooperation succeeds where confrontation fails', *Business and Social Review*, no. 54, pp. 27–9.

—— (1986a) 'The Nestlé boycott: implications for strategic business planning', *Journal of Business Strategy*, vol. 6, no. 4, pp. 12–20.

—— (1986b) *Shell US South Africa strategy. Prepared for: the Shell Oil company for use in the U.S. & for the development of global coordination within the Royal Dutch Shell Group*, Pagan International, Washington, DC, (the *Neptune Strategy*).

—— (1992) 'Rio outcome? – paperwork', *Washington Times*, 13 September.

—— (1996) 'Corporate strategies for effective crisis management: corporate decision making and corporate public policy development. A participant's response', in S.P. Sethi, P. Steidl-Meier and C. M. Falbe, *Scaling the Corporate Wall: Readings in Business and Society*, Prentice Hall, Upper Saddle River, NJ.

Pallister, D. (2003) 'Firms on the frontline, Rubicon International', *Guardian*, 10 December, <www.guardian.co.uk/world/2003/dec/10/politics.iraq1>.

Pattakos, A.N. (1978) 'Memorandum for the Director', Defense Communications Agency to the Joint Chief of Staffs, Washington DC, 16 January, <http://tinyurl.com/6grrlu2>.

—— (2001) 'Do OPSEC and risk management mesh?' *Security Management Online*, November, <www.securitymanagement.com/library/view_nov01.html>.

Penman, A. (2009) 'Ban for firms that blacklist unions', *Daily Mirror*, 7 July, <http://blogs.mirror.co.uk/investigations/2009/07/ban-for-firms-that-blacklist-u.html>.

Perlez, J. and R. Bonner (2005) 'Below a mountain of wealth, a river of waste', *New York Times*, 27 December, <www.nytimes.com/2005/12/27/international/asia/27gold.htm>.

—— (2006) 'New York urges U.S. inquiry in mining company's Indonesia payment', *New York Times*, 28 January, <www.nytimes.com/2006/01/28/international/asia/28indo.htm>.

Pickerill, J. (2002) *Cyberprotest, Environmental Activism Online*, Manchester University Press, Manchester.

—— (2006) 'Radical Politics on the Net', *Parliamentary Affairs*, vol. 59, no. 2, pp. 266–82.

Picking, Ch. (2006) Freedom of Information request. Answer from Police Constable 2497, Freedom of Information Officer for the Thames Valley Police, 15 May.

Pilger, J. (1998) *Hidden Agenda*, Vintage, London.

Platoni, (2002) 'Kernels of truth', *East Bay Express*, San Francisco, 29 May, <www.eastbayexpress.com/news/kernels_of_truth/Content?oid=283704>.

Policy Exchange (2011) Ideas Space. The Rise of Street Extremism: Will law breaking, direct action and violence succeed? 10 January, Mercer's introduction starts at 7 minutes into the film <www.policyexchange.org.uk/events/event.cgi?id=285>.

Post, J.E. (1985) 'Assessing the Nestlé boycott: corporate accountability and human rights', *California Management Review*, no. 2, pp. 113–31.

PowerBase (2009a) *Andura Smetacek*, <www.PowerBase.info/index.php/Andura_Smetacek>.

—— (2009b) *Bivings*, <www.PowerBase.info/index.php/Bivings>.

—— (2009c) Channapatna S. Prakash, <www.powerbase.info/index.php/Channapatna_S._Prakash>.

—— (2009d) *Jay Byrne*, <www.PowerBase.info/index.php/Jay_Byrne>.

—— (2009e) *Mary Murphy*, <www.PowerBase.info/index.php/Mary_Murphy>.

Pratt, R. (1997) *In Good Faith: Canadian Churches Against Apartheid*, Canadian Corporation for Studies in Religion, Wilfrid Laurier University Press, Waterloo.

Purkitt, H.E. and S.F. Burgess (2005) *South Africa's Weapons of Mass Destruction*, Indiana University Press, Bloomington, IN.

Quist, D. and I. Chapela (2001) 'Transgenic DNA introgressed into traditional maize landraces in Oaxaco, Mexico', *Nature*, 29 November, London, vol. 414, pp. 541–3, <www.nature.com/nature/journal/v414/n6863/full/414541a.html>. Republished at <www.mindfully.org/GE/GE3/Chapela-Transgenic-Maize-Oaxaca-Nature29nov01.htm>.

Ragan Interactive Public Relations (2000) 'From the front: PR pros share their lessons to handle rogue web sites and assaults on their brands', *Monthly Newsletter for Web Professionals from the World Organisation of Webmasters (WOW)*, December, vol. 3, no. 16, <http://web.archive.org/web/20010709010308/www.joinwow.org/newsletter/16/in/>.

Rampton, S. (2002) 'Spinning the web', *PR Watch Quarterly*, first quarter 2002, vol. 9, no. 1, <www.prwatch.org/prwissues/2002Q1/web.html>.

Raney, R.F. (1999) 'Incognito spinmeisters battle on-line critics: when a company's product is under fire, one option is to plant a defender in the chat room', *New York Times*, 14 October, <http://tinyurl.com/3enzrpj>.

Redflags.info (2011) 'Liability risks for companies operating in high-risk zones', www.redflags.info.

Renfro, W.L. (1993) *Issue Management in Strategic Planning*, Quoru, Westport, CT.

Revolutionäre Aufbau (2000a) *Die Gruppe 2, ein nachrichtendienstliches Project des Agenten Manfred Schlickenrieder*, <www.libertad.de/inhalt/spezial/gruppe2/pdf/gruppe2.pdf>.

—— (2000b) *Gedanken, Reflexionen, Selbstkritik*, December 2000, <www.libertad.de/inhalt/spezial/gruppe2/ab_reflektion.shtml>.

—— (2006) *Was will der revolutionäre Aufbau Schweiz?*, 4 December, <www.aufbau.org/index.php?option=com_content&task=view&id=19&Itemid=60>.

—— (2011) Die Enttarnung des Agenten Manfred Schlickenrieder, <www.aufbau.org/index.php?option=com_content&task=view&id=22&Itemid=32>.

Richter, J. (1991) 'Public relations, politics and public pressure: recovering the history of corporate propaganda', MA Thesis, Institute of Development Studies, The Hague.

—— (1998) *Engineering of Consent: Uncovering Corporate PR*, Corner House, Briefing no. 6, Sturminster Newton.

—— (2001) *Holding Corporations Accountable: Corporate Conduct, International Codes, and Citizen Action*, Zed Books, London.

Ridgeway, J. (2008) 'Black ops, green groups. Why did a private security firm spy on Greenpeace and other environmental outfits?', *Mother Jones*, 11 April, viewed 20 June 2009, <www.motherjones.com/environment/2008/04/exclusive-cops-and-former-secret-service-agents-ran-black-ops-green-groups>.

Roddick, A. (2001) Roddick's retort, letter to the editor, *Sunday Times*, 24 June.

Rositzke, H. (1977) *The CIA's Secret Operations*, Readers Digest Press, New York, NY.

Rowell, A. (1996) *Green Backlash: Global Subversion of the Environmental Movement*, Routledge, London.

—— (2002a) 'Seeds of dissent, anti-GM scientists are facing widespread assaults on their credibility. Andy Rowell investigates who is behind the attacks', *Big Issue South West*, 15–21 April, no. 484, republished at <http://ngin.tripod.com/280402a.htm>.

—— (2002b) 'Dialogue, divide and rule', in E. Lubbers (ed.), *Battling Big Business*, pp. 33–43.

—— (2003) *Don't Worry, It's Safe To Eat: The True Story of GM Food, BSE and Foot and Mouth*, Earthscan Publications, London.

Rufford, N. (1999) 'Cloak and dagger Ltd: former spies of the Cold War era engage in industrial espionage', *Management Today*, 1 February, p. 9.

Runderkamp, L. and F. Salverda (1987) 'De Neptunus strategie', documentary, *Gouden Bergen*, VPRO, October, tape and transcript.

Salleh, A. (2002) 'Mexican maize madness', ABC Science, Part I – The war of words, <www.abc.net.au/science/slab/mexicanmaize/default.htm>, Part II – The devil in the detail, <www.abc.net.au/science/slab/mexicanmaize/part_two.htm>.

Salmon, C. (1989) 'Milking the deadly dollars from the third world', *Business & Society Review*, no. 68, pp. 43–8.

Sassen, S. (1996) *Losing Control? Sovereignty in an Age of Globalization*, Columbia University Press, New York, NY.

Saunders, E.W. (1980) *Internal memo to Nestlé's managing director Arthur Fuhrer in August 1980, Nestlégate – US boycott – Conclusions based on US visit, August 2-4*, released by ICCR, New York, NY. Reproduced version with annotations in Baby Milk Action Coalition (1981) *Nestlégate Memorandum: Secret Memo Reveals Corporate Cover-up*, Cambridge.

Scahill, J. (2007) *Blackwater: The Rise of the World's Most Powerful Mercenary Army*, Nation Books, New York, NY.

Schampers, B. (1995) 'Twijfels rond Gentse gifgasexpert Heyndrickx. Twee jaar geëist tegen vermaarde professor,' *Brabants Dagblad*, 5 May.

Schlesinger Jr., A.M. (1977) 'Introduction,' in H. Rositzke, *The CIA's Secret Operations*, Readers Digest Press, New York, NY.

Schlosser, E. (2008) 'Burger with a side of spies', *New York Times*, 7 May, viewed 20 April 2009, <www.nytimes.com/2008/05/07/opinion/07schlosser.html?_r=1>.

Scott, L. and P. Jackson (2004a) 'The study of intelligence in theory and practice,' *Intelligence and national security*, vol. 19, no. 2, pp. 139–69.

—— (2004b) *Understanding Intelligence in the Twenty-first Century: Journeys in Shadows*, Routledge, London.

Seelye, K. (2006) 'Mining Company Notes U.S. Review of Payments to Indonesian Military', *New York Times*, 19 January, <http://tinyurl.com/65x6rlw>.

Sethi, S.P. (1981) 'Unlikely prostitution', *Business & Society Review*, issue 37, Spring.

—— (ed.) (1987) *The South African quagmire: In Search of a Peaceful Path to Democratic Pluralism*, Ballinger Publishing Company, Cambridge, MA.

—— (1994) *Multinational Corporations and the Impact of Public Advocacy on Corporate Strategy: Nestlé and the Infant Formula Controversy*, Kluwer Academic Publishers, Boston, Dordrecht and London.

Seymour, M. and S. Moore (2000) 'Brent Spar: learning effective communication the hard way', *Effective Crisis Management: Worldwide Principles and Practice*, Cassel, London. Republished version *The Crisis Manager*, November, <www.bernsteincrisismanagement.com/nl/crisismgr010901.html#3>.

Shah, S. (2007) 'BAE paid agency to spy on peace group', *Independent*, 19 April, <http://tinyurl.com/7guvgbh>.

Shorrock, T. (2008) *Spies for hire, the secret world of intelligence outsourcing*, Simon & Schuster, New York, London and Toronto.

Shulsky, A. and G. Schmitt (2001) *Silent Warfare: Understanding the World of Intelligence* , second revised edition, Brassey's, Washington, DC.

Silverberg, L.G. (1941) 'Citizens' committees: their role in industrial conflict', *Public Opinion Quarterly*, March, vol. 5, no. 1, pp. 17–37.

Singh, J.A. (2008) 'Project Coast: eugenics in apartheid South Africa', *Endeavour*, vol. 32, no. 1, pp. 5–9.

'Smetacek, A.' (2000) 'A plea to help stop eco-terror', list server 20 July, AgbioView, <www.agbioworld.org/newsletter_wm/index.php?caseid=archive&newsid=483>.

—— (2001a) 'Ignatio Chapela – activist FIRST, scientist second', 29 November, list server AgBioView, <www.agbioworld.org/newsletter_wm/index.php?caseid=archive&newsid=1268>.

—— (2001b) 'More evidence that Chapela was coordinating with activists', list server, 30 November, AgroBioView, <www.agbioworld.org/newsletter_wm/index.php?caseid=archive&newsid=1270>.

—— (2002a) 'Watch out Greenpeace, Melchett has joined the dark side', list server 5 January, AgBioView, <www.agbioworld.org/newsletter_wm/index.php?caseid=archive&newsid=1300>.

—— (2002b) *Make José Bové serve his time. Petition to the French Government*, July, <www.petitiononline.com/cinagro4/petition.html>.

Smith, R.M. (2003) *From blackjacks to briefcases: a history of commercialized strikebreaking and union busting in the United States,* Ohio University Press, Athens, OH.

Smith T. and D. Katzin (1987) *The Shell Game: Shell Oil's Secret Plan to Counteract the Anti-apartheid Boycott*, Interfaith Center on Corporate Responsibility, New York, NY, September.

Sparks, S. (1987) 'South Africa U.S. clergy group linked to Shell Oil', *IPS News*, 7 October.

SpinWatch.org (2011) An open letter to Bob Lambert, 20 October, <http://tinyurl.com/d9nrecu>.

Sriramesh, K. and D. Verčič (2003) *The Global Public Relations Handbook: Theory, Research, and Practice*, Lawrence Erlbaum Associates, Mahwah, NJ.

Stauber, J. and S. Rampton (1995) *Toxic Sludge is Good For You. Lies, Damn Lies and the Public Relations Industry*, Common Courage Press, Monroe, ME.

—— (1996) 'Women and children first: on the frontline of the chlorine war', *PR Watch Quarterly*, vol. 3, no. 2, documents, <www.prwatch.org/prwissues/1996Q2/women.html>.

—— (1998) *Mad Cow USA: The Unfolding Nightmare*, Common Courage Press, Monroe, ME.

—— (2001) *Trust Us, We're Experts: How Industry Manipulates Science and Gambles with your Future*, Penguin Putnam, New York, NY.

—— (2003) *Weapons of Mass Deception: The Uses of Propaganda in Bush's War on Iraq*, Penguin Putnam, New York, NY.

—— (2004) *Banana Republicans: How the Right Wing is Turning America into a One-party State*, Penguin Putnam, New York, NY.

—— (2006) *The Best War Ever: Lies, Damned Lies, and the Mess in Iraq*, Penguin Putnam, New York, NY.

Steel, H. and D. Morris (1996) *Notice of intention to apply for leave to issue 'third party proceedings' against Anthony Pocklington, Brian Bishop and Allan Clare, enquiry agents formerly employed on behalf of McDonald's*, 28 June 1996, <www.mcspotlight.org/case/trial/intention.html>.

Stepanek, M. (2000) 'Now, companies can track down their cyber-critics', *BusinessWeek Online*, 7 July, <www.businessweek.com/bwdaily/dnflash/july2000/nf00707g.htm>.

Strehle, R. (2000) 'Die grünen Krieger bespitzelt', *Weltwoche*, no. 49, 7 December, <www.libertad.de/inhalt/spezial/gruppe2/ww4900.shtml>.

—— (2000/2001) Interview on the Swiss local radio station Lora, *Offener Politkanal: Rote Welle*, a programme produced by Aufbau.org (see www.lora.ch), 17 December. Tape 1: Raw tape of the interview. Tape 2: three subsequent editions of the Rote Welle program, all about the exposure of Schlickenrieder, 7, 14 and 21 January 2001.

Swanson, P. (2002) *Fuelling Conflict: The Oil Industry and Armed Conflict*, Fafo Report, Oslo, viewed 29 September 2009, <www.fafo.no/pub/rapp/378/index.htm>.

Taylor, M. and P. Lewis (2009) 'Secret police intelligence was given to E.ON before planned demo. Secret police intelligence passed to firm. Emails show civil servants passed data on protesters to security officials at E.ON', *Guardian*, 20 April, <www.guardian.co.uk/uk/2009/apr/20/police-intelligence-e-on-berr>.

Taylor, P. (2002) 'Hired spy stopped Newbury protest', documentary, *True Spies: It Could Happen to You*, BBC, November, <http://news.bbc.co.uk/1/hi/programmes/true_spies/2405325.stm>.

Tedlow, R.S. (1976) 'The National Association of Manufacturers and Public Relations during the New Deal', *Business History Review*, vol. 50, no. 1, pp. 25–45.

Tefft, S. (ed.) (1980) *Secrecy: A Cross-cultural Perspective*, Human Sciences Press, New York and London.

Terry (2005) 'The enemy within', list server, 27 July, Indymedia.uk, <www.indymedia.org.uk/en/2005/07/319686?c=on>

Thomas, M. (2007) 'Martin and me', *Guardian*, 4 December, <www.guardian.co.uk/world/2007/dec/04/bae.armstrade>.

Thomas, R. (2004) Letter from the Information Commissioner to CAAT, 20 December, <www.caat.org.uk/about/spying/201204letter.pdf>.

—— (2005) Letter from the Information Commissioner to CAAT, 8 February, <www.caat.org.uk/about/spying/080205letter.pdf>.

Tiller, F. (1996) *Witness statement for the defence, investigator for firm hired by McDonald's,* 15 March, <www.mcspotlight.org/people/witnesses/publication/tiller_francis.html>.

—— (1997) 'McDonald's spy Fran Tiller on infiltration and subterfuge, Big Mac style', in F. Armstrong, *McLibel: Two Worlds Collide*, documentary, 53 minutes, One-Off Productions, London. Transcript of the full interview, <www.mcspotlight.org/people/interviews/tiller_fran.html>.

Time (1938) 'Self-evident subtlety', 1 August, <www.time.com/time/magazine/article/0,9171,771150,00.htm>.

Toffler, A. (1980) *The Third Wave*, Morrow, New York, NY.

—— (1990) *Power Shift: Knowledge, Wealth, and Violence at the edge of the 21st century*, Bantam, New York, NY.

Travis, A., P. Lewis and M. Wainwright (2011) 'Clean-up of covert policing ordered after Mark Kennedy revelations. Home Office minister Nick Herbert says Acpo will lose control of three teams involved in tackling "domestic extremism"', *Guardian*, 18 January, <www.guardian.co.uk/uk/2011/jan/18/covert-policing-cleanup-acpo?INTCMP=SRCH>.

Trewavas, A. (2002) 'Subject: commentary on Chapela', list server, 22 February, AgBioView, <www.agbioworld.org/newsletter_wm/index.php?caseid=archive&newsid=1363>.

Truth and Reconciliation Commission (1998) *Special investigation into Project Coast, the South African chemical and biological warfare programme, final report presented to President Nelson Mandela on 29 October 1998*, vol. 2, chapter 6, <www.fas.org/nuke/guide/rsa/cbw/2chap6c.htm>.

TU Delta (1996) De Brent Spar, of de boodschap die niet overkwam, vol. 41, no. 26, 22 February, <http://tinyurl.com/68cqrpp>.

Tulder, R. van and A. van der Zwart (2003) *Reputaties op het spel, maatschappelijk verantwoord ondernemen in een onderhandelingsmaatschappij*, Het Spectrum, Utrecht.

UCATT (2010) 'New blacklisting regulations won't stop outrageous practice', press release, 2 March, <https://www.ucatt.org.uk/content/view/843/30/>.

United Methodist Church (2004) *The Book of Discipline*, Abingdon Press, Nashville, TN.

University of Notre Dame (1988) *Journal of the Faculty Senate Meeting*, 11 October, <http://facultysenate.nd.edu/meetings/documents/minutes1988-89_000.pdf>.

Verhille, P. (1998) 'Putting the pressure on, the rise of pressure activism in Europe', paper presented at the Putting the Pressure On Conference, Brussels, 4 June.

Vidal, J. (1997) *McLibel*, Macmillan, London.

Volkskrant (1987) 'Raad van Kerken verontrust na gesprek katholieken met Shell', 13 October.

Walker, M. (1986) 'The cost of doing business in South Africa, anti-apartheid coalition boycotts Shell', *Multinational Monitor*, vol. 7, no. 7, 15 April, <www.multinationalmonitor.org/hyper/issues/1986/0415/walker.html>.

Wallraff, G. (1985a) *Verslaggever van Bild*, Van Gennep, Amsterdam.

—— (1985b) *Ik (Ali),* Van Gennep, Amsterdam.

—— (1987) *Opening van zaken, over spionnen, infiltranten en lastercampagnes*, Van Gennep, Amsterdam.

Washington Post (1982) Editorial: 'Revisiting the Formula Fight', 5 November.

Washington Times (1993) 'Obituaries Rafael D. Pagan, 67, adviser to 5 presidents', 5 May, p. B6.

Wazir, B. (2000) 'Eating the greens: electronics giants such as Sony are using the internet to hit back at troublesome eco-warriors', *Observer*, 1 October, <www.guardian.co.uk/technology/2000/oct/01/sony.gadgets>.

Webster, B. (2008) 'Spy caught by anti-aviation group was "more Austin Powers than 007"', *The Times*, 8 April, <http://business.timesonline.co.uk/tol/business/industry_sectors/transport/article3701838.ece>.

Wedel, J. (2004a) 'Blurring the state–private divide: flex organisations and the decline of accountability', in M. Spoor (ed.), *Globalisation, Poverty and Conflict: a Critical Development Reader*, Kluwer Academic Publishers, Dordrecht and Boston, NY, pp. 217–35, <http://janinewedel.info/scholarly_Kluwer.pdf>.

—— (2004b) 'Flex power: an influential band of policy brothers', *Washington Post*, 12 December, p. B04, <www.washingtonpost.com/wp-dyn/articles/A56845-2004Dec11.html>.

—— (2009) *Shadow Elite: New Agents of Power and Influence*, Basic Books, New York, NY.

Whitaker, J.S. (1988) 'Review of "The South Africa quagmire: in search of a peaceful path to democratic pluralism. Edited by S. Prakash Sethi"', *Foreign Affairs*, vol. 66, no. 4, p. 891, <http://tinyurl.com/69bfpuy>.

Wilensky, H.L. (1967) *Organizational Intelligence*, Basic Books, New York, NY.

Willcock, J. (1998) 'People & Business', *Independent*, 14 August.

Windsor, C. (1999) 'Charles: my fears over the safety of GM foods', *Daily Mail*, 1 June, p.1, Republished at <www.ncbe.reading.ac.uk/NCBE/GMFood/charles.html>.

—— (2000) 'Respect for the earth', *Reith lectures 2000*, BBC, <http://news.bbc.co.uk/hi/english/static/events/reith_2000/lecture6.stm>.

Wilton Park (2005) *Annual Report & Accounts 2004/2005*, presented to the House of Commons, 20 July, <www.official-documents.gov.uk/document/hc0506/hc02/0234/0234.pdf>.

Wrigley, C. (1990) *Lloyd George and the Challenge of Labour: The Postwar Coalition, 1918–1922*, Harvester, New York, NY.

Lord Young (2010) Blacklisting outlawed, press release Department for Business, Innovation and Skills, 2 March, <www.direct.gov.uk/en/Nl1/Newsroom/DG_185922>.

Young, T.R. (1971) 'The politics of sociology: Gouldner, Goffman, Garfinkel', *American Sociologist*, 6, pp. 276–81.

Zöllner, S. (2004) 'Das West Papua Netzwerk im Visier des Bundes-Nachrichten-Dienstes (BND)', *Westpapua rundbrief Wuppertal*, October, <www.west-papua-netz.de/upload/rundbrief_32.pdf>.

Index

Compiled by Sue Carlton

6I intelligence agency 184–5, 193
7 Medical Battalion 187

ABC 3
Abu Jamal, Mumia 150
Action Directe (France) 138
activist groups
    impact of infiltration and espionage
        5–7, 10, 96, 107, 172, 177–8
    and security awareness 5, 6, 7, 156,
        205
activist intelligence 5, 16, 22, 45,
        79–80, 201–2
    and regulation 202–3
    research into 12–13, 20, 136–7, 206
    and resistance 201–2
    and secrecy 195–7, 200
    see also covert corporate strategy;
        private intelligence agencies
AgBioWorld 127–8, 131
    AgBioView discussion forum 124–7,
        129, 131
agents provocateurs x, 154–5, 159,
        172
Agir Ici 171
Aldrich, Renu 119, 120, 121, 122
Altstedder, Norman 73
American Iron and Steel Institute 31,
        32
Amnesty International 171
ANC (African National Congress) 11
Angell, Philip 130
Angola 61, 184, 187–8, 189
Angst, Carl 48
Animal Liberation Front 100, 102
animal rights activists xi–xii, 83, 85,
        88, 99–101, 103–5
Animal Rights National Index (ARNI)
        xi–xii, xiii, 85, 86–7, 100, 104,
        105, 194
anti-apartheid campaign 60, 61, 66,
        69–70, 73, 75, 189, 204

anti-communism 11, 27, 44, 183–6,
        191, 193, 200
    see also West European Defence
        Association (WEDA)
apartheid 3, 45, 60, 63, 75
Armed Forces Communication
        Electronics Association (AFCEA)
        174–5
Armstrong, James (Jim) 66, 67, 68–9,
        71–2, 73
Aronoff, Craig 15
Ascherson, Neal 151
Associated Industries of Cleveland
        29–30
Association of Chief Police Officers
        (ACPO) xi, xiii, 43, 108, 194
Attac Switzerland 58–9
Auerbach, Jeff S. 30–1

Baader–Meinhof group *see* Rote
        Armee Fraktion
Bank für Gewerkschaft 148
Barbie, Klaus 183
Barlow Lyde & Gilbert 87, 90
Baskin, Otis W. 15
Basson, Dr Wouter 187, 188
Battling Big Business (Lubbers) 7–9
Baynes, Andrew 113
Beck, Ulrich 16, 198
Becks 148
Bell, R. (Justice) 84, 92, 97
Benson, Matthew 131
Bergoff Brothers and Waddell 25–6
Berkman Institute of Internet and
        Society 117
Bernays, Edward 26, 81
Bernhard, Prince (Netherlands) 188,
        190
Bernstein, Carl 204
Bethlehem Steel 33
Biddick, Kathleen 73
Big Issue 128

Bindman and Partners 167
biotech industry 111–12, 123–5, 127,
    129–30, 131, 133
    see also genetic engineering;
    Monsanto
Bishop, Brian 88, 90, 91, 93, 94–5, 96,
    97, 99, 104–5
Bivings 109, 110, 112, 122–34
    creation of fake online identities
    124–6, 131, 132, 133
    fake identities denial 112, 128–9,
    133–4
    viral marketing 112, 130–3
Bivings, Gary F. 128
Bivings-Woodell Inc. 123
Black, Pete 108
blacklisting 23, 35, 36, 37–8, 39, 40,
    41–3, 44
    and cybersurveillance 118, 121, 133
Bleifuss, Joel 78
blurring boundaries 11, 135, 199
    see also grey intelligence
Body Shop 143, 144, 168
Boesak, Alan 66
Botha, Pieter Willem 190
Botswana 190
Bowan, Harry 25–6
Bowerfind, Edgar S. 32
Boyling, Jim 101
BP
    and Greenpeace protests 145, 147,
    198
    and Hakluyt 135, 142, 144, 145,
    146, 157
    and Koeppler Appeal 186
brand identity 8
Bray's detective agency xv–xvi, 181,
    182
Brent Spar crisis (1995) 8, 110–11,
    143, 145, 197
Brett, Richard 39
British Aerospace (BAe)
    and advanced warnings of direct
    action 167, 168–70, 174
    bribes from Saudi royal family 191
    and sale of Hawk aircraft to
    Indonesia 159, 162, 165, 169
    undermining public protest 144–5,
    162, 169–70, 198, 200

warned about road protesters 178,
    179
    see also Threat Response
    International (TRI)
Brodeur, Jean-Paul 7, 19
Brooke, Charlie 99, 102
Brouwer, Rev. Arie 66
Bundesnachrichtendienst (BND) 148,
    155
Burdett, Robert (formerly Boiteux) 183
buro Jansen & Janssen 2, 5, 6, 46,
    136, 160, 205, 206, 210
BusinessWeek 116, 119, 120
BVD (Dutch Secret Service) 4
Byrne, Jay 131–2

C&A, and child labour 4–5
C2i International xiv
Campaign against Arms Trade (CAAT)
    10, 11, 159–78, 190, 191, 193
    exposure of Hogbin 172–5, 176–7
    openness 167
    Rapid Response Network 169
    'snowball' strategy 169
    undermined 144–5, 167, 172
Campaign for Nuclear Disarmament
    (CND) 179, 180, 185, 191–3
Campbell, Patrick xv
Campbell, Philip 130
capitalism 36–7, 44, 47, 50, 154, 156
Caprim Ltd 39–40
Carroll, Terry 86–7
Carter, Stacy M. 78–9
Castro, Rev. Emilio 66, 73–4
Cazalet, Sir Peter 142
Cellules Communist Combattantes
    (CCC) (Belgium) 138
Center for Democracy and Technology
    117–18
Chalfont, Lord 184, 185, 193
Chamberlain, Phil 40, 41
Chapela, Ignacio 124, 125, 129, 130
Charles, Prince of Wales 111–12
Chase, W. Howard 14
Chemical and Biological Medical
    Treatments Symposia (CBMTS)
    186–7
chemical and biological warfare
    (CBW) 186–8
Chlorine Chemistry Council (CCC) 79

Christian Democratic Party (Christen-Democratisch Appèl) (Netherlands) 67

Church Committee (US) 108, 199–200

Church of England 68

CILIP magazine 139

Cioka, Henry 48

citizens' committees 32–3, 63–4

civil society 46, 198, 199, 202, 203

Clancy, David 41

Clare, Allan 84, 88, 90, 91–2, 93, 94, 95, 96–8, 105–6

Clark, David 167

Clarke, Andrew 100

Clean Clothes Campaign 4–5

Clean Investment Campaign 168

Climate Camp xii

Coal and Iron Police Acts (1865 and 1866) 25

Coalition for Peace through Security 185, 192

Coalition on Southern Africa (COSA) 65

COINTELPRO (Counterintelligence Programme) 200

Cole, Chris 169

Communist Party 38, 192

community building 63–4

Competitive Enterprise Institute (CEI) 127

Confederation of British Industry (CBI) 43

Conko, Gregory 127–8

construction industry, and blacklisting 40, 41–3

Consulting Association 40, 42

containment 49–51, 54, 80, 116

Convention on Biological Diversity (UN-2002) 125

Coroners and Justice Act (2009) 43

corporate social responsibility (CSR) 8, 59, 64, 80, 196–7

Costain 42, 179, 181

counterstrategy 8, 14, 80, 109, 111, 114, 124, 133, 144–6

covert corporate strategy 5, 16, 79–80, 201–2

    consequences/deaths resulting from 13, 30, 59

and continuum in undermining resistance 191–4, 199

denials and damage control 112, 114–15, 119–21, 128–9, 133–4, 146–7

in the past 23–44

and regulation 202–3

research into 9–10, 12–13, 20–2, 136–7, 206

and secrecy 195–200, 201

use of internet 109–10, 111, 133–4

and violence 24, 25, 26, 30, 32–3

    see also activist intelligence; issue management (IM); *Neptune Strategy*; private intelligence agencies

Crawford, Holly 17

Cronin, Blaise 17

Crooke, Ian 189, 190

Crozier, Brian 184–5, 193

CyberSleuth 109, 116–19, 134

    PR Newswire's denial of 119–21

cybersurveillance 10, 109–34

    and civil liberties 117–18, 120, 121–2

    impact on activists 118

    security software 119–20

    see also internet

Daily Mail xi

Daily Mirror 39

Data Protection Act (1984) 38, 42

Davey, Brian 187, 188

Dearlove, Richard 141

Defence Manufacturers Association (DMA) 168, 185

Defence Systems and Equipment international fair (DSEi) 175

Deffenbagh, Rev. Ralston 71

Delborne, Jason 129, 132

Dell, Michael S. 132

democracy 9, 26, 27, 32, 36, 181, 202

    secrecy as threat to 1, 138, 195–200

Dempsey, Jim 117–18

Denel 176

Deutsche Telekom 147

Dev Sol (Devrimci Sol-Revolutionary Left) (*now* Revolutionary People's Liberation Party Front-DHKP/C) (Turkey) 154–5

DeWitt, DeAnne 122

Dezenhall, Eric 81
dialogue 9–10, 45, 49, 60, 69, 80, 197–8
  see also divide and rule strategies
Diederichs, Otto 139–40, 149, 155–6
DIGITALEUROPE 112–13
Dimock, Andrew 132
Dinan, William 35, 36
dioxin 79
Disarm DSEi campaign 175, 177
divide and rule strategies 48–58, 64–5,
  76, 78
Dorouba (Black Panther) 150
Dover, Rob 20, 193
Dow Chemicals 127
Duchin, Ron 78–9
Dutch Council of Churches 67

Earth First! (EF!) xiii, 180
Earth Watch 143
East Timor 159, 165
Ebener, Martin 147
Ecologist 126, 128
Economic League (formerly National
  Propaganda) 11, 23, 35–44, 85
  blacklisting 35, 36, 37–8, 40, 41–3,
    44, 118
  legacy of 37–44
economic warfare 17–18
Edelman 48
electronic industry, toxic waste from
  109, 112–14, 198
Ellis, Stephen 188, 190
Ellison, Graham 19
Employment Relations Act (1999) 43
Engels, Friedrich 16
engineering of consent 15–16, 69–70,
  80, 195, 198
environmental movement xii–xiii,
  xv–xvi, 43, 112–14, 123–5, 194,
  197
  see also Brent Spar crisis; Friends of
    the Earth; Greenpeace; road
    protests
E.ON xii–xiii, 194
Ernst & Young 117
espionage
  impact of 5–7
  and strikebreaking 28–30
  see also cybersurveillance;
    infiltration; surveillance

Ethical Investment Research Service 40
European Information and
  Communication Technology
  Industry Association (EICTA)
  112–15
  denial and damage control 114–15
European Network Against Arms
  Trade (ENAAT) 170–2, 175–6
European Round Table 186
Eurosatory international arms fair
  (1998) 170–1
Evans, Dick 162
eWatch 109, 111, 115–22, 133–4
  see also PR Newswire
Exxon-Mobil 144

Farleigh Projects 39
Faulds, Eric 110
Fife, Maria 39
Financial Times 140, 141, 142
First World War 23, 26, 36, 37
flex power 19–20, 199, 201–2, 203
Foot, Paul 39
Fossey, Alan 162, 166
Frank, Donovan (District Judge) 117
Franks, Adrian (Adrian le Chêne)
  160–1, 170–2, 176, 182, 183
Freedom of Information Act 43, 106,
  107
Freeport 148
Friends of the Earth 113, 143, 148
Fuehrer, Alan 62–3

Gane, Barrie 180, 182
Garland, David 12
Garnier-Lançot, Monique 184
Gartner Consulting 118–19
Geddes, Sir Auckland 38
General Motors 29, 34
genetic engineering 8, 10, 122, 130,
  133, 198
  cattle drug rBGH 126
  GM seeds and food 100, 110,
    111–12, 131, 204–5
  cross-pollination 123–4, 129
  see also Mexican maize
    controversy; Monsanto
German secret services 139–40
  see also Bundesnachrichtendienst;
    Landesamt für Verfassungsschutz

Gerson, John 142
Gifford, Tilly xiv–xv
Gill, Martin 203
Gill, Peter 20–2, 133, 201
Gladwin, John 68
Glencore 147
Global Open xiii, 194
globalization 1, 9, 11, 14, 18, 157, 202
Graig, Cameron H. 120
Granowitz, Rabbi A.M. 33
Gravett, Paul 102
Great Depression (1930s) 23, 27
Great Steel Strike (1919) 26–7
Greenpeace 113, 114–15, 145–7, 153, 198
   see also London Greenpeace
Greenpeace Germany 136, 145, 146–7
grey intelligence 11, 18, 135, 157, 202
   see also blurring boundaries
Group 4 xvi, 180–1
gruppe 2 143, 149, 150–1
Guardian xvi, 40, 41, 100–1, 128–9, 177, 185
Guerrant, David 47

Hackney and Islington Animal Rights Campaign 102, 105
Haden Young 40, 41
Hakluyt 10, 135, 138, 140–8, 156–8, 197, 205
   board of directors 157
   denial and damage control 146–7, 158
   and Greenpeace Germany 146–7
   intelligence used for counterstrategy 144–6, 156
   see also BP; Schlickenrieder; Shell
Hakluyt Foundation 141–2, 157
Hakluyt, Richard 140–1
Hall, Sir Reginald 38
Hamdan, Fouad 146–7
Hamilton, George xv
Hanks, John 188
Hanley, Jeremy 167
Hardy, Stan 39, 40
Harknett, Julie 106–7
Hart, Jerry 203
Hartley, Gerald 88
Hawk fighter jets
   damaged by activists 168, 169
   sale to Indonesia 159, 163, 165, 169

Heath, Robert L. 14, 15
Hester, Lex 151
Heyndrickx, Aubin 187–8
Highways Agency 180–1
Hill & Knowlton 11, 27, 28, 31–2, 33–4, 48
Hill, John 11, 27–8, 37, 81
Hodges, Robert 182
Hogbin, Martin 162, 165–6, 172–7
Hollingsworth, Mark 39
Holmes, Sir Peter 142
Hoogenboom, Bob 18, 108, 135
Hooker, Michelle 90, 91, 93, 94–5, 98–100, 101–3, 105
Howarth, David xii
Hudson, Kate 192
Hughes, Mike 38
Hull Against Hawks 162, 169

Independent Police Complaints Commission 101
Indonesia 159, 163, 165, 167, 169, 171
industrial munitions 24, 28, 30
INFACT (Infant Formula Action Coalition) 50, 54, 55, 56
infant formula industry 4, 45, 47
infiltration 2, 9–10, 22, 138
   BAe and CAAT 159–78, 190
   impact of 5–7, 10, 96, 107, 172, 177–8
   and law breaking 96–8
   McDonald's and London Greenpeace 82–107
   Nestlé and Attac Switzerland 13, 58–9
   and provocation x, 101, 154–5, 159, 170–2
   of road protests 178–82
   and rules 137–8
info-cleansing 116, 120
Infonic 109, 111, 112, 113, 114–15, 133–4, 198
Information Commissioner's Office (ICO) 40, 41, 42–4, 173, 174, 175, 177
information wars 16–20
Inside EAP Weekly Report 113–14
Inside PR 123

intelligence, state–private cooperation x–xi, xii, xiii, 18–20, 23, 44, 81, 83, 85–7, 89, 105–8, 118, 140
Inter Press Service (IPS) 113
Interfaith Center on Corporate Responsibility (ICCR) 45–6, 50, 60, 66–7, 68, 70, 77
International Baby Food Action Network (IBFAN) 59
International Barometer 62–3
International Business Research 120
International Day of Action against McDonald's 82, 89
International Federation of Chemical, Energy, Mine and General Workers' Unions (ICEM) 148
International Nestlé Boycott Committee 47
internet 109–34
   see also cybersurveillance; online discussion groups
Internet Crimes Group (ICG) 120, 121
investigative journalists 12, 20, 39, 46, 62, 134, 204, 206
   and use of deception 136–7
Irian Jaya 148
Irving, Gordon xiii
issue management (IM) 14–15, 21, 48, 49, 76, 196, 202
ivory and rhino horn smuggling 188–91

Jackson, Peter 20
James, Christopher 140, 141, 142
Jane's Weekly 187–8
Jellicoe, George, Earl 141
Jensen, Paul 74
Johnson, Doug 54, 56
Johnston, Les 19–20

Karataş, Dursun 154
KAS Enterprises 188–90
Katzin, Donna 65, 68–9
Kaunda, Kenneth 190
Kennedy, Mark ('Mark Stone') x–xi, xii, xiii, xvi, 12, 101, 194, 203, 205
Kent, Bruce 192
Kenya 190
Kerr, Ian 40, 41–2, 43
King, Justin xiv

Kings Investigation Bureau 87–8, 97
Kingsnorth power station xii
Klar, Christian 149
Klein, Naomi 7–8
'Knotter, Marcel' (pseudonym) *see* Oosterbeek, Paul
Knowlton, Donald 27, 81
Koeppler Appeal 186
Kommunistischen Studentenbund (Communist Student Union) 149
Krikke, Hans 4
Krug, Stefan 145
Kruszewska, Iza 114
Kumleben Report 189–90

La Follette Committee 28, 29, 31, 32, 33, 34
La Follette, Robert 24, 28, 33, 34
Labour movement, campaign against 37–8
Labour Party, and Trotskyist Militants 185
Lambert, Robert 83, 85, 100–1, 102–3, 205
Landesamt für Verfassungsschutz (LfV) 148, 155
Lang, Ian 141
Lattimore, Dan 15
Lauterbach, Vreni 150
Le Chêne, Evelyn 44, 159–63, 182–94, 210
   and access to CAAT's computers 166–7
   anti-communism 11, 44, 183–6, 193, 200
   and continuum in undermining resistance 11, 191–4, 200
   counterstrategies used against CAAT 168–70
   and daily reports on CAAT 163–5
   disapproval of activists 165
   and Hogbin 173–4
   interest in chemical and biological warfare (CBW) 186–8
   and road protests xvi, 178–80
   and surveillance of CAAT activists 165
   undercover in Southern Africa 11, 188–91
   see also Threat Response International (TRI)

Le Chêne, Pierre 182–3
LeagueWatch 39
Lee, Ivy 81
Leeming, Rod xiii, 194
Lewis, Julian 185, 192–3
Lewis, Mike 177
libel laws 9, 82–3, 86, 87, 150, 197, 205
Liberia 148
Libertad 152
Liberty xvi
Lipski, Roy 112, 114
Little Steel 27–8, 30, 31
lobbying 9, 20, 48, 113, 127, 196
    advanced warnings about 144–5,
        159, 167–8
London Greenpeace 82–108, 194
    annual Fayre 91, 93, 102
    group meetings 89–90, 93–4
    impact of infiltrators 93–4, 107
    infiltrators unaware of each other 94
    letters and photos stolen 95, 96–8,
        107
    libel case against 82–7, 197
    linked with animal rights movement
        103–5
    McDonald's issue low on agenda
        92–3
    suspicions about infiltrators 95–6,
        107
London Metropolitan Police 108
    cooperation with McDonald's 11,
        83, 85, 105–7, 194
    see also Animal Rights National
        Index
Love, Dr James 120

Macdonald Douglas 185
McDonald's 11, 44, 205
    cooperation with police 11, 83, 85,
        105–7, 194
    infiltration of London Greenpeace
        82–106
        continuing after writs served 98–9
        investigators breaking law 96–8
        justifications given 103–5
        reporting arrangements 103
    libel case against London
        Greenpeace activists 82–7, 197
    see also Animal Rights National
        Index

McGinty, Mike 162
McIvor, Arthur 35, 36
Maclay, Michael 142–3
Maclean, Sir Fitzroy 142
MacLeod, Jack M. 75
McSpotlight.org website 84, 85
Madagascar 148
Major, John 163
Malan, General Magnus 189, 190
Malloy, Rev. Edward A. 73
Management Today 140
Mandela, Nelson 187, 189
Mandelson, Peter 43
Marianist Brothers and Priests
    (Baltimore) 52
Märkische Phasen 147
Marx, Gary T. 137, 201, 204
Marx, Karl 16
Marzullo, Sal 71, 72
Matthews, Jonathan 124, 125–6, 128
Maucher, Helmut 48
Mauthausen concentration camp 183
May, Simon 111
Memorial Day Massacre (1937) 24,
    27, 34
Mercer, Paul 191–3, 194
Methodist Task Force (MTF), to
    examine Nestlé's practices 49, 50,
    51, 52, 55, 56
Mexican maize controversy 123–5,
    129, 132
MI5 37
MI6, former members of 140, 141,
    142, 144, 180
Militant Tendency 185
Miller, Dan 35, 36
Miller, Karen S. 27
Miller, W.H. 14
Millgate, Heather xiii
mining companies 25, 148
Mirren, Helen 167–8
Monasterio, Fernando Ortiz 124
Monbiot, George 128
Mongoven, Biscoe & Dutchin, Inc.
    (MBD) 78–9
Mongoven, Jack 51, 52, 54, 57, 65,
    76–8, 157
Monhaupt, Brigitte 149

Monsanto 8, 111–12, 198, 204–5
  and Competitive Enterprise Institute
    (CEI) 127
  internet strategy 112, 122, 123–9,
    131, 133
    creation of fake identities 10, 110,
      124–6, 133
    fake identities denial 128
  see also biotech industry; genetic
    engineering
Montague, Peter 78
Morris, Dave 83, 85, 89, 91, 92, 95,
  103–6
Motor Products strike (1953) 30
Multinational Monitor 52, 53, 58
'Murphy, Mary' (pseudonym) 124–6,
  128, 129, 132
Muskie, Edmund S. 53, 54
  see also Nestlé Infant Formula Audit
    Commission (NIFAC)

Namibia 61, 189, 190
National Association of Manufacturers
  31, 32
National Congress of Parents and
  Teachers 64
National Council of Churches 50, 55,
  66
National Council for Civil Liberties 39
National Council for Civil Protection
  185–6
National Domestic Extremism Team xi
National Extremism Tactical
  Coordination Unit xi
National Labour Relations Board (US)
  29
National Propaganda 36
  see also Economic League
National Public Order Intelligence Unit
  (NPOIU) xi, 194
NATO (North Atlantic Treaty
  Organization) 139, 183, 193
Nature journal 123–5, 130
neoliberalism 1, 11
Neptune Strategy 45–6, 60–76, 146,
  204
  intelligence gathering and
    assessment 61, 62–3
  leaked to press 45, 60, 68, 73–4, 78
  and religious groups 66–9, 71

strategy for schools 63–4, 70, 198
  target groups 61, 63–4, 66, 74
  and university campuses 69–73, 80
  see also Shell
Nestlé 4, 10, 45–59, 73, 76, 77–8,
  79–81
  attempts to influence students 53
  boycott renewed (1988) 58
  end of boycott (1984) 56–7
  hiring of Rafael Pagan 47–8
  infiltration of Attac Switzerland 13,
    58–9
  relations with religious groups 50–2
  strategies for breaking boycott
    48–58
  strategies revisited for Neptune
    Strategy 60, 63–4, 66, 68
  unsuccessful PR strategy 47–8
  and WHO codes 51–2, 53, 57, 59,
    64, 80
Nestlé Coordination Centre for
  Nutrition (NCCN) 48, 49–50,
  51, 52, 57
Nestlé Infant Formula Audit
  Commission (NIFAC) (Muskie)
  53–4, 57–8, 80, 197
Nestlé News 53
New Deal reforms (US) 23, 26
New Statesman 123
New York Herald Tribune 32
New York Times131 118
Newbury bypass protests xvi, 159,
  178–82
Newsnight (BBC) 128
Next 5 Minutes conference (1999) 7
NGO Strategy 113–15
Nichols, Nick 81
Nicholson, Sidney 85–7, 89, 90–1, 97,
  103–4
Nigeria 8, 111, 143, 144, 197
Noar, Michael 42
Northern Alliance for Sustainability
  (ANPED) 114
Northwest Airlines (NWA) 116–18,
  198
Norton-Taylor, Richard 39
Notre Dame University 53, 72–3
Novartis (now Syngenta) 130
NRC Handelsblad 188
Nutricia (now Numico) 4

Ogilvy & Mather 58
online discussion groups 110, 115,
    117–18, 120, 122, 132
    and anonymity 118, 120, 121, 122,
    132, 134
    fake identities 10, 110, 124–9, 132,
    133
    and viral marketing 130–3
    see also cybersurveillance; internet
Oosterbeek, Paul ('Marcel Knotter')
    2–5
OPEC oil embargo (1979) 61
Operation Gladio 193
Operation Lock 188–91
    military training for anti-poaching
    teams 189–90
O'Reilly, Conor 19
Organic Consumers Association 131
Organisation for the Prohibition of
    Chemical Weapons (OPCW) 187
Orwell, George 122
Osler, Dave 40

Pagan International (PI) 57, 60, 62, 65,
    66, 68–9, 73, 77–8
Pagan, Rafael D. Jr. 76–81, 200
    as founder of International
    Barometer 62–3
    and Nestlé 45, 46, 47–58, 76, 77,
    197
    and Shell 45–6, 60–76, 78, 79–81,
    198
Pattakos, Arion N. 77, 157
peace movement 191–3
    links with Communist Party 192
    links with road protest movement
    179–80, 193
    see also Campaign for Nuclear
    Disarmament (CND); Coalition
    Against Arms Trade (CAAT)
Pearl, Steve xii
Philip Morris 127
Phythian, Mark 21–2
Pinkerton, Allan 24
Pinkerton's National Detective Agency
    11, 24, 28, 34, 182
Pinkerton's Protective Police Patrol 11,
    23, 24–5
Pirelli 147
Plane Stupid xii, xiv–xv

Ploughshares Movement 169
Pocklington, Antony 89, 90, 91–2, 93,
    95, 105
police
    dealing with Newbury bypass
    protesters 178–9
    recruiting activists xiv–xv
    selling information x–xi
    see also Animal Rights National
    Index; London Metropolitan
    Police
Policy Research Associates 185, 192
Pollard, Sir Charles 181, 182
Post, Rev. Avery 66
PR Newswire 119–21
Prakash, Dr C.S. 127–8, 130, 131
Preston, Paul 87, 103–4
Preus, David 66, 71
Printers Ink 31
Privacy and Electronic
    Communications Regulations 43
private intelligence agencies 158
    background of investigators xiii, xiv,
    10, 18, 85–6, 141, 157–8
    cooperation with state sector x–xi,
    xii, xiii, 18–20, 23, 44, 81, 83,
    85–7, 89, 105–8, 118, 140
    methods of information collection
    9–10
Pro K 150
Project Coast 187
propaganda 26–8, 31–5
    see also Economic League; issue
    management (IM); public
    relations (PR)
PRwatch.org 79
public opinion, manipulation of 31–5
public relations (PR) 8–9, 13–14, 16,
    31–5, 59, 196, 197
    and online strategy 122–3
    see also issue management (IM);
    propaganda
Purves, Sir William 142

Quist, David 123, 129, 130

Radcliffe-on-Soar power station xii
Raffe, Gerry 48
Rainforest Action Network 180
Rampton, Richard 88, 103

Rampton, Sheldon 79
Rapporti Sociali 154
rBGH (genetically engineered cattle drug) 126
Reclaim the Streets 100
Red Brigades (Brigate Rosse-Italy) 138–9, 149, 150
regulation, of intelligence agencies 202–3
Reliance Security 182
Renfro, William L. 15, 16
Representation of the People Act (1918) 36
Republic Steel Corporation 28, 30–1, 32
research
    collecting data 204, 206
    and regulation of private intelligence 202–3
    and resistance 20–6
    use of deception 136–8
Revolutionäre Aufbau 135–6, 139, 145, 148, 149, 152, 154, 155–6
Reynolds, Mike 141, 145, 146
Rich, Mark 147
Richter, Judith 15–16, 201
Rifkind, Malcolm 141
Rio Tinto 147, 148
risk 16, 23, 124, 198
risk assessment 1, 180
Risk and Crisis Analysis 182, 190
Rispens, Jan 145
road protests xv–xvi, 159, 178–82
Robert Bishop Ltd (part of Westhall Services) 88
Roddick, Anita 144
Romero, Luciano Enrique 13
Rooijen, Martin van 67, 75
Rote Armee Fraktion (Red Army Faction-RAF) 135, 138, 148, 149, 151
Rote Hilfe (Red Help) 149
Rowell, Andy 124, 126, 128
Royal Dutch Shell, response to exposure of *Neptune Strategy* 74–5
Rubicon 182
Rufford, Nicholas 140
Russell, Jack 88, 89
Russian Revolution (1917) 36

Saro-Wiwa, Ken 111, 143, 144, 145, 197
Saunders, Ernest 48
Savimbi, Jonas 11, 184, 187–8
Scales, Prunella 167–8
Schlickenrieder, Manfred 135–6, 138–40, 143–57
    as agent provocateur 154–5
    career background 148–9
    disseminating printed material for groups 150
    documentary making 143–4, 149–50
    exposure 139, 144, 146–7, 148, 150, 151, 152, 155
    and Greenpeace 145–7
    intelligence files 136, 138–40, 147, 152–3, 154, 207–9
    work highly valued 153–4
    working methods 149–52, 156
    see also Hakluyt
Schulz, Adelheid 149
Scott, Len 20
secrecy 21, 80, 107, 108, 158, 195–6, 199–200, 204
Securitas 58, 59
Setchell, Anton xii
Sethi, S. Prakash 45, 46, 48, 50, 54, 56, 57, 70–3, 78
Shell 8, 10, 78, 79–81
    and anti-apartheid campaign 60–1, 69–70
    Brent Spar crisis (1995) 8, 110–11, 143, 145, 197
    damage control 73–6, 197
    divide and rule strategies 64–9
    links with Hakluyt 142, 143–4, 146, 157
    online strategy 111
    and Pagan 45–6, 60–76, 78, 79–81, 198
    relations with religious groups 66–9
    role in South Africa 60–1, 63–5
    and Sullivan Principles 64, 71
    see also Neptune Strategy
Shephard, Geoff 100, 102
sickout, airline employees 10, 116–18
Siebelt, Peter 3
Silicon Valley Toxics Coalition 113
Silverberg, Louis 32–3, 34–5

Skinner, Ted 116–17, 119
Small, Mark 115
'Smetacek, Andura' (pseudonym)
  124–6, 128, 132
Smith, Robert Michael 25
Smith, Tim 68–9
Soberon, Jorge 125
Sokolsky, George 32
Sony 113, 114–15, 198
South Africa 60–1, 63, 64, 66, 67, 68,
  189–90, 198
  post-apartheid 65, 70–3
  see also anti-apartheid campaign;
  apartheid
South African Defence Force (SADF)
  187, 189
South African National Union of
  Mineworkers (NUM) 60–1
Special Branch 181, 194
  cooperation with McDonald's xii,
  11, 83, 85, 86–7, 100–6, 107–8,
  157
  see also Animal Rights National
  Index
Spedding, Sir David 141, 142
SpinWatch.org 7, 100, 205, 206
Stark, Holger 149
Stauber, John 79
Stauffacher, Andrea 149, 150
Steel Corporation 26–7
Steel, Helen 83–5, 87, 89, 91–2, 93–4,
  95–6, 97, 98, 103–6
steel industry (US) 23–4, 26–7
  and manipulation of public opinion
  31–5
Steinbacher, Res 149, 150
Stena Dee oil installation 145
Stepanek, Marcia 119
Stephens, Mark 145–6
Stewart, Tom 73
Stirling, Sir David 188, 190
'Stone, Mark' (pseudonym) see
  Kennedy, Mark
Strauss, Robert 74
Straw, Jack 167
Strehle, Res 147
strikebreaking 24, 25–6
  and espionage 28–30
Sullivan Signatory Group, Principles
  64, 71

Sunday Times
  exposure of Schlickenrieder 144,
  146–7
  exposure of spy files on CAAT 10,
  11, 159, 161, 162, 165, 168,
  172–3, 176–7
  and spying on road protesters 178,
  180
surveillance 21, 23
  and blacklisting 37–8
  and corporate strategy 9, 22, 44,
  79–80, 195
  resistance to 201
  see also cybersurveillance;
  infiltration
Swaziland 190

Tanzania 190
Tarmac 181
Taylor, Peter 181–2
teachers, and Shell strategy 63–4, 70,
  198
Teamsters Local 2000 117
Tefft, Stanton 199
De Telegraaf 3–4
Temps Présent (Swiss TV programme)
  58, 59
Thames Valley Police xvi, 181–2
Thatcher, Margaret 184
Thomas, Mark 177
Thomson, Basil 38
Threat Research and Analysis Group
  (Walmart) 118
Threat Response International (TRI)
  159–82, 204
  spying on CAAT 159–78
    access to CAAT's computers
    165–7
    counterstrategies used against
    CAAT 168–70
    files and reports 44, 159, 162–5,
    178
    giving advanced warnings on
    lobbying 167–8
    information on planned direct
    action 168–70
    surveillance of CAAT activists
    165
  spying on road protests 159, 178–82
  see also Le Chêne, Evelyn

Tiller, Frances 88–9, 90, 91, 92, 93, 94
Time 32
The Times 180, 185
Tobias, Ken xiv
Toffler, Alvin and Heidi 16–18, 108, 157
Tokra Limited xiii
trade unions
    blacklisting in UK 38, 40–4
    Pagan's anti-union strategy 63, 74, 80
    rising membership in UK 36
    and role of Shell in South Africa 60–1, 63
    union busting in US 24–6, 28–9, 34
Tremayne, Charles 39
Trewavas, Anthony 125
Truth and Reconciliation Commission 187
Tutu, Desmond 66, 72
Twyford Down road protest xv–xvi

UCATT (construction workers' union) 43
Ullrich, Richard 52
union busting 24–6, 28–9, 34
Unita (Angola) 184, 187–8
United Methodist Church (UMC) 49, 50, 51–2, 55–6
    Task Force (MTF) 49, 50, 51, 52, 55, 56
United Mine Workers of America (UMW) 60
universities
    influence of corporations 129–30
    targeted in *Neptune Strategy* 69–73, 80
Unrepresented Nations and Peoples Organization (UNPO) 148
Up Against The Wall 118
US Environmental Protection Agency 79

Valentine, Detective Sergeant 106
Vericola xiii
viral marketing 10, 112, 130–3

Wachem, Lodewijk Christiaan van 75
Wagner Act (1935) 27, 28
Wainwright, Alan 40–1
Wallraff, Gunter 136
Walmart 118
Washington Post 54–5
Waste from Electrical and Electronic Equipment (WEEE) (EU directive) 112
'Waste Paper Man' *see* Oosterbeek, Paul ('Marcel Knotter')
Watergate 204
WebWatch 120
Wedel, Janine 19, 20, 158, 199, 201
Wemos 4
West European Defence Association (WEDA) 183–5, 191, 192, 193
West Papua Network 148
What's Wrong With McDonald's? (leaflet) 82–3
whistleblowers 6, 12, 38–9, 40–1, 159, 162, 204, 206
Whitaker, J.S. 72
White Plains conference (1987) 71, 72
Wijngaarden, Marq 155
Williamson, Craig 190
Wilson, Woodrow 26
Wilton Park International Association 186
Winder, Jack 39
Wogaman, Philip 56
Wolpe, Howard 72
Woodward, Bob 204
World in Action (Granada TV) 39
World Health Organization (WHO), infant formula code 4, 47, 51, 53, 57, 59, 64, 80
World Wide Fund for Nature (WWF) 188

Young, Lord 43

Zambia 190
Zee, Wim van der 67
Zeigler, Todd 128
Zimbabwe 190
Zöbel, Gunter 147